India-China Relations

Politics of Resources, Identity and Authority

K.R. Gupta

ATLANTIC

PUBLISHERS & DISTRIBUTORS (P) LTD

Published by
ATLANTIC
PUBLISHERS & DISTRIBUTORS (P) LTD
7/22, Ansari Road, Darya Ganj, New Delhi-110002
Phones : +91-11-40775252, 23273880, 23275880, 23280451
Fax : +91-11-23285873
Web : www.atlanticbooks.com
E-mail : orders@atlanticbooks.com

Branch Office
5, Nallathambi Street, Wallajah Road, Chennai-600002
Phones : +91-44-64611085, 32413319
E-mail : chennai@atlanticbooks.com

Printed in India at Nice Printing Press, A-33/3A, Site-IV,
Industrial Area, Sahibabad, Ghaziabad, U.P.

Preface

Not much has changed in the rhetoric of India-China relations since Mao Zedong, founding father of the People's Republic of China who ruled China as the Chairman of the Communist Party of China from its establishment in 1949 until his death in 1976, speaking in 1951 in honour of the first anniversary of Indian constitution, declared that 'excellent friendship' had existed between the two countries 'for thousands of years'. Yet few of the lofty proclamations made by Chinese and Indian leaders over the years truly reflect the reality of relations between the two giants of the Asia. It is surprising that two neighbouring states with such a rich and sometimes fractious history, including a border conflict in 1962, should have what appears to be a largely reactive relationship. But neither has developed a grand strategy about the other. An unshakeable and largely unprofitable preoccupation with the past on the Indian side and an equally intense preoccupation with domestic consolidation on the Chinese side, have left the relationship under-tended. It might best be one of geostrategic competition qualified by growing commercial cooperation.

China is a more fraught subject in Indian national debates than India is for China, which does not appear to feel threatened in any serious way by India, while India at times displays tremendous insecurity in the face of Chinese economic success and military expansion. To outsiders, India and China show some striking similarities. Both are ancient civilisations reincarnated as modern republics in the mid-twentieth century and are now rising powers. Both have nuclear weapons, burgeoning economies, expanding military budgets and large reservoirs of manpower, and seem to be vying for influence in the Indian Ocean, the Persian Gulf, Africa, Central and East Asia. Yet little attention is paid to the relationship between them. Most attention has been focused on China's relations with the United States, Japan and East Asia or India's relations with Pakistan, South Asia and the

United States. Whereas China-United States ties are often cast as one-to-one contest for global preeminence, moreover, the India-China relationship is more often seen in terms of the countries' interactions with extraneous actors such as the United States, Pakistan and other South Asian nations. It is also defined by contrasting polities and models of development, with the parties silently competing not just for capital, resources and markets, but also for legitimacy in the arena of great and emerging global powers.

The book *India-China Relations: Politics of Resources, Identity and Authority* draws on evidence from interactions between India and China over the years to make an empirical case for the existence and impact of asymmetrical perceptions of threat and friendship between the two countries. The major issues of India-China relations, including the boundary problem, the nuclear issue, the Tibet issue, water diplomacy, regional competition and cooperation, and India-China relations in the global context, have been examined in this book. The book highlights the asymmetry of the threat perceptions between India and China and has explained the interactions of India-China relations. The India-China relations are constrained by the asymmetry between their threat perceptions. Due to the asymmetry in perceptions of threat, India has tried to reduce the sense of insecurity by adopting some countermeasures, such as developing nuclear weapons, allying with other countries, and undermining China's influence. However, India is also very cautious and avoids angering China. On the other hand, China is in favour of the status quo, and feels no urgent need to sort out the boundary disputes. China has ignored the asymmetry and does not want to share India's expectations and concerns. Thus, the asymmetry has made it difficult for India and China to forge shared knowledge and to set a common agenda around which their expectations could converge.

The book will be useful to the students and researchers of Political Science and International Relations. It will also be useful to all those who are interested and want to explore India-China relations.

K.R. Gupta

सत्यमेव जयते

Contents

Preface ... *iii*

1. A Brief History of India-China Relations ... 1
2. India-China Relations in Pre-Independence Era ... 24
3. India-China Relations in Post-Independence Era ... 37
4. India-China Border Disputes ... 51
5. The Tibet Issue ... 72
6. The Nuclear Dimension ... 84
7. The Water Diplomacy ... 103
8. Pakistan as a Factor in India-China Relations ... 122
9. Cyber Warfare Doctrine ... 136
10. Defence Cooperation and Military Engagement ... 141
11. Comprehensive Trade and Economic Cooperation ... 160
12. Regional Competition and Cooperation ... 234
13. India and China in the Global Arena ... 264

CHAPTER 1

A Brief History of India-China Relations

India and China, the two giants of Asia with oldest and living civilization of the world, have a lot in common, and in fact they have had the longest uninterrupted history as a nation. Sindhu and Ganges gave birth to Indian civilization, which influenced South and Southeast Asia. Similarly, Huang He (Yellow River) and Chang Jiang (Yangtze River) gave birth to the Chinese civilization, which influenced Northeast and Southeast Asia. Both India and China have a considerable influence on world economy due to their bigger geographical area and population. They have got independence in the same century (India on 15th August 1947 and China on 1st October 1949), but the manner in which freedom was won speaks volumes about their policies. India won freedom after a prolonged non-violent struggle, on the other hand, Chinese independence was a result of a never seen before military backed aggression. An analysis of India-China bilateral relation also determines the policies adopted by the respective countries in terms of dealing with international order. Traditionally China has used a confrontationist approach, for example, its actions in the South China Sea, its conflicts with South Korea and Taiwan, its role in the Vietnam-Cambodia-Laos conflict, *etc.* On the other hand, India has never been pro-active in declaring war with any of its neighbours. Even in the case of China, India (Pt. Jawaharlal Nehru to be specific) tried its best to assuage Chinese apprehensions. As a nation that was struggling to grapple with the task of nation building, India saw in China an ally thanks to its socialist ideologies. Pt. Nehru also believed in socialist policies, much to the angst of his political contemporaries. China's breaking of the Panchsheel policies was a setback from which India unfortunately never recovered.

Existing in close proximity for thousands of years, the ancient civilizations of India and China had surprisingly little political interaction for most of that time. However, the twentieth century saw tensions between the two increased over disputed borders and geopolitical competition for power, influence, resources, and markets. As ancient civilizations, India and China coexisted in peace and harmony for millennia, but as postcolonial modern nation-states, except for a very short period of bonhomie in the early 1950s, relations between the two Asian giants have been marked by conflict, containment, mutual suspicion, distrust, and rivalry. Just as the Indian sub-continental plate has a tendency to constantly rub and push against the Eurasian tectonic plate, causing friction and volatility in the entire Himalayan mountain range, India's bilateral relationship with China also remains volatile and ridden with friction and tension.

During the 1950s the relations between India and China were cordial, based on the peaceful coexistence, but the Tibet issue, followed by a border dispute poisoned the climate of India-China entente cordiale. Pt. Nehru's policies of no-dispute and no-negotiation policies finally led to a war in 1962. From then on, India-China relations entered an era of cold war which lasted nearly for 20 years. However, during the era of Rajiv Gandhi (1988), the tension between the two countries was minimized and initiatives were taken for improvement in the relations. Since the end of cold war, the relations between the two countries have steadily improved, and also strengthened in various fields of mutual interest. The regular visits between the heads of state and officials have strengthened the relations and various issues including the border issue have been in the discussion for resolution by mutual cooperation.

Over the past six decades relation between India and China has undergone dramatic changes—ranging from the 1950s with a deep hostility in the 1960s and 1970s to a rapprochement in the 1980s and a readjustment since the demise of Soviet Union. The post-cold war era has offered enormous opportunities to India and China to move in the direction of a productive relationship. Both the neighbours have realized the imperative need for cooperation in diverse areas, especially in the trade and economic domains, in the long-term interest of peace and stability in Asia as well as for faster economic development and prosperity at home. The fast-changing economic and strategic milieu punctuated by uncertainty brought about by globalization in macrocosmic terms, has created challenges as well as opportunities for both the neighbouring countries to free themselves of 'historical baggage' in terms of bilateral relations.

Historical and Cultural Legacies

The reliable literature records of India-China interface could be traced from Han Dynasty (206 BC — 220 AD). The first information is provided by Sima Qian (135 BC — 86 BC), father of Chinese historiography, in his masterpiece *Shiji* (Records of the Grand Historian). He has narrated that people in the Shu (another name of Sichuan, Southwestern Chinese province) were wearing clothes that were brought from Shendu (Sindhu from India). Later Ban Gu (32 AD — 92 AD), Chinese historian, politician, and poet best known for his part in compiling the Book of Han, the second of China's 24 dynastic histories, writes about Kashmir (Jibin State) in his book *Qian Hanshu* and talks about state of affairs there, its weather and products like pearls, corals, lapis lazuli, *etc.*

From the above-mentioned facts, it could be established that by 4th to 5th century AD there was already a sea route between India and China; and India supplied the trade items that were in demand in China and available only in India. According to literary sources, imported items transported from India to China included coral, pearls, glass and fragrances. On the other hand, silk appears to be the major item transported from China to India. Trade relations further developed during Tang Dynasty (618 AD — 907 AD), Song Dynasty (960 AD — 1279 AD), and Yuan Dynasty (1279 AD — 1368 AD). By this time, maritime activities were intense and it has been found in various sources that in Guangzhou (Canton) there were ships of Indian, Persians, and Sri Lankan merchants. Meanwhile, Indian astronomy, colander, medicine, music and dance, sugar manufacturing technology, *etc.*, made their way to China. Chinese silk products remained popular among the trading items. Historical literature and archeological discoveries have established that there was a continuous flow of cross-cultural currents between India and China. The two elements of the exchange between India and China could be categorized as material exchange and spiritual cultural exchange. This two-faceted exchange was carried through the following four routes of communication:

(a) The Central Asian Route (or Silk Route),

(b) Assam-Burma and Yunnan Route (or Southern Silk Route),

(c) Tibet-Nepal Route, and

(d) The Sea Route (or Maritime Silk Route).

The Central Asian Route was the main overland route though this was not the earliest one to be discovered. This route was especially vital for the traders and missionaries from China to India and vice versa. The route started from Chang'an passed through Dunhuang and Kashgar. From Dunhuang, it bifurcated into Northern and Southern route. The Northern route passed through the oasis between the Northern edge of Taklamaken Desert and the Tianshan mountain ranges. The Southern route ran through the Southern edge of the desert and Kunlun Mountain. These two smaller routes further merged at Kashgar in Xinjiang autonomous region. The route further splits into two from Kashgar—the Northern route passed through Kokand and Samarkand (now in Kirghizstan) and Southern route which ran through modern Bectria and merged with the Northern branch at Merv in Margiana (present Turkmenistan). From Bectria, the route ran through Kapisi and Kabul to Peshawar and Taxila. From Taxila it was connected to Mathura and Ujjain. Another route from Kashgar ran through Gilgit in Kashmir. Assam-Burma and Yunnan route originated in Chengdu, Sichuan province of China and entered Dali, Baoshan and Tengchong of Yunnan province. From Yunnan it passed through the Northern part of Burma and entered Assam in the Northeast of India. The Southern silk route further ran through Bengal and then finally merged with the Central Asian route. It is believed this was earliest route for the India-China interface. The Tibet-Nepal route was more difficult to access than the central Asian and Southern Silk route. This route came into being in the late 7th century.

India and China have the quality of resilience that has enabled them to survive and prosper through the ages and against the odds. During the past three thousand years, each of the Asian countries—some situated on the continental landmass, others being islands off the Asia mainland—has at some stage been directly influenced by one or both of these two great civilizations. Both have long and rich strategic traditions. Both Kautilya's *Arthashastra*—a treatise on war, diplomacy, statecraft, and empire; and Sunzi's (Sun Tzu's) *Sunzi Bingfa*—the art of war, were written over two thousand years ago in India and China, respectively. The traditional Chinese concept of international relations was based on concentric circles from the imperial capital outward through variously dependent states to the barbarians. It bears remarkable resemblance to the Indian concept of mandala or circles as outlined in *Arthashastra*, which postulated that a king's neighbour is his natural enemy, while the king beyond his neighbour is his natural ally. The Chinese dynasties followed a similar policy of encircling and attacking nearby neighbours and maintaining friendly relations with more distant kingdoms. Much like imperial China, tribute, homage, subservience, but not annexation, were the rightful fruits of victory in ancient India.

Political contacts between ancient India and China were few and far between. In the cultural sphere, it was mostly a one-way—from India to China. Hindu and Buddhist religious and cultural influence spread to China through Central Asia, and Chinese scholars attended Indian Universities at Nalanda and Taxila. Though Indian and Chinese civilizations reacted to one another during the first few centuries of the Christian era, the process of religious-cultural interaction ceased after tenth century BC, coinciding with the Islamic invasions in India. Since then, the two neighbours lived as if they were oblivious to each other's existence for over a thousand years, until the advent of the 19th century, when both came under the influence of European powers. Before the age of European colonization, India accounted for about 25 percent of the world's manufactured goods and China for about 33 percent. China under the Song and Qing dynasties was the world's superpower. Under the Guptas and Mughals, India's economic, military, and cultural prowess was an object of envy. Then in a complete reversal of fortune, both the mighty Asian civilizations declined, decayed, and disintegrated and were finally conquered by European powers.

Early Contacts: Before the Christian Era

It is exactly not known when contact or cultural exchange between India and China actually began. But it is assumed that ancient Indians had known China since no later than the 4th century BC. Some Indian literatures such as *Ramayana*, *Mahabharata*, and *Arthashastra* had mentioned Cina (present day China) more than once. In the *Arthashastra*, which was written around 4th century BC, Chinese silk was mentioned, indicating that there was silk trade between India and China. In ancient times, both countries divided the sky into 28 constellations in the same order, demonstrating mutual exchanges in the field of astronomy.

Before the Christian era, cultural exchange between India and China is characterized by a combination of trade and efforts to establish contacts with each other. According to *Shiji* (Records of the Grand Historian), Zhang Qian (unknown — 114 BC) started his journey for the Western Regions in 135 BC on a diplomatic mission and came back 13 years later. In Bactria (present day Iran and Afghanistan), he found cloth produced in Sichuan and rods made of Qionglai bamboo. Local people said such articles were from merchants who came from Sichuan and were doing business in India. When the Emperor Wu of Han (Liu Che, 156 BC — 87 BC) came to know about this, he sent envoys several times to Southwestern China to look for the passage to India, but was obstructed by local people. The passage through which Zhang Qian journeyed to the Western Regions was known as 'Silk Route'. With this route being opened, an increasing number of envoys were sent from China to India. According to Biographies of the Dayuan of *Shiji* when Zhang Qian was on his second trip to the Western Regions, he sent his deputy envoy to India. After Zhang Qian, in the first century BC, China on an average sent seven or eight missions to the Western Regions every year, with each mission consisting of more than 100 persons and taking eight or nine years to accomplish a round trip. Due to frequent contacts Chinese got a lot of information about India. In the section on "Biographies of Western Regions" in *Shiji*, the geographical position, products, traditions, *etc.* of some Indian places and their relationship with the Han Dynasty were recorded. In Southwestern China, the "Dian-Mian Route" (Yunnan-Burma) had existed for long as a route to India through which private trade activities were carried out. Moreover, in the 2nd century BC, there was also a sea route between India and China, which was known as "South Sea Route". In the section on Geography in *Han Shu* (Book of Han), a clear sea route from Guangdong to Kanci (present day Kanchipuram) as well as a specific shipping schedule was recorded. At that time, goods shipped to India from China mainly included gold and silk fabrics and those from India to China mainly consisted of gem, crystal and glassware.

Interactions Driven by Buddhism: Between 1st to 6th Centuries AD

This phase of India-China interactions is characterized by a combination of material and spiritual exchanges and the entry of Buddhism into China. In the 1st and 2nd centuries AD, the Silk Route had been interrupted from time to time, but the South Sea Route was available uninterrupted. In the year 59 AD, the King of Kanci sent people to bring a rhinoceros from China; the King of Gandhara (present day Kandahar in Afghanistan) sent a white elephant to China; and in the year 87 AD, Kushan King offered lions to China.

The most significant event in the history of India-China cultural exchange was the entry of Buddhism into China around the beginning of the present era. Initially, Buddhism won imperial recognition and was accepted by a few noblemen, who took Buddha as a god and worshipped him together with Laozi (an ancient Chinese philosopher and writer; a deity in religious Taoism and traditional Chinese religions). Later on, the followers of Buddha began to increase. According to the 6th century AD work, *Memoirs of Eminent Monks*, the first Indian monks went to China were Kasyapa Matanga, Dharmaratna and then An Shigao (prince of Parthia) and Lokaksema (from Gandhara). Other Indian monks then went to China and were engaged mainly in translating Buddhist sutras. In the 1st century AD, China built its first Buddhist temple, *i.e.*, White Horse Temple and the first sutras were translated into Chinese. In the 2nd century AD, Zhai Rong became a legendary figure in the Buddhist history of China. He was in-charge of land and water transportation in Guangling (present day Yangzhou of Jiangsu Province) and Danyang (in Jiangsu Province) and spent a large amount of money and material to build copper Buddha statues, pagodas and temples. Within his jurisdiction, those listening to and studying Buddhist scriptures would be exempted from compulsory labour service and more than 5000 families were converted into Buddhists. On Buddha's birth festival, he would provide a grand feast along the road attracting nearly 10,000 people to dine and celebrate.

From 220 to 580 AD, cultural exchanges had greatly developed with increasing movement of people and trade between India and China. The most prominent feature of this period was the large-scale eastward movement of Buddhism which was associated with a great number of Indian monks going to China to preach. According to *Memoirs of Eminent Monks*, there were as many as 30 or 40 monks who translated sutras, preached Buddhist teachings, and brought into China the knowledge and techniques related to Indian astronomy, calendar, medicine, architecture, painting, sculpture and so on.

In the 3rd century AD, Chinese began to go westward to seek the *dharma*. Zhu Shixing set out in 260 AD and crossed the Gobi Desert to arrive at Khotan which was near India and had many Indian residents. There he found a sutra in Sanskrit and asked someone to bring it back to China, while he remained in Khotan. About 20 years later, Dharmaraksa went to the Western Regions for Buddhist sutras and there he visited various kingdoms and collected many sutras. He was said to have learnt as many as 36 languages. Later he took 165 Sanskrit sutras back to China and translated them and preached Buddhist doctrines in Dunhuang, Chang'an, and other places. In the 4th century AD, Kumarajiva was a representative of such pilgrims. At the age of nine, he went from Kucha (an ancient Buddhist Kingdom located on the branch of the Silk Route that ran along the northern edge of the Taklamakan Desert in the Tarim Basin and south of the Muzat River) with his mother to study *dharma* in India and began the return journey at the age of 12. In 385 AD, he went to Liangzhou in Gansu Province. In 401 AD, Yao Xing, the Emperor of Later Qin (366 — 416 AD), invited him to Chang'an and gave him the status of Teacher of the State. Thereafter, he settled in Chang'an, translating sutras and setting up a translation workshop, where he translated more than 300 volumes of sutras. He had 3000 followers whom he used to preached Buddhist texts.

Faxian along with nine other fellow students came to India to seek the Buddhist Vinaya. Some of them returned midway, some fell sick and died, and some permanently settled in India. But, Faxian visited holy places in India, studied *dharma* and gathered and transcribed sutras. Around 414 AD, he went to Sri Lanka, Java, and other places and returned to China by sea route. Later, he wrote a memoir known as *A Record of Buddhism Kingdoms* (also, known as *Biography of Faxian*) and translated many sutras.

Political Contacts: During 3rd to 6th century AD, more frequent contacts were made between Indian and Chinese states. In 428 AD, the Emperor Wen of Song received a letter of credence from Candrapria, the King of Kapilavastu. In 502 AD, the Emperor Wu of Liang received an official letter from the Gupta King which was recorded in Chinese official documents. The southern states of China mainly maintained contacts with the southern kingdoms of India via the maritime route. According to *Wei Shu* (classic Chinese historical text complied by Wei Shou from 551 to 554 AD and is an important text describing the history of the Northern Wei and Eastern Wei from 386 to 550 AD), from 451 to 521 AD, envoys along with some merchants from across India came to the Northern Wei, at least, 27 times and the Northern Wei also sent envoys to India several times, mainly to the Kingdoms in the North of India through the Silk route. During this period, Indian envoys and merchants took to

China many rare objects and animals while the Chinese exported to India mainly silk and silk products.

Technologies: Indian envoys, merchants and monks brought with them the knowledge of astronomy, calendar and medicine into China along with sutras. The book *Sui Shu* (official history of Sui dynasty written by Wei Zeng) mentions a number of books in its bibliographical section on astronomy and the calendar, such as *Longshu Pusa Yaofang* (Nagarjuna Prescriptions) as well as books on medicine and fitness regimen, such as *Longshu Pusa Yangxingfang* (Nagarjuna Mind Cultivation). These books were available in China and had an impact on Chinese astronomy, calendar and medicine. According to the *Memoirs of Eminent Monks* (Vol. IV), Yu Fakai was a follower of Jivaka Komarabhacca (a famous physician in ancient India and was personal physician of Indian King Bimbisara and Gautama Buddha) and had also a good knowledge of acupuncture. He combined the traditional Chinese medicine with Indian medicine. Tao Hongjing (also known as Tongming was a polymath Chinese author, scholar, calligrapher, alchemist, pharmacologist, and astronomer during the Northern and Southern dynasties) introduced Indian theories in his works on medicine.

Translations: For propagating Buddhism into China, it was necessary to translate sutras into Chinese. During the initial period, Indian monks as well as Chinese were involved in translation of sutras into local languages. During the 1st to 3rd centuries AD, most important translators were Dharmaraksa, Vighna, Zhu Luyan, Zhi Qian, Kang Senghui, Baiyan, Samghavarman, Tan Di, Nie Chengyuan, Zhi Qian, and many others. Among all these, Dharmaraksa was the most important translator and he translated Mahayana sutras in Chinese, several of which had profound effects on East Asian Buddhism. During the 4th to 6th centuries AD, there were Dao'an, Srimitra, Boyuan, Buddhabhadra, Dharmanandi, Samghabhuti, Samghadeva, Samgharaksa, Zhu Fonian, Dharmayasa, Kumarajiva, Punyatara, Dharmaruci, Vimalaksa, Buddhayawa, Buddhabhadr, Dharmaksema, Faxian, Gunavarman, Xie Lingyun, Zhimeng, Sanga Gendun, Gunabhadra, Paramartha, Bodhiruci and Narendrayasas. Dao'an and Kumarajiva were the most important among the above-mentioned translators who not only translated many classic volumes but also proposed their own translation theories.

Architecture: During the period of 3rd to 6th centuries AD, many Buddhist temples were built in China. In 247 AD, during the region of Sun Quan, the Jianchu Temple was built in Nanjing. Many Buddhist temples were built in Guangdong, Zhejiang, Jiangsu, Jiangxi, Hunan, Hubei and Sichuan while in the North, according to *Chongkan Luoyang Jialan Ji* by Xuan-zhi Yang, in Luoyang alone there were 42 Buddhist temples in the 3rd century AD. In the Northern Wei Dynasty, as many as 1367 Buddhist temples were built. Buddhist temples in China formed a unique school of architecture by combining the traditional Chinese style and artistic characteristics of Indian buildings. The pagoda (a tiered tower with multiple eaves) was a form of building structure learned from India and later on Chinese constructed various forms of pagoda. Similarly, cave temples originated in India and spread to the Xinjiang region in China in about the 3rd century AD and then were introduced into the heartland of China, reaching the peak of development in the period from the 4th to 9th centuries AD. For example, Kizil Grottoes in Xinjiang, Dunhuang Mogao Grottoes and Majishan Grottoes in Gansu, Yungang Grottoes in Shanxi and Longmen Grottoes in Henan were all constructed during this period. These grottoes were influenced by Indian architecture, sculpture, painting and so on. These Buddhist temples were a place for cultural activities as well as a seat of learning and practice by followers. During a Buddhist event, a grand celebration would be held and there would be acrobatics, dancing and singing as well as a procession of Buddha figures. Chinese learnt these practices from India.

Literature: During the period of 3rd to 6th centuries AD, following the introduction of Buddhism into China, there appeared a number of ghost stories, which were called "supplemental textbooks for Buddhism" by Zhou Shuren (with pen name Lu Xun), a leading figure of modern Chinese literature. These stories not only introduced to Chinese the Buddhist outlook on world, life and morality and a way of thinking but also testified to the rich imagination and literary creation of ancient Indians.

Drawing and Painting: Following the introduction of Buddhism into China, new subjects and skills were introduced to Chinese drawing and painting. Between 3rd to 6th centuries AD, there were a number of painters who were good at painting Buddhist pictures, *e.g.*, Cao Buxing, a native of Wuxing (present day Huzhou of Zhejiang Province), under the influence of Indian sculpture, drew vivid folds on the clothes of human figures, that seemed to come alive; Dai Kui (poet, painter and musician, and was one of the first to establish the tradition of scholarly amateur painting), a native of Suxian of Anhui Province, drew many figures of Buddha and carved a 60 feet tall wooden Amitabha (the Buddha of Infinite Light); Gu Kaizhi (also, known as Changkang), a native of Wuxi, caused a great sensation by his painting of Vimalakirti on the wall of Waguan Temple in Nanjing, capital of China's Eastern Jiangsu Province; Zhang Sengyao (a famous Liang dynasty painter), a native of Suzhou in Southeastern Jiangsu Province of East China, was good at painting Buddhist figures and often went to temples to paint murals. Zhang Sengyao once produced a painting on the door of a temple, which, from the distance, appeared to be in relief, while from nearby it appeared smooth and even. This skill was exported to China from India.

Music and Dance: This period saw the emergence of Buddhist music in China, largely due to Cao Zhi (also, known as Zijian), prince of the state of Cao Wei in Three Kingdoms period of China. In 230 AD, Cao Zhi adapted and composed the Prince Ode and other pieces of music. In the 6th century AD, the Emperor Wu of Liang reformed the court music, added much Buddhist content and ordered the musician Shen Yue to compose Buddhist music and play it at the royal court.

Heightened Political, Cultural and Commercial Contacts: Between 6th to 10th Centuries AD

In 618 AD, with the rise of Tang Dynasty a powerful and prosperous era began in China. During the rule of this dynasty, China adopted a policy of opening to the outside world. It was the period when a large number of Indians came to China to trade, live, or serve in an official capacity. Enthusiasm for both Buddhism and political contacts was the main characteristic of that period.

During the Tang Dynasty the number of pilgrims to India rose to a peak level. According to the *Buddhist Monk's Pilgrimage of Tang Dynasty* by Yi Jing (originally named Zhang Wenming), from 641 to 691 AD, more than 40 Chinese monks visited India. This did not include the famous names such as Faxian (who travelled by foot from China to India, visiting many sacred Buddhist sites in what are now Xinjiang, Pakistan, India, Nepal, Bangladesh and Sri Lanka), Xuanzang (monk, scholar, traveler and translator who travelled to India and described the interaction between Chinese Buddhism and Indian Buddhism during the early Tang Dynasty), Hui Ri, Han Guang, Wu Kong and Zhi Xuan. This rising passion for Buddhism in the Tang Dynasty promoted cultural exchange between India and China and quickened the fusion of the Chinese culture with the Indian culture. Chinese Buddhism became more mature and different sects arose, *e.g.*, San-ron-shu (Three Sastras), Tiantai, Hosso-shu (Dharmalaksana), Avatamsaka, Vinaya, Dhyana, Pure Land and Esoteric Buddhism.

During this period, Buddhism was also introduced into Tibet. In the first half of the 7th century AD, Songtsan Gampo unified the greater part of the Qinghai-Tibet Plateau and founded the Tubo Kingdom with Lhasa as the center. He successively married the Princess Bhrikuti of Nepal and the Princess Wencheng of the Tang Dynasty and built Buddhist temples for them. In 755 AD, the young Trisong Detsen succeeded to the throne. He was the son of Me Agtsom and the 37th Emperor of Tibet. When he grew up, he began to believe in Buddhism, inviting Santaraksita (abbot of Nalanda) and Padmasambhava (founder of the Nyingma school of tradition) from India and building temples. To propagate Buddhism in Tibet, Trisong Detsen invited masters from India including, among others, Dharmakirti (a Buddhist philosopher from Nalanda, one of the key scholars of epistemology in Buddhist philosophy and one of the primary theorists of Buddhist atomism) and Vimalamitra (his teachers were Buddhaguhya, Jnanasutra and Sri Simha, and was supposed to have vowed to take rebirth every hundred years), to teach Buddhism and 12 Indian monks to preside over the Tibetans' monastic ceremony. However, since the Tibetan Bon faith was still powerful, in 836 AD, some of its more powerful adherents began to eradicate Buddhism which consequently nearly became extinct in Tibet. This period was known as the first propagation of Tibetan Buddhism. Around the 7th century AD, Theravada Buddhism expanded from Burma into southern Yunnan but soon disappeared due to wars and ensuing chaos. After the 8th century AD, Buddhism began to spread in the Nanzhao area of Yunnan and developed quickly.

Political Contacts: The *Sui Shu* (Book of Sui Dynasty), in the section on Western Regions, referred that the Emperor Yang of Sui of the Sui Dynasty sent Wei Jie, Du Xingman and others to visit kingdoms in the Western Region and there they obtained besides sutras, agate cups and other things. According to *Tang Shu* (Book of Tang Dynasty), *Tongdian* (Chinese institutional history and encyclopedia text covering a panoply of topics from high antiquity through the year 756 AD) and *Cefu Yuangui* (largest encyclopedia compiled during the Chinese Song Dynasty), the Tang Dynasty had many contacts with Indian states while the Indian rulers also sent many envoys to China. According to *Jiu Tang Shu* (Old Book of Tang), Shiladitya sent envoys to China in 641 AD and the Emperor Taizong of the Tang Dynasty wrote him a letter along with an imperial jade seal. The Tang empire also sent many envoys to India, and among them, Wang Xuance (diplomat and the ambassador) was the most reputed and he was sent to India by Tang Taizong in response to Harshavardhana's sending an ambassador to China. Wang Xuance visited India three or four times and wrote Zhongtian Zhuguo Xingji (also known as Wang Xuance Xiguo Xingzhuan) consisting of ten volumes, with three volumes of maps and charts and covering religion, geography, politics, law, arts and customs.

Drawing and Painting: Chinese painting was enriched and diversified during the Tang Dynasty. There were many great masters with new schools constantly emerging, distinctive styles being established and exotic skills being assimilated. For example, Yuchi Yiseng, a Khotanese nobleman and painter (Khotan was an ancient Iranic Saka Buddhist kingdom located on the branch of the Silk Road that ran along the Southern edge of the Taklamakan Desert in the Tarim Basin, present day Xinjiang in China), was recommended to visit Chang'an by the King of Khotan and was highly appreciated by the imperial court. At that time, his murals could be seen in the big temples of Chang'an and Luoyang. Wu Daozi (also known as the "Sage of Painting") was a native of Yuxian of Henan and his legendary life was recorded in many documents. He used to do paintings at temples and his famous painting, "Birth of Gautama Buddha", portraying Suddhodana and Maya Devi carrying the newly born Siddhartha to the Mahesvara can still be seen.

Music, Dance and Drama: In its music section, the *Sui Shu* mentioned that in 581 AD the royal court of the Sui Dynasty put in place seven ensembles with Indian music as one of them and that 30 years later, there were nine ensembles with Indian music still being in the group. During the Tang Dynasty, Buddhist music became very popular and many forms of music could be traced to India. Also, some musical instruments were introduced from India. According to the fifth volume of the *Life of Xuanzang* (Xuanzang was famous for his sixteen-year pilgrimage to India and he was also a translator of Buddhist scriptures), when meeting with Xuanzang Indian ruler Shiladitya asked about the musical composition *Qin Wang Po Zhen Yue* (Prince Qin Breaking through the Enemy Array) indicating that Chinese music was well recognized in India as well.

Cultural exchanges between India and China resulted in the birth of Chinese dance and drama and their enrichment. During the 9th century AD, Buddhist temples became places for cultural events and entertainment. Big temples, such as the Da Ci'en (mercy and kindness) temple, had their own theatre for music, dance and acrobatic performance.

Literature, Astronomy and Mathematics: During the Tang Dynasty, some great poets, such as Li Bai, Du Fu, Bai Juyi, Liu Yuxi and Han Yu, had close contacts with monks from India. There were also *Tang Chuan Qi* (form of short story in the classical language developed in the Tang Dynasty) in which traces of Indian influence could be found. Under the influence of Buddhism, the Tang period saw a new genre of literature, known as Bianwen. It was believed that reciting Bianwen on the Buddhist stories of gods and ghosts such as Xiangmo Bianwen and Mulian Jiumu Bianwen disseminated the concepts of karma and samsara. It has had a profound influence on later generations of Chinese writers.

Some Buddhist texts had subject matter related to astronomy and calendar. *Su Yao Jing* consisted of two volumes and offered a detailed introduction of the Indian knowledge system on constellations, stars, the zodiac and astrology. It is an important reference work for the study of ancient Indian and Chinese astronomy and calendar. According to Calendar-I of *Jiu Tang Shu* (Old Book of Tang), Volume 32, during the reign of the Empress Wu Zetian, Gautama Luo created the Guang Zhai Calendar, and during the region of the Emperor Xuanzong, Yi Xing produced the Da Yan Calendar; all of which were influenced by ancient Indian astronomy and calendar. In the 8th century AD, three families from India served as court astronomers. They were Kasyapa, Kumara and Gautama. According to written records and archaeological information, Gautama family members lived in China for five generations in the sequence of Gautama Yi, Gautama Luo, Gautama Siddha, Gautama Zhuan and Gautama Yan. Gautama Yi had gone to China from India in the early Tang Dynasty, four subsequent generations also served as royal astrologers in the Tang Dynasty. Among these five generations, Gautama Siddha was the most famous and compiled the 120-volume *Treatise on Astrology of the Kaiyuan Era*, introducing various astrological theories and schools in ancient China and recording Chinese observation of heavenly bodies and their knowledge about the universe. Navagraha Calendar, translated by him in 718 AD, is also of great research value because, with the translation of the Navagraha Calendar, Chinese began to know of Indian arithmetic. It showed how to write Indian numerals and listed 10 numbers from zero to nine, *i.e.*, the predecessors of the current numerals 0 to 9.

Technologies and Medicine: The technique of making cane sugar was known to Indians from ancient times. According to some literatures translated around the 5th century AD, India's technology of making can sugar had already been introduced into China at that time. According to the Biography of Xuan Zang (volume IV) in the sequel of *Memoirs of Eminent Monks*, the Taizong Emperor sent Wang Xuance to India to study the boiling technique of sugar. The Mahabodhi Temple sent two craftsmen and eight monks to visit to China with Wang Xuance and help China with sugar manufacturing. The paper-making technique may have had links with India. In the middle of 2nd century AD, paper was already in use in Khotan (present day Xinjiang). It is very close to India and so it is possible that Indians might have known paper at that time. In the 7th century AD, Yi Jing came to India and found that paper was used here. It is assumed that paper making technique was brought into Tibet in the middle of 7th century AD and later from there it came to India. Indians learned the technique of making silk from China.

Ophthalmology was practiced in ancient India. During the Tang Dynasty, oculist-monks from India used the so-called 'Gold Grate Method' to cure cataract and Bai Juyi (poet and Tang Dynasty government official) and Liu Yuxi (poet, philosopher and essayist active during Tang Dynasty) both wrote poems to praise this technique. A medical practitioner Sun Simiao wrote two books—*Qian Jin Yao Fang* and *Qian Jin Yi Fang*, the former included recipes compiled by him based on historical documents and private prescriptions in the year 652 AD, and the latter was composed 30 years later on the basis of his medical practice. In the book *Qian Jin Yao Fang*, Sun cited medical theories in Buddhist texts, thinking that people would not fall ill if four elements inside their bodies, *i.e.*, earth, water, fire and wind were coordinated while lack of coordination would lead to illness. The *Qian Jin Yi Fang* had a number of Indian prescriptions, some of which used Indian medicinal herbs. Wang Tao was another medical doctor who adopted the "four elements" theory and included many Indian prescriptions.

Linguistics, Lexicography and Translations: Indians had paid attention to the study of phonetics for long and there were already grammar books and a highly scientific alphabet system in ancient India. Buddhist culture from India, to some extent, promoted linguistics in China and had a significant impact, especially in respect of phonology, syntax and lexicography. The term "Zimu" (letter) first appeared in sutras translated in the early 5th century AD and was also recorded in *Xitan Ziji* by the monk Zhiguang in the Tang Dynasty. This implied that "Zimu" was directly related to the spread of Sanskrit.

For understanding Sutras, Chinese monks compiled some dictionaries among which *Yiqiejng Yinyi* (A Phonetic and Semantic Dictionary for all Buddhist Sutras), consisting of 25 volumes, was compiled by Xuan Ying around the year 648 AD. This book explained terms chosen from 450 Buddhist Hinayana texts with many quotations from ancient Chinese books. Huilin in his 100 volumes *Yiqiejing Yinyi* (Pronunciation and Meaning in the Complete Buddhist Canon) selected terms from 1300 Buddhist texts to annotate them with a great number of quotations from ancient Chinese books. To facilitate translation of sutra, Chinese-Sanskrit dictionaries were compiled. For example, Yijing compiled the *Fanyu Qianziwen* (A Thousand Sanskrit Words) using Sanskrit to explain 1000 Chinese characters. Indian monks were also involved in compiling Chinese-Sanskrit dictionaries. For example, the one-volume *Tangfan Shuangyu Duidui Ji* was compiled by Antatabodha and Pragunamishash, the two Indian monks.

From the late 6th to early 7th centuries AD, Yan Cong and Dharmagupta were the main translators. Yan Cong, in addition to presiding over the translation workshops in the Sui Dynasty and compiling *Zhong Jing Mulu*, also translated 23 sutras. In the early Tang Dynasty, Prabhakaramitra of Nalanda went to China. In the 629 AD, the Emperor Taizong decreed sutras to be translated at Da Xing Shan Temple, with Prabhakaramitra as the chief translator.

Frequent Contacts Across the Sea: Between 10th to 17th Centuries AD

During 10th to 17th centuries AD, cultural exchanges between India and China continued to deepen. Cultural activities driven by Buddhism had weakened and the practice of Chinese seeking to find the dharma in India was about to come to an end. But, sea-borne traffic and booming trade had reached to a very high level during this period. According to the records of *Fo Zu Tong Ji* (A General History of Chinese Buddhism), from 972 to 1053 AD, some Indian monks went to China to translate and preach sutras, but no more thereafter. Also, the era of Chinese monks' westward pilgrimage was nearing to an end. According to *Fo Zu Tong Ji*, in 966 AD, Emperor Taizu of the Song Dynasty arranged for 157 pilgrims to be sent to India. This was assumed to be the last officially sponsored pilgrimage. A century later, Fan Chengda wrote *Wu Chuan Ji* on the basis of available information and recorded the journey of one of these pilgrims, Jiye, who returned to China in 976 AD. But even later, other pilgrims came back from or went to India, indicating that travel then was quite convenient.

With the Muslim invasion of India in the 11th century AD, Buddhism had declined to a very low level. On the other hand, during the reign of Emperor Renzong of the Song Dynasty, pilgrimages from China to India, that lasted six centuries, virtually ceased. However, these activities continued in Tibet. From the late 10th to late 15th centuries AD, Tibetan Buddhism had its "second propagation" and its leading sects such as Nyingma, Ganden, Sakya, Kagyu and Gelug, had been formed. An Indian scholar Smriti Jnana Kirti, master of pancavidya and esoteric Buddhism, went to Tibet in the latter half of the 10th century AD and disseminated Buddhism there, translated many tantric texts and wrote *Yu Yan Men Lun*, a Tibetan grammar book. Rinchen Zangpo was one of the most important figures in the revival of Tibetan Buddhism. He came to India three times and successively studied under 75 scholars. Back in Tibet, he translated 50 sutrayanas and 108 tantrayanas. Atisa, a Theravada preacher at Vikramshila, was invited to expound Buddhism in Tibet in 1043 AD. He had many followers and his *Pu Ti Dao Deng Lun* (A Lamp for the Enlightenment Path) had a great influence in Tibet.

From 10th to 17th centuries AD, Indian astrology, hetuvidya, medicine, phonology, literature, arts, language and writing, all had a significant impact on Tibet. In the same era, esoteric Buddhism in the Dali Kingdom (Yunnan) and Theravada in South Yunnan also developed rapidly. After the middle of 10th century AD, Neo-Confucianism gained prominence, evolving and absorbing Buddhist thinking in its course. In the field of literature, Zhi Guai and Chuanqi novels (Song Dynasty), Zaju Opera (Yuan Dynasty) and vernacular novels (Ming Dynasty) assimilated Buddhist ethics and recalled and retold the golden days of Buddhist pilgrimage. Cave temples continued to be built and paintings still preserved many Buddhist themes in China.

Political Contacts: During 10th to 17th centuries AD, political and diplomatic contacts between Indian states and China were by and large maintained through the sea route. For example, according to the *Song Shi* (History of the Song Dynasty) and *Fo Zu Tong Ji* (A General History of Chinese Buddhism), in 1015 AD, the Chola ruler sent envoys to China with Sanskrit Sutras and a letter from King Rajaraja. South Indians rulers came to know about the Song Dynasty through merchants coming by sea. According to *Song Shi* (History of Song), South Indian and North Indian states sent envoys to China many times and they usually brought along them gifts, such as pearl, ivory, medicine, spice and so on. Yuan Dynasty left several records concerning maritime contacts with Indian states. During the region of Kublai Khan (the fifth Khagan of the Mongol Empire, reigning from 1260 to 1294; founded the Yuan Dynasty in China as a conquest dynasty in 1271, and ruled as the first Yuan emperor until his death in 1294), diplomatic contacts between India and China were most prolific. According to *Yuan Shi* (History of the Yuan Dynasty), from 1272 to 1294, Yuan Dynasty sent envoys to India 11 times while various Indian kingdoms sent envoys to China 13 times. In the early 15th century AD, China further extended its maritime navigation and Zheng He's (a Chinese mariner, explorer, diplomat, and fleet admiral during China's early Ming Dynasty) seven expeditions to the Western Ocean served to expand India-China interaction. Zheng visited several places in India. Fei Xin, Ma Huan and Gong Zhen, who had accompanied Zheng in these expeditions, wrote *Xing Cha Sheng Lan* (The Description of the Starry Raft), *Ying Ya Sheng*

Lan (The General Survey of the Ocean Shores) and *Xi Yang Fan Guo Zhi* (The Annals of Foreign Nations in the Western Ocean), respectively. Around the same time, Hou Xian visited India several times on a diplomatic mission. According to *Xing Cha Sheng Lan*, *Ying Ya Sheng Lan* and *Ming Shi*, Ming Dynasty had contact with many Indian kingdoms or places, such as Delhi, Jaunpur, Bengal, Vijayanagar, Cochin, Kollam, Cail (on the East coast of South India), Comorin, Chola (on the Southwest coast of India), Calicut, and the Andaman and Nicobar Islands.

Commodity Trade: Through the sea route bulk commodity exchange began between India and China. According to *Zhu Fan Zhi* (The Barbarian Countries) by Zhao Rukuo of the Song Dynasty, in the port of Quanzhou there were many foreign merchants, including those from India and Indian monks preaching Buddhism. At that time Quanzhou became the centre of commerce as well as religious activities. According to *Ling Wai Dai Da* by Zhou Qufei of the Song Dynasty, Gulin (present day Kollam in Kerala) at the Southern end of the West coast of India also had close connections through sea route with China. During the Yuan Dynasty, Wang Dayuan (a traveler from Quanzhou, China) made two major trips on ships to investigate the seas South and West of China, first setting out in 1330 AD and returning four years later. He sailed along the South China Sea and visited many places in Southeast Asia and reached as far as South Asia, landing in Bengal, Sri Lanka and India. The second voyage he started in 1337 AD and returned back two years later. He visited many places in India and after returning to China, in 1349 AD, he completed *Dao Yi Zhi Lue*—this book offers a detailed introduction to various places in India and is of great help to understand maritime culture exchange between the Yuan Dynasty and Indian states. Whatever places he visited, he would pay attention to the geography, soil, produce, trade, race, and customs. At that time, India was known for gems, pearls, cotton cloth, linen, medicine, spice, *etc.*, while China was mainly known for silk, coloured silk satin, cloves, cardamom, blue-and-white porcelain, white porcelain, *etc.* Ma Huan (pen name Mountain-Woodcutter, was a Chinese voyager and translator who accompanied Admiral Zheng He on three of his seven expeditions to the Western Ocean) in his book *Yingya Shenglan* provided detailed information about the countries visited by him over the course of Zheng He's treasure voyages. For example, about Cochin, he recorded information about its people's dress, houses, social structure and professions of five classes of the population, the king's beliefs, religion, climate, weights and measure, currency, marriage and funeral ceremonies, farm and livestock produce, as well as on its trade with China. He had also mentioned that Zheng He had erected a monument in Calicut in 1407 AD and provided the text of the inscription.

Medicine: The sea route facilitated the bulk movement of medicines and related materials during the period 10th to 17th centuries AD. The *Yuan Shi* (History of Yuan) recorded details of medicine sent as tribute by Indian states to China. The *Ming Shi* (History of Ming) had a list of tribute items from Bengal to China, including frankincense, pine resin, five-spice powder, *etc*. The books *Xing Cha Sheng Lan* (a historical work written by Fei Xin who had served as a soldier in the third, fifth, and seventh treasure voyages under the command of Admiral Zheng He) and *Xi Yang Fan Guo Zhi* (a report submitted by Ming Dynasty envoy Chen Cheng to the Yongle Emperor about the eighteen countries and territories he visited as a member of an embassy contingency to the kingdom of Timurid in Central Asia) mentioned that Indians were very fond of musk from China and that Chinese traded musk with them. The *Compendium of Materia Medica* (a Chinese herbology volume) compiled by Li Shizhen during the Ming Dynasty contains valuable information about medical exchanges between India and China. It is a work epitomizing the materia medica known at that time and introduced and verified many medicines from India and by using many quotations from Buddhist texts, provided their Sanskrit names. It is too extensive to be compared to any similar book from the past. It also included some Indian prescriptions, explained the preparation of medicines and evaluated their efficacy, indicating that these prescriptions then were in actual use. Some prescriptions required Indian medicinal materials, and this could be taken as evidence that several Indian recipes had been assimilated into traditional Chinese medicine.

Entry of Western Powers: During the mid-14th to mid-17th centuries AD, the major trading companies of Western powers, such as those of Portugal, Holland and Britain gradually penetrated the intra-Asian trade and started to control the silk trade between India and China. Western merchants took India as an intermediate station, through which they transported large amounts of raw silk from China to Europe. Although, a large amount of raw silk was imported to India from China during this period, it was mainly for re-export to Europe, and local sales in India were quite limited. According to the records found in the *Ying Ya Sheng Lan* and other Ming era works, Indian states were already able to manufacture silk, and therefore, people were using silk products there.

During the late Ming period, the Dutch East India Company established bases for trade with China in Southeast Asia and Taiwan and used to purchase large amount of Chinese porcelain at very low prices which they would first transport to the Southeast coast of India, and then ship to Europe. Due to this, large amounts of Chinese porcelain could be found in different places in India, not just in the coastal regions but also in the interior regions, such as in Assam in Northeast India. At that time, it had become a fashion among the rulers, courtiers and high officials of various Indian states to collect Chinese porcelain articles. In India tea was brought from China. Early Ming records, such as the works of Ma Huan, Fei Xin and Gong Zhen who had visited to the West together with Zheng He, have not any reference to Indians drinking tea, while on the contrary, there are records of other beverages consumed by Indians such as cow milk, rose water, mulse and all kinds of wine. Ma Huan's *Ying Ya Sheng Lan* said categorically that "no tea was sold in the Indian market", while the records of Western countries also said that there was no tea drinking custom in India. Therefore, it is established that tea drinking was introduced in India only under the influence of the large amounts of tea shipped through India from China to the West by the British and Dutch East India Companies.

CHAPTER 2

India-China Relations in Pre-Independence Era

India and China share plenty of common concerns and stances on a variety of important issues concerning world peace and development right from pre-independence era. A look at Indian and Chinese independence struggles shows that the anti-imperialistic efflorescence of the Indian and Chinese people manifested in a major way as a challenge to the colonial order for the first time during the First War of Independence (1857-59) in India and the Taiping Uprising (1850-64) in China. The reaction of Indian and Chinese people against their common enemy (Britishers) was the same. For the first-time Indian soldiers were stationed in China and switched over to the Taipings (Taiping Rebellion, radical political and religious upheaval that was probably the most important event in China in the 19th century. It lasted for some 14 years, 1850-64, ravaged 17 provinces, took an estimated 20 million lives) and fought shoulder to shoulder against imperialists and Qing Government. It was due to the synergy between the cultures of India and China that the nationalists and revolutionaries of India and China developed deep mutual contact that turned into friendship amidst their anti-imperialist struggle. India and China became the natural allies and used various ways to remove the intruder. They supported Bal Gangadhar Tilak (first leader of the Indian Independence Movement), who carried out activities like Shivaji's commemorative meetings as far as Tokyo to make the Indian voice of anti-imperialism reach outside India. Besides, the nationalists like Ananda Mohan Bose (co-founder of Indian National Association—one of the earliest Indian political organizations, and a senior leader of the Indian National Congress), Rash Behari Bose (a revolutionary leader against the British Raj in India, one of the key organizers of the Ghadar

Mutiny and later, the Indian National Army), Manabendra Nath Roy (an Indian revolutionary, radical activist and political theorist), Abdul Hafiz Mohamed Barakatullah (an Indian revolutionary with sympathy for the Pan-Islamic movement), Lala Lajpat Rai (also known as Punjab Kesari), and many others outstanding pioneers of Indian freedom movement maintained good contracts and friendship with Sun Yat-sen (a Chinese physician, writer, philosopher, calligrapher and revolutionary, the first president and founding father of the Republic of China) who whole heartedly supported the Indian cause and rendered all possible help to them.

With the rise of Mahatma Gandhi in Indian politics, the entire Indian freedom movement turned into a mass movement, which had caught the attention of Chinese rulers. Mahatma Gandhi took spiritual world order or spiritual management of society and worked to bring in order through civilized means such as Satyagraha and Ahimsa. He made nonviolence his principle creed and never compromised with it. He also opposed Japanese attack against China during the Second World War in an open letter to Japanese people saying how he "intensely disliked it", criticizing the move by saying "Japan has descended to imperial ambition". Chinese people had upheld him as a symbol of Eastern civilization who manifested himself to represent this civilization in various shapes and forms. The Chinese media had also paid utmost attention and widely covered the Indian freedom struggle in various newspapers and journals.

A new chapter was written in the history of India-China relations during the War of Resistance and Second World War. So long as China suffered at the hands of Japanese, the reverberation affected India too. India dispatched a medical mission to China in 1938 to help them in their War of Resistance. Jawaharlal Nehru made bonds of friendship even stronger when he visited China in 1939. The period from 1905 to 1947 was the period when both the people of India and China rendered support and sympathy to each other in their common struggle for independence from Britishers. It was the demand of time that India and China should necessarily come nearer to each other for the vast and tremendous potentials of economic cooperation in the New World after the war.

Forging New Connections in Modern Times: Between 18th Century AD to 1949

Interactions between India and China continued based on trade, but under new conditions of nationalism and anti-imperialism. Technological and other changes helped to bring India and China closer in some respects, while political developments in some cases led to new strains in their relations. Western colonialism and imperialist expansion in this part of the world had affected the age-old relationship between the two countries and civilization in many ways. On the other hand, this was also an era in which political activists, intellectuals, writers and artists in both the countries sought to rediscover each other in the new conditions of social, political, technological, and economical transformations.

Trade: During this era, overland trade between India and China continued, and there was the trans-Karakoram trade between Punjab, Ladakh and Kashmir in Indian side and the oasis towns such as Kashgar and Yarkand in Xinjiang in Chinese side. There was also trade between Kashmir and other parts of Northern and Northeastern India with Tibet. However, the volume of overland trade was not large because it was carried out in physically very difficult conditions using mules and ponies over the high mountain passes. Also, trade was vulnerable to changing political conditions in this region. In spite of all these things, overland trade between these regions persisted right until the middle of the 20th century AD.

Due to spectacular growth of the tea trade between China and Europe, maritime trade between India and China had revived. There was a flourishing intra-Asian maritime trade before and after the arrival of European traders in the Eastern waters in the 16th century AD. The commercial connection between India and China was maintained through the larger intra-Asian trade. However, from the last quarter of the 18th century AD, there was a huge increase in the direct trade between the emerging port of Bombay on the West coast of India and Guangzhou (port city Northwest of Hong Kong on the Pearl River) based on the export of raw cotton and later, opium from India to China. These exports were carried both by the British East India Company as well as by private Indian and Western traders.

Starting from the late 19th century AD, one of the major export from India to China was of manufactured cotton yarn. Indian cotton yarn had displaced British yarn from the Chinese market, and from about 1880 to 1905 almost completely monopolized the Chinese market for imported cotton yarn. The export of cotton yarn to China played a major role in stabilizing the growth of the emerging modern textile industry in India. However, during and after First World War, Chinese cotton yarn industry developed rapidly and by 1929, China was exporting cotton yarn to India.

In the middle of 19th century, the volume of goods imported to India from China was much less than that of goods exported to China from India. Therefore, China faced a huge trade deficit, which required silver to pay for the balance. India mainly exported cotton, opium, wheat and jute to China; whereas the main goods of China were raw silk, porcelain, tea and medicinal materials, mainly exported to Britain, France, Netherland, Spain and USA. During the period 1834 to 1845, the annual average value of the goods imported from China by India was only (1/80)th of the value of the goods exported from India to China. The goods imported from China included raw silk, tea, porcelain, rock candy, white sugar, alum, satin, camphor, paper, *etc.* During 1864 to 1891, the annual total volume of direct trade between India and China was on an average 27.77 million haikwan tales (a unit of value formerly used in China for reckoning customs duties and is equal to 1.20666 troy ounces of fine silver). In 1926, the total volume of trade between the two countries reached 95,113,114 haikwan tales, of which the total value of goods exported to China from India was 79,191,013 haikwan tales. During this period, India exported mainly cotton, rice and cotton yarn to China. Besides these, China also used to import flour, sugar, coal, kerosene, cement, jute and various kinds of cloth from India. On the other hand, imports from China included silk, tea, beans, eggs, peanuts, cowhide, sesame,

China wood oil, coal, cotton yarn, pig iron, *etc.* It should be noted that while cotton yarn had earlier been exported from India to China, during this period China began to export cotton yarn to India.

Transmission of Art: A by-product of the 19th century AD trade between India and China was the transmission of some artistic and cultural influences from China to India. However, compared to the pre-modern period, this transmission of Art was on a small scale. Traders from Bombay used to import from China silk cloth with the fine silk embroidery which was a specialty of Guangzhou (a sprawling port city Northwest of Hong Kong on the Pearl River). This had influenced the style of particularly women's and children's clothing among the Parsis. The characteristic gara sarees, with their distinctly Chinese style embroidery, were a product of the fusion of Chinese and Indian styles. The tanchoi type of silk brocade weaving in India was also learned and adapted from Chinese weavers. Chinese porcelain and furniture were also greatly appreciated and used in India. Indian also learnt portrait painting and the art of reverse glass painting from Chinese.

Diasporas: The overland and maritime trade led to the exchanges of people between India and China. Traders from Punjab used to stay in Xinjiang only for the duration of the trading season. However, many Kashmiris migrated to Xinjiang and settled down there, eventually losing their contacts with their native places and even languages and becoming a part of local community. Financiers and moneylenders from Shikarpur in Sindh (in present day Pakistan) could also be seen in the main towns of Southern Xinjiang. The maritime trade led to groups of merchants from India reaching on the Chinese coast. They were mainly from Parsi community, Baghdadi Jewish community based in Bombay and some Muslim Bohra and Ismaili traders. With the opening of treaty ports (the name given to the port cities in China and Japan that were opened to foreign trade by the unequal treaties with the Western powers) after the First Opium War and the growth of Hong Kong as a port, many of Indian merchants took up more or less permanent residence in China. From the import-export trade, their interests diversified to include other lines of business in eastern China's port cities, such as banking, real estate, manufacturing, and share brokerage. In the 20th century AD, a large number of people from the Marwari and Sindhi communities went to Hong Kong and China's port cities. Another group of Indians who went to China and stayed on there were policemen and watchmen, especially from Punjab. The policemen were mainly based in Hong Kong and in the foreign concessions at Shanghai, Guangzhou, Tianjin, Hankou and so on, whereas the Indian watchmen were more widely dispersed among smaller towns as well. At one time, they accounted for approximately half of the Indians in Eastern China. This group, along with the merchants in Western China and in the Chinese ports, were mostly repatriated to India during the 1930s and 1940s.

A large number of Chinese also came to India, but they were mainly concentrated in and around Calcutta and Bombay. However, it was only in Calcutta that their numbers grew large enough to form a Chinse settlement in India. The first Chinese known to have settled in India in this period was Yang Dazhao (Tong Atchew) who received a grant of land from the British authorities in Bengal to set up a sugar mill at the end of the 18th century AD. Thereafter, more Chinese continued to arrive in India throughout the 19th century AD. Chinese were also brought to Assam to work on the tea plantations that the British established. Their skills in tea cultivation and processing were used to develop an extensive tea industry in India. From the early 20th century AD, due to turbulent conditions in China, large numbers of Chinese including women and children came to India. But, after the war between India and China in 1962, large numbers of Chinese went back, and their population dwindled in India.

The Ports of Hong Kong, Shanghai and Bombay: These three mega port cities of Asia developed to a large extent due to the India-China connection. Indian merchants played a significant role in the early growth of Hong Kong. Among the well-known individuals and families from India who can be considered among the builders of Hong Kong were the Sassoons (Baghdadi Jewish descent from Mumbai), the Ruttonjees (Parsi family from Mumbai), the Kadoories (originally Mizrahi Jews from Baghdad, established in Mumbai), Paul Chater (British businessman of Armenian descent from Kolkata), H.N. Mody (Parsi businessman from Mumbai) and so on. Many of them not only became business tycoons, but also played a key role in the development of the infrastructure, education and in the governance of Hong Kong. The Sassoons were a prominent part of the Shanghai business community and owned several landmark buildings on the Shanghai waterfront. Mumbai's growth as India's leading commercial, shipping, industrial and financial centre was greatly linked to the trade with China. Many of Mumbai's prominent citizens in the 19th century AD, including Sir Jamsetjee Jejeebhoy (1st Baronet, a Parsi-Indian merchant and philanthropist, made a huge fortune in cotton and opium trade to China), were either directly involved in trade with China, or else came from families that were involved in it. The accumulation of capital through trade with China played a significant role in the early development of modern industries in India and in the development of Bombay's urban infrastructure in the 19th century AD.

Prominent Visitors: In the modern times, the first official mission from China to India came about when China sent a six-person delegation on a visit to India from March to September 1879. Huang Maocai, a member of the delegation, wrote several books about his experiences in India, including *Yin Du Zha Ji*, *You Li Zou Yan* and *Xi Jiao Shui Dao*. In July 1881, the Qing Dynasty sent two representatives, Ma Jianzhong and Wu Guangpei, to India to negotiate with the British Indian Government about matters related to opium trade. After returning to China, Ma Jianzhong wrote an account of his visit, *Nan Xing Ji* and Wu Guangpei wrote his own account of visit entitled *Nan Xing Ri Ji*. Later, Chinese envoys Xue Fucheng and Huang Zunxian visited India en-route to Europe and wrote about it. In 1893, Swami Vivekananda, one of the most prominent philosophers of modern India, went to China. He was one of the earliest Indian public figures to do so in this period. He wrote about China and expressed sympathy and friendship with Chinese people, predicting a great future for them. Kang Youwei, an influential

Chinese scholar and leader of the 1898 reform movement, was forced to leave China and live in exile after the suppression of the movement. During his exile, he came to Darjeeling in 1901 and stayed for one-and-a-half years, touring around India. He analysed Indian conditions of that time in his Travel Notes and book, *Xu Mi Xue Ting Shi Ji*.

Rabindranath Tagore had perhaps the greatest impact on China in the modern era. Chinese literary circles had a fascination for Tagore and, therefore, numerous articles about him and translations of his work were published in Chinese. In April 1924, in response to an invitation from his admirers in China, Tagore paid a 50-day visit to China. During his stay in China, he went to Hong Kong, Shanghai, Hangzhou, Nanjing, Jinan, Beijing, Taiyuan and Haikou. He cultivated deep friendships with celebrated Chinese thinkers, writers and artists, particularly with Chinese poet Xu Zhimo who acted as his translator. The relationships Tagore formed with Chinese intellectuals, writers and artists had a deep impact on him and on his sense of affinity with China.

Nationalist and Anti-imperialist Links: The imperialist expansion of Western powers had victimized both India and China, although in different ways and to a different extent. This served as the basis for new kinds of ties based on a shared anti-imperialism to emerge in this period between the two neighbouring countries. The earliest recorded instances of cooperation between India and China against foreign imperialism involved soldiers from the British Indian forces sent to help suppress the Taiping Rebellion in the middle of the 19th century AD. Several Indian soldiers had crossed over to the side of the rebels and fought alongside them.

In the first half of the 20th century AD, the pace of nationalist and anti-imperialist movements in both India and China picked up. During this period, China and Chinese political leaders had provided a haven to several exiled Indian political activists and nationalist organisations. One of the most prominent of these was the Ghadar Party (also known as Pacific Coast Hindustan Association, formed in 1913 in the United States) whose activities in China spanned the years from World War I to the 1930s.

The Ghadar Party had mobilized the support of Indian soldiers and policemen in the service of the British in China towards Chinese people. This had some impact among Indian forces in China during 1925 to 1927 when the Nationalist Revolution in China was reaching a peak. Dr. Sun Yat-sen, the leader of China's Republican Revolution of 1911, had great concern for and interest in the cause of Indian freedom from colonial rule. He met many Indian students and revolutionaries, both in China and Japan, and tried to assist them. At the same time, he was also an inspiration for many Indian nationalists in India.

From the late 1920s, the Indian National Congress and its leaders had concerns with Chinese people and they were constantly monitoring the situations in China. They sought to build links with a broad spectrum of Chinese nationalists and, also, publicly condemned the use of Indian troops against the Chinese. Pt. Nehru had written repeatedly about the prevalent conditions in China and expressed much appreciation for its ancient civilization. Chinese people also began to learn about the progress of the national movement of India. In the 1920s, Mahatma Gandhi was already a well-known figure in China and from the 1920s to the 1940s, 27 books about Gandhi and his thoughts were published in China, including four editions of his autobiography. Many articles were written on the Non-Cooperation Movement and other developments regrading freedom struggle of India. For example, the Oriental Magazine of China alone had published around 60 to 70 such articles and for some time even had a regular column on "Gandhi and New India".

Asian Renaissance: During the early years of the 20th century AD, particularly among intellectuals in India and China, a consciousness of the oneness of Asia and the virtues of eastern civilization developed. This helped in awakening of the people of India and China who were languishing under colonial or imperialist domination. Prominent Chinese personalities, such as Sun Yat-sen, Zhang Taiyan, Liu Shipei, Liang Qichao, Li Dazhao, *etc.*, sought to build this kind of consciousness of Asian unity in their speeches and writings. On the other hand, Pt. Nehru and exiled Indian nationalist Raja Mahendra Pratap were among those who fervently espoused the cause of Asian solidarity. However, the great poet Rabindranath Tagore was the most notable Indian personality who had espoused the cause of Asian solidarity. His visit to China in 1924 was part of his quest to revive the ancient links between the two great Asian civilization India and China. He set up an institute for Chinese studies at the Visva-Bharati University in Santiniketan, West Bengal. The discourse on Asia and Asianism had helped to stimulate interest and awareness among Indians and Chinese about each other's countries.

Indian-Chinese Studies: The systematic study of Indian studies in China and Chinese studies in India began in the 20th century AD. In 1916, Xu Jishang started teaching Indian philosophy at Peking University, Beijing. From 1917 to 1924, Liang Suming also taught Indian philosophy there. In 1922, Tang Yongtong returned from United States after studying Eastern and Western Philosophies, Sanskrit and Pali at Harvard University and began to teach the history of Chinese Buddhism and Indian Buddhism among other courses. Chen Yinque who was a Chinese historian, scholar and fellow of Academia Sinica, considered one of the most original and creative historians in 20th century China, returned to China to teach after mastering Sanskrit and Pali abroad. Many Chinese students including some monks came to study in India. Some of the Chinese scholars who came to India during this period included Xu Jishan (1919), Xu Dishan (1926, 1934), Jim Kemu (1941), Wu Xiaoling (1942), Xu Fancheng (1942), Chen Hansheng (1944), Chang Renxia (1945) and Chen Hongjin (1945).

In 1942, the National School of Oriental Languages was established at Yunnan in Southwestern China offering for the first time a course in the Hindi language, besides courses on Indian history, religion and society. In 1946, the Department of Oriental Languages was established at Peking University which taught Indian languages. In 1949, the National School of Oriental Languages was incorporated into Department of Oriental Languages at Peking University.

Rabindranath Tagore was very interested to set up a centre for the study of China and Chinese civilization in his world famous Visva-Bharati University at Santiniketan in West Bengal. He met a young Chinese scholar Tan Yunshan in Singapore in 1927 and invited him to visit Visva-Bharati University. Tan Yunshan came and stayed on in Visva-Bharti to start teaching Chinese language and he became Tagore's main collaborator and assistant in setting up the first centre for Chinese studies in modern India. He went to China to raise financial and other support for the project of setting up such a centre and, finally, the centre was inaugurated on 10th April 1937. With the assistance given by the Nationalist Government, the Sino-Indian Cultural Society and other supporters in China, the Cheena Bhavana at Visva-Bharti was established with its own unique building and a library consisting of a large number of Chinese works. In the 1930s, Raghu Vira who began to study Chinese culture and the history of the India-China relationship and developed academic links with China, founded the International Academy of Indian Culture in New Delhi for Chinese studies. In 1938, he wrote *Ramayana in China*. In the late 1930s, Fergusson College in Pune started a centre for China studies. Scholars Bapat and Gokro had made a comparative study of Sanskrit, Pali, Chinese and Tibetan Buddhist texts. However, Prabodh Chandra Bagchi was one of the most prominent Indian scholars of China studies of this period. He obtained his master's degree from Calcutta University and studied Chinese under the guidance of the French sinologist Sylvain Levy. During 1945 to 1956, he taught and did research at Visva-Bharati University. He wrote many important works on various aspects of the cultural interaction between India and China through history. He also went to China in 1947 and taught there briefly and visited again in 1952.

World War II: Indian public opinion was against the invasion of China by Japan in the 1930s. Indian leaders had organized various activities to protest the Japanese aggression. Apart from writing and speaking against the Japanese aggression, they also organized various actions to show their sympathy and support for China including the collection of funds and organizing "China Days" to popularize the Chinese resistance among the Indian public. In 1939, Pt. Nehru also visited China's wartime capital Chongqing. But, the best-known instance of cooperation between India and China during the Second World War was the dispatch of the Indian Medical Mission to China to assist the Chinese war effort. The Indian Medical Mission was formed in August 1938, and included five doctors M.M. Atal, M.R. Cholkar, D.S. Kotnis, B.K. Basu and D. Mukherjee. Carrying much needed medical equipment, they went to Yan'an in February 1939 and worked under very difficult conditions to provide medical care to the resistance fighters and local people. Dr. Basu and Dr. Kotnis stayed on even when the other members of the mission came back to India. Dr. Kotnis was appointed as the Director of the Dr. Bethune International Peace Hospital.

During World War II, when Japan occupied almost all of the Eastern China, India became of great strategic importance to China as a supply and communication route for the Nationalist Government headed by Chiang Kai-shek which had to shift its headquarters from Nanjing to Chongqing in Western China. This was because after the Japanese invasion of Burma in the middle of 1942 cut off the supply routes to Southwestern China through that country. For the rest of the war, the Stilwell Road from Ledo in Assam to Yunnan, the Calcutta-Kunming oil pipeline and the "Hump" air route which saw hundreds of planes carrying goods and passengers between airfields in Eastern India and Southwest China, played a very important role in the so-called "China-Burma-India" theatre of war. The route from Kalimpong in North Bengal to Tibet and Yunnan was also used to transport civilian goods. During the War, thousands of Chinese soldiers also received training at Ramgarh (in present day Jharkhand) to fight Japanese forces in Burma.

During the Second World War, the Indian national movement was approaching to a climax. Top leaders of the Indian National Congress including Mahatma Gandhi and Pt. Nehru were arrested and jailed by the Britishers. Much against the wishes of the British Prime Minister Winston Churchill, Chiang Kai-shek (head of the Nationalist Government in China) and his wife paid a visit to India in 1942 and met both Gandhi and Pt. Nehru. Chiang Kai-shek tried to persuade the British Government to agree to the demands of the Indian nationalists for political power. While leaving India, he broadcasted his message to the Indian people expressing sympathy for their objectives.

Establishment of Diplomatic Relations: During the Second World War, it was decided that diplomatic envoys would be exchanged between the British Government of India and the Nationalist Government in China. The first three envoys from India were K.P.S. Menon, K.M. Panikkar and Zafarullah Khan, and first three envoys from China were T.K. Tseng, Lo Chia-lun and Shihhua. Initially, the Indian envoys were stationed in Chongqing but with the end of the War, the Indian embassy was shifted to Nanjing which once again became the headquarters of the Chinese Government. After India became independent in August 1947, the status of the envoys on both sides was raised to that of Ambassador—this was the beginning of the diplomatic relations between the modern states of India and China.

CHAPTER 3

India-China Relations in Post-Independence Era

The gradual Westward expansion over the centuries under Mongol and Qing dynasties extended China's influence over Tibet and parts of Central Asia (present day Xinjiang, an autonomous territory in Northwest China). On the other hand, India's boundaries shrank following the 1947 partition that broke up the subcontinent's strategic unity that went back to more than two thousand years to the first Mauryan Empire (322 BC – 185 BC). As a result of Chinese occupation of Tibet in 1950, India and China came into close physical contact for the first time and clashed. India's partition in 1947 and Chinese occupation of Tibet in 1950 have allowed China to extend its reach and influence into a region where it had, in terms of history and civilization, previously exercised no influence at all.

India was the first country in non-communist block to recognize China after it got independence on 1st October 1949 in the culmination of Chinese Civil War (1945-49) and establish diplomatic relations with it. Pt. Nehru greeted the birth of communist China in October 1949 with great pomp and, in a rare gesture, India displayed excessive zeal in prompting China's membership in the United Nations. Pt. Nehru did not share the American perception that communism was a threat to world peace and stability. On the contrary, he believed that Western hatred of communism might boomerang, since nationalism in China was stronger than communism. He was convinced that Chinese nationalism played a far better important part than communism and that Chinese civilization was too old to succumb completely to Marxist dogma.

Pt. Nehru's belief seemed to be true as the early phase of India-China relations was marked by a close warm friendship, despite China's military takeover of Tibet in 1950 and India's providing asylum to Dalai Lama and his countless Buddhist followers. Although Indian government did not register a serious protest with Beijing, opposition leaders in parliament criticized Pt. Nehru's policy on the Tibetan issue but he remained unmoved and preferred to deal with monolithic China diplomatically by keeping it in check and isolating it from USSR rather than coming into open confrontation with it. This strategy paid off and India was able to maintain peace and tranquility on its Northeastern borders for over a decade.

At Peking, on 29th April 1954, India and China signed an agreement on trade and intercourse between the Tibet region of China and India, and had an exchange of notes. India thus signed away all its inherited privileges in Tibet by virtue of earlier pacts. This agreement is also known as *Panchsheel.*

Panchsheel: It is also known as the Five Principles of Peaceful Co-existence, which were first formally enunciated in the Agreement on Trade and Intercourse between the Tibet region of China and India signed on 29th April 1954, which stated, in its preamble, that the two Governments have resolved to enter into the present Agreement based on the following principles:

(a) Mutual respect for each other's territorial integrity and sovereignty.
(b) Mutual non-aggression.
(c) Mutual non-interference.
(d) Equality and mutual benefit.
(e) Peaceful co-existence.

Two months later, during the visit of Premier Zhou Enlai to India, he and Pt. Nehru issued a joint statement on 28th June 1954 that elaborated their vision of *Panchsheel* as the framework, not only for relations between the two countries, but also for their relations with all other countries, so that a solid foundation could be laid for peace and security in the world. *Panchsheel*, as envisioned by its creators, gave substance to the voice of newly established countries who were seeking the space to consolidate their hard-won independence, as it provided an alternative ideology dedicated to peace and development of all as the basis for international interaction, whether bilateral or multilateral. The two leaders also expressed the hope in the Joint Statement that the adoption of *Panchsheel* will also help in creating an area of peace which as circumstances permit can be enlarged thus lessening the chances of war and strengthening the cause of peace all over the world.

The vision of *Panchsheel* caught the imagination of the people of Asia and the world, and was incorporated into the Ten Principles of International Peace and Cooperation enunciated in the Declaration issued on 18th April 1955 at Bandung Conference of 29 Afro-Asian countries. The universal relevance of *Panchsheel* was emphasized when its tenets were incorporated in a resolution on peaceful co-existence presented by India, Yugoslavia and Sweden, and unanimously adopted on 11th December 1957, by the United Nations General Assembly. In 1961, the Conference of Non-Aligned Nations in Belgrade accepted *Panchsheel* as the principled core of the Non-Aligned Movement. Down the years, the ethos of *Panchsheel* continued to be reflected in the world events even if there was no conscious attribution, finding expression in the position of the developing countries in the North-South dialogue, and in other groupings. The timeless relevance of *Panchsheel* is based on its firm roots in the cultural traditions of its originators, two of the world's most ancient civilisations. The linkage that was established by the spread of Buddhism in China laid the historical basis for the formulation of the principles of *Panchsheel* by India and China.

The five Principles of Peaceful Coexistence and the Bandung Conference were highlights of India-China cooperation during the initial period of 1950s. However, by late 1950s, serious differences between the two states had begun to surface, particularly over the un-demarcated border. China refused to acknowledge the British demarcation of the India-China border, *i.e.*, McMahon Line, which demarcates Arunachal Pradesh to be a part of India.

The first Premier of the People's Republic of China, Zhou Enlai refused to accept the McMahon Line as the final line of the border demarcation between India and China. To counter the Indian claim that Beijing had, in the past, never contested the legality of McMahon Line, China argued that Tibet was not a sovereign state and therefore did not have the power to conclude treaties with the British. Moreover, China regarded the disputed Aksai China area as part of the Chinese province of Sinkiang and not Tibet. Chinese maps showed some 65,000 sq. km. of the territory South of the Line as part of the Tibet Autonomous Region, known as South Tibet, in China. However, China recognized a Line of Actual Control which closely approximates McMahon Line in the Eastern part of its border with India, according to a 1959 diplomatic note by the Premier Zhou Enlai. On the contrary, India contested that Chinese maps had never shown Sinkiang to extend South of the Kuentun range, which separated it from Tibet. Ultimately, border clashes led to a full-scale India-China war in October 1962 and armed skirmishes in 1967 and 1987.

Between 1962 and 1969, India-China relations remained in a deep freeze. Cheered by its easy victory over India, China initiated a vitriolic and vituperative propaganda against India, which intensified India's suspicion over China even further. India's mistrust over China was further confirmed when China befriended Pakistan and started to extend military and political support to it. On the contrary, China saw Indo-Soviet friendship as an anti-China ploy. In the wake of humiliating defeat, when India accorder high priority to its armed forces, China accused India of militarism. When India sought support from the USA and Soviet Union for strengthening its armed forces, India was leveled as a stooge of the US imperialism and Soviet revisionism and social imperialism.

From the middle of 1966 onwards, the internal conditions of both the neighbours, India and China, were in a state of continuous flux. China was in the cobweb of socio-economic upheaval and acute leadership struggle during the Cultural Revolution phase of 1966-69. On the other hand, India was in the hand of a new Prime Minister, Mrs. Indira Gandhi who was an untried and untested leader. Besides she had to face many problems, like famines due to widespread drought. Parliamentary elections of 1967 severely weakened the central leadership, as Mrs. Gandhi returned to power with reduced majority. During the phase of Cultural Revolution, Chinese foreign policy remained dormant, but this did not stop the Chinese from extending its support to the so-called national liberation movement in the third world by exhorting them to replace the legitimate regimes. Accordingly, China started to exploit two basic weaknesses of the Indian administration.

(a) The inability to integrate the tribal people of the Northeast into the mainstream of India.

(b) The failure to ameliorate the condition of the rural peasantry and landless labours in the lower Ganges Valley.

Sensing the weaknesses of Indian administration as an opportunity, China openly supported Naga and Mizo insurgents and encouraged them to rise in revolution against India. The Naxalbari uprising in West Bengal catered a golden opportunity to the Chinese to recommend the Maoist path for the Indian revolutionaries. India-China relations further attenuated in June 1967 with the expulsion of two Indian diplomats from Beijing on alleged charges of espionage activities. On 11th September 1967, Chinese troops attacked Indian troops on the Sikkim border across the Nathu La and opened heavy mortar and artillery fire. After repeated Indian protest and proposal for ceasefire, by 15th September 1967, there was a virtual cessation of all hostile activities. Again, Chinese troops fired heavily on the Indian positions at Cho La on 1st October 1967 and both the sides suffered casualties. All these led to deterioration in the relations between the two countries. However, Mrs. Gandhi kept striving to normalize relations with Beijing and, by the end of 1967, in a discussion on external affairs she replied, "China continues to maintain an attitude of hostility towards us and carries anti-Indian propaganda not only against the Indian Government but also against the whole of our democratic functioning and even our national integrity. But, I would like to say that we do not harbor any evil intention towards the Chinese people, and we do hope that a day will come when they will also realize that it is in the interests of all the countries of Southeast Asia that we should be friends and that each country should be able to devote its strength to solving the very major problem of combating poverty and backwardness."

Mrs. Gandhi adopted a flex approach regarding relations with China and tried to establish healthy relations with it. In an address to parliament on 20th February 1970, the President of India Mr. V.V. Giri reiterated his government's desire to conduct its relations with China on "the principle of mutual respect of each other's sovereignty and territorial integrity and non-interference. We expect China to respect our rights to pursue own domestic affairs and foreign policy."

During the 1970s, China not only supported the military junta and its role in East Pakistan but also tried discreetly to moderate Yahya Khan's brutal policy towards East Pakistan. China alleged that "Weighted down with difficulties at home and abroad, the reactionary Indian Government has embarked on a mad course of arms expansion and war preparations to carry out an expansionist policy towards its neighbor." It continued to step up friendly acts with Pakistan against India. Despite virulent anti-Indian Chinese propaganda, India played cool and maintained a low profile, and took the initiative to start dialogue with China, when its ambassador in Moscow met twice with his Chinese counterpart in May 1971, to discuss the terms of restoration of diplomatic representation to the Ambassadorial level. After a period of 14 years from India-China war, India's normalization of relations with Beijing ultimately resulted in the restoration of diplomatic relations with China in 1976. One of the senior members of the Indian Foreign Service, K.R. Narayanan who later became the President of India, was accredited India's Ambassador to Beijing in 1976. It was a pragmatic step towards putting India-China relations back on an even track.

The 1977 parliamentary elections paved the way for the formation of Janata Party-led government under the leadership of Morarji Desai, who was a strict disciplinarian and true Gandhian. Desai continued with the legacy of normalizing relations with China and sent his foreign minister, A.B. Vajpayee, to China in 1979 to carry forward the process of rapprochement. During the visit, Vajpayee broached the contentious border issue with Chinese leaders. Deng Xiaoping, Chinese revolutionary, politician, and paramount leader of the People's Republic of China from 1978 until his retirement in 1989, told Vajpayee to avoid bringing the issue on which both countries differed sharply into the discussion. Deng said, "We should have common ground while resolving differences. As for the boundary question, we can solve it through peaceful consultation. This question should not prevent us from improving our relations in other fields."

India-China relations entered into a new phase with the path-breaking visit of Prime Minister Rajiv Gandhi to Beijing on 19th December 1988. His visit saw a significant improvement in India-China relations, which became more cordial that at any time since mid-1950s. This visit was judged a success by both sides, because it was the first visit by an Indian Prime Minister to China since Pt. Nehru's 1954 visit and it helped balance the score in terms of summit visits. Rajiv Gandhi indicated India's willingness to increase consultation and cooperation with China on a range of international issues, such as the creation of a New International Economic Order, disarmament, and pollution. India's willingness to cooperate with China on such global issues represented acceptance of Chinese proposal that had been on the table since the early 1980s. The idea behind such macro diplomatic cooperation was that, as large developing countries with long histories, India and China shared many important characteristics and common interests. Moreover, by cooperating on these issues, the two countries could create an important atmosphere conductive to better bilateral relations.

During his visit, Rajiv Gandhi set the tone by declaring, "It is now time to look to the future, I have come to renew an old friendship". Deng Xiaoping responded by saying, "China and India should forget the unpleasant past and set their eyes on future." Premier Li Peng was Rajiv Gandhi's major interlocutor during the visit, and their discussion focused on the substantive issue of the border, Tibet, bilateral relations, and international situations. He also accepted an invitation to play a return visit to India.

During Rajiv Gandhi's visit the two countries had in-depth discussion on the India-China border questions and agreed to settle it through peaceful and friendly consultations. In December 1988, India and China decided to set up a Joint Working Group (JWG) on the boundary issue headed by Foreign Secretary on the Indian side and a Vice-minister of Foreign Affairs on the Chinese side. The JWG had following two important functions.

(a) The JWG was to make concrete recommendations for the overall solution of the boundary question.

(b) The JWG would ensure the peace and tranquility on the Line of Actual Control.

The two countries also agreed to develop relations in other fields and set up a joint group on economic relations and trade, as well as science and technology. They signed three accords on cultural, scientific, and technological cooperation as well as civil aviation.

Following Prime Minister Rajiv Gandhi's China visit, the Chinese Premier Li Peng paid a return visit to India on 11th December 1991. The joint statement issued at the end of the visit stressed that the boundary questions should not affect the development of bilateral relations. The JWG on the boundary questions should step up its work, and peace and tranquility should be maintained along the Line of Actual Control pending the final settlement of the boundary questions. Indian President R. Venkataraman paid a state visit to China in May 1992 and Vice-President K.R. Narayanan in October 1994. Between December 1988 and June 1993, six rounds of JWG meetings on the border issues were held.

Progress was made in reducing border tension through Confidence Building Measures (CBMs), including mutual troop reductions, regular meetings of local military officers and advance notification of military drills and exercises. After an interval of more than 30 years, border trade between India and China resumed in July 1992 and both the countries reopened their consulates in Mumbai and Shanghai in December 1992. Indian defense minister Sharad Pawar visited China in December 1992, when the two defense establishments agreed to develop academic, military, scientific and technological cooperation. In 1993, the two countries agreed to open an additional border trading post.

In September 1993, Prime Minister P.V. Narasimha Rao visited China and concluded an Agreement on Maintenance of Peace and Tranquility in Border Areas along the Line of Actual Control. In December, in the same year, a senior level Chinese military delegation made a six-days goodwill visit to India for fostering CBMs between the defence forces of two countries. In 1994, the two countries signed a number of agreements and MoUs, such as Agreement on Avoiding Double Taxation, Agreement for Cooperation on Health and Medical Science, MoUs on Simplifying the Procedure for Visa Application and Banking Cooperation, *etc.* In the beginning of 1994, Beijing announced that it not only favoured a negotiated settlement on Kashmir but also opposed any form of independence for the region.

President of the People's Republic of China, Jiang Zemin visited India in November-December 1996. This visit was notable for the agreement on CBMs in military field in the border areas along the Line of Actual Control, which covered troop reduction and weapons limitation along the borders. Both countries reaffirmed in the agreement that neither side would use force against the other by any means or seek unilateral military support for them. The leaders of both countries agreed to establish constrictive and cooperative partnership between India and China into 21st century, on the principles of *Panchsheel.* Four other accords reached during the visit were those relating to maritime transport, cooperation in combating narcotic drug trafficking, improving communication across the border, and maintenance of the Consulate-General of India in Hongkong Special Administrative Region.

Growing Engagement in Diverse Spheres: From 1949 to Till Date

On 1st October 1949, People's Republic of China (PRC) came into existence and on 1st April 1950, India and PRC established diplomatic relations. India was the first country outside the socialist group of countries to establish an embassy in the PRC. On the first official reception of Indian embassy, on the occasion of India's Republic Day in Beijing, on 26th January 1951, Chairman of PRC, Mao Zedong personally attended the function and spoke warm words about India-China friendship. Since then, the relations between India and China have had some ups and downs but currently they are on a path of rapidly growing interaction in multidimensional spheres.

India and China were at high in their bilateral diplomatic engagement in the middle of 1950s. Premier Zhou Enlai (first Premier of the PRC, serving from October 1949 until his death in January 1976) visited India during 25-28 June 1954, while Prime Minister Pt. Nehru visited China during 19-30 October in the same year. Both the visits were highly appreciated by the public in both countries. Premier Zhou Enlai again visited India in 1956 and 1960. Due to these visits of head of states of both the countries, trade had begun to pick up again from 1951 and, on 29th April 1954, the two countries signed the "Agreement on trade and intercourse between the Tibet region of China and India". The first-ever trade protocol was also signed by both the countries. In this period, the main imports from China were rice, sorghum, soybean, raw silk, machinery, transformer, wool, caustic soda and paper, while India mainly exported to China jute, rice, beans, tobacco leaf, chemicals, medicine, mica, electric fans, woolen fabrics and machinery. The preamble to the 1954 trade agreement contained the formulation of the Five Principles of Peaceful Coexistence, which were intended to set a principled foundation for the peaceful relationship between India and China.

Through most part of the 1950s, regular educational, cultural and scientific/technical exchanges between India and China which had been stepped up from the 1940s, continued. Many high-level delegations were exchanged between the two countries. Noted Indian artists like Beohar Rammanohar Sinha (known as a cultural ambassador of India and also known for his illustrations in the original final manuscript of Constitution of India, including the complete Preamble-page) and the scholar-philosopher Rahul Sankrityayan (known as the father of Hindi

Travelogue, played a pivotal role to give travelogue a 'literature form') visited China and interacted with their counterparts there. Indian films, such as *Awaara* and other films starring Raj Kapoor, were very popular among Chinese people.

Unfortunately, developments leading up to the 1962 border clash between India and China, and its aftermath led to a disruption in the normal interaction between them for several years. A few attempts were made in the 1970s to revive contacts, particularly through Dr. B.K. Basu who had been the part of the Indian Medical Mission to China during the World War II. After returning from the Indian Medical Mission to China, Dr. Basu again visited China several times from the middle of 1970s to the middle of 1980s and when he died, his ashes were scattered both in India and China as per his wishes. During this period, a few other goodwill and informal exchanges also took place, but contacts remained limited although preparations were being made for revival of relations. In 1979, Foreign Minister Atal Bihari Vajpayee became the first high level Indian dignitary to visit China after many years. During early 1980s, Indian and Chinese leaders met each other on the sidelines of various international summits. The visit of Prime Minister Rajiv Gandhi to China on 19th December 1988, marked the resumption of high level ties and a significant step towards normalization of relations between these two countries. Apart from meeting the Chinese Premier Li Peng, Rajiv Gandhi also met Deng Xiaoping and other important Chinese leaders, and signed agreements on science and technology cooperation, civil air transport and cultural exchange and cooperation. Thereafter, exchange of visits by the top dignitaries of both countries developed rapidly and has become the regular task. Following are some of the important such visits that have taken place in subsequent years—Premier Li Peng (1991), President R. Venkataraman (1992), Prime Minister Narasimha Rao (1993), President Jiang Zemin (1996), President K.R. Narayanan (2000), Premier Zhu Rongji (2002), Prime Minister Atal Bihari Vajpayee (2003), Premier Wen Jiabao (2005, 2010), President Hu Jintao (2006, 2012), Prime Minister Manmohan Singh (2008, 2013), President Pratibha Devisingh Patil (2010), Premier Li Keqiang (2013), Premier Xi

Jinping (2014, 2016), Foreign Minister Wang Yi (2014), Army Chief Bikram Singh (2014), Vice-President Li Yuanchao (2015), and Prime Minister Narendra Modi (2015). During these visits, a very large number of agreements have been signed between the two countries to enhance their levels of cooperation in diverse spheres, including the maintenance of peace on the borders.

In recent times, the relations between India and China have reached to a significant level due to the spectacular increase in economic and commercial interactions. Direct trade was resumed in 1977 and agreements were signed to enhance trade and commerce between the two countries. The total trade volume between India and China was under US$ 3 billion in 2000, but this figure soared astronomically to over US$ 60 billion by 2010, making China India's largest trading partner and making India China's seventh largest export destination. This marked a new phenomenon in the relations between India and China in the modern times. India's exports to China include iron ores, slag and ash, cotton yarn and fabrics, copper, gems, chemical products, *etc.* On the other hand, India's imports from China include parts of nuclear reactors and boilers, electrical machinery, iron and steel, organic chemicals and fertilisers, *etc.* However, at present, the balance of trade is in favour of China. Many Indian companies and banks have set up their offices or branches in China including Bharat Forge, Sundram Fasteners', Adani Global, Ashapura Minechem, Dr. Reddy's Laboratories, Electrosteel Integrated, ESSAR, Ispat Industries, Jindal Steel & Power, JSW Steel, Reliance, Sasken Communication Technologies, Suzlon Energy, TCS, BHEL, TATA Sons, Matrix Pharma, BEML, ESSEL Packing, Godrej & Boyce, Zee TV, GENPACT, Liaoning Birla Carbon, Apollo International, Ashok Leyland, Aurobindo Pharma, Infosys, Lupin, State Bank of India, Bank of India, Union Bank of India, Allahabad Bank, Bank of Baroda, ICICI Bank, Axis Bank, *etc.* Similarly, many Chinese companies and banks have set up their offices or branches in India including Sino Steel, Shougang International, Baoshan Iron & Steel, Sang Heavy Industry, Sino Hydro Corporation, Huawei Technologies, ZTE, TCL, Haier, Shanghai Electric, Harbin Electric, TBEA Energy, Chenguaing Bio-Tech India,

YAPP India Automotive Systems, XINDIA Steels, Nippon Paint, WISCO, Xiaomi, Oppo Electronics, Vivo, OnePlus, Industrial & Commercial Bank of China, HSBC Bank, *etc*. Both the countries are also exploring the ways to encourage investment in setting up industrial parks in each other's countries.

Along with the growth of economic ties between the two countries, the number of Indian and Chinese visiting each other's countries, and also living and working there has also grown considerably. Indian visitors include students, traders and businessmen, and professionals spread across many provinces of China. Tens of thousands of Chinese have also visited India over the last decade. Many come to visit the places of Buddhist pilgrimage in India. Many Chinese are also working as software professionals, chartered accountants and entrepreneurs in India. The development of people-to-people contacts has reached levels unprecedented in India-China relations although the number is still small given the size of China and India and their populations. The visit of Prime Minister Rajiv Gandhi to China in 1988 gave a boost to cultural exchanges between India and China, and since then many cultural delegations have been exchanged. Festivals of India and China have been organized in each other's countries. Notable examples of cultural cooperation included the construction with Indian assistance of a Buddhist temple of Indian style in Luoyang and the establishment of a Xuanzang Memorial Hall at Nalanda, the site of the famous educational centre visited by Xuanzang (a Chinese Buddhist monk, scholar, traveler, and translator who travelled to India in the seventh century and described the interaction between Chinese Buddhism and Indian Buddhism during the early Tang Dynasty). The Cultural Exchange Programme launched after the visit of Premier Wen Jiabao to India in December 2010 triggered activity in various spheres including exchanges of visits of writers and performing artists, archaeologists, archivists, and others as well as the organizing of film festivals and other cultural festivals as well as youth delegations and sports and media exchanges. Academic exchanges between scholars from India and China are also increasing steadily and cover diverse branches of knowledge. Indian yoga, food, fashion and films are gaining popularity in China. On the other hand, the popularity of Chinese language course, Chinese martial arts and certain forms of Chinese medicine is increasing in India.

An important trend of growing cooperation between India and China can be seen at regional and global forums. The most important achievement in this regard was the joint statement issued on the eve of Premier Wen Jiabao's visit to India in April 2005. The statement established a Strategic and Cooperative Partnership for Peace and Prosperity, indicating that both sides would regard their relations not merely from a bilateral perspective, but from a larger global strategic perspective. There would be greater cooperation and coordination between India and China on the issues concerning international trade, regional security, maritime security, environmental problems and so on. The growing economic and military strengths of India and China has increased their roles and responsibilities in the international affairs. It has also generated greater interest globally in the relationship between India and China.

CHAPTER 4

India-China Border Disputes

India is China's second largest neighbour sharing a little over 4000 km. land border which stretches from the barren Aksai Chin plateau in the west (administered by China but claimed by India as part of the Ladakh district of Jammu and Kashmir) through the former kingdom of Sikkim in the middle section, and across to the eastern Indian state of Arunachal Pradesh (administered by India but claimed by China as 'South Tibet').

The origins of border dispute stem from a combination of difficult terrain, nascent survey technology, the absence of a functioning Tibetan state and the craft of British Imperial map, making writ large. In 1914, at the Anglo-Tibetan Shimla Conference, the British colonial authorities drew the McMahon Line (named after the chief negotiator Sir Henry McMahon), which established the boundary between British India and Tibet. Although, Chinese representative were present at Shimla, they refused to sign or recognize the accords on the basis that Tibet was under Chinese jurisdiction and therefore did not have the power to conclude treaties.

Currently, India and China dispute over a land area of about 125000 sq. km., which can be divided into the eastern, middle and western sectors. The eastern sector includes the McMahon Line which runs from the tri-junction between India, China and Bhutan from the west to Brahmaputra River in the east, largely along the crest of the Himalayas. This section is now called the Indian State of Arunachal Pradesh and occupies about an area of 90000 sq. km. having a population of over a million people. The middle sector starts from the tri-junction between the Southwestern of Ngari Prefecture, Tibet, La Dvags and Punjab to the tri-junction between China, India and Nepal. It length is about 450 km. long, with about 2000 sq. km. of land under dispute. The disputed area in the middle sector on the other hand is much smaller, involving only several pockets. The western sector starts with the pass of Karakoram in the North to the tri-junction between Tibet's Ngari Prefecture, La Dvags and Himachal Pradesh, running along 600 km. The disputed area, known as Aksai Chin, occupies about 33500 sq. km. of land and is now controlled by China. India's claim to the area is largely based on the "Johnson Line". In 1846, Great Britain annexed Kashmir which played a critical role in the British strategy for securing the northern frontiers of India. To advance its border claims, in 1865, W.H. Johnson, a civil servant with the Survey of India who was sent to survey the area, proposed the "Johnson Line", putting Aksai Chin in Kashmir. While Aksai Chin is a virtually uninhabited bleak barren plateau, it is of high strategic value to China as it is a vital passage point between Tibet and Xinjiang.

India-China border disputes are complex historical issues. As both countries cannot agree on border delimitation, the India-China border has never been officially drawn. When India came under British rule, it began to advance the two countries' traditional border to the Chinese side. During the 1913-14 tripartite conference involving a Tibetan delegate, a representative of Chinese central government, and Sir Henry McMahon, a foreign secretary of the British Indian Government, a secret bilateral agreement was signed with the Tibetan representative on a new border line, also known as the McMahon Line. The Chinese central government rejected the accord and their plenipotentiary, and the Tibetan government later disputed the legality of the McMahon Line. Furthermore, the McMahon Line was initially rejected by the British-run Indian Government as incompatible with the 1907 Anglo-Russian Convention. However, the British began using the McMahon Line on the Survey of India maps in 1937, and officially published the Shimla Accord in 1938. During the Second World War and immediately after that, the British made extensive effort to expand their control towards the claimed McMahon Line. By the time India gained independence on 15th August 1947, the McMahon Line had become India's Northeast border.

India inherited the British territorial policy, including the McMahon Line as the legitimate border. After the newly established People's Republic of China took over Tibet in 1951, India felt threatened by the Chinese military presence in Tibet and quickly extended administrative and military control in the eastern sector. In the same year, India took control of the Tawang, a centre of Tibet's Buddhist culture with one of the biggest Tibetan monasteries outside Lhasa. It is also a holy site as it was the birthplace of the sixth Dalai Lama in the seventeenth century. While the Tibetan Government fiercely protested India's move, the Chinese central government remained silent on the issue and this silence was perceived by India as an indication that the newly founded People's Republic of China (PRC) was willing to accept the McMahon Line.

After taking control of Tawang, the India-China border became quite again, and both the countries had undertaken substantial efforts in building infrastructure roads and check-posts and sending out patrol and survey teams. In 1954, two countries signed an agreement on trade and intercourse across Tibetan borders. This was the first document whereby both India and China enunciated the so-called "Five Principles of Peaceful Coexistence". In the agreement, India surrendered various rights and privileges over Tibet, which the British had induced Tibet to grant, without any mention of the border issue in the agreement. While China back then felt it was better to postpone discussions on the border issue, India's interpretation of the agreement was very different, believing that the two countries had agreed that there was no border dispute between them. However, from China's perspective, there was no trade-off between Tibet and the border, real or imagined, and the Chinese position has steadfastly remained that India's recognition of China's sovereignty over Tibet, and China's acceptance of the former colonial McMahon Line were not connected issues.

But, later on, Pt. Nehru announced that the two countries' borders were drawn and there should be no further disputes on the border issue. He recommended a system of check-posts to be set up along the entire border. Furthermore, after establishing a presence in the border areas, India claimed that certain sections of the McMahon Line should be modified, placing it further north into China's side. This eventually led to first India-China military clash in August 1959 at Longju. Yet both countries' border dispute did not start in the eastern sector along the McMahon Line. Instead, the first border dispute occurred in the middle sector in 1954 when India occupied several posts. In 1958, China's ambassador to India at the time sent two memos to the Indian Foreign Ministry calling for an immediate withdrawal of Indian troops from the disputed areas and the resumption of negotiations. Later, greater tensions occurred in the western sector because, between 1953 and 1957, China had undertaken massive projects for road construction to support its presence in Tibet. One important project started in 1953 was to convert the old caravan route in Aksai Chin from Xinjiang into a motorable road, which was finally completed in September 1957.

On 18th October 1958, India sent a memo to the Chinese Government, officially claiming Aksai Chin as Indian territory. In this memo to Zhou Enlai, the first Premier of the People's Republic of China, Pt. Nehru wrote, "There can be no question of these large parts of India (shown as within China on the Chinese map) being anything but India and there is no dispute about it". In January 1959, Zhou's reply highlighted following points:

(a) Both countries' borders had never been formally demarcated.

(b) Border disputes do exist between India and China.

(c) Aksai Chin was China's land and had always been under Chinese jurisdiction.

(d) Through the McMahon Line was illegal, China would consider accepting it if it could legitimize the McMahon Line while India waived or sharply modified its claim to Aksai Chin.

The proposal of Zhou was rejected by Pt. Nehru who insisted on sending Indian troops into all territories claimed by

India. After Kongka Pass incident, Zhou visited India hoping to solve the border disputes peacefully through negotiations. During the meeting, Zhou made China's proposal explicit for the first time—reciprocal acceptance of present actualities in both sectors and constitution of a boundary commission. However, India rejected the proposal, claiming that there should be no compromise, no standstill agreement and no negotiations. After the failed summit, while India began to implement its Forward Policy between 1961 and 1962, China for its part attempted to increase its military forces in the disputed areas by setting up check-posts and enhancing border patrols. Tensions continued to rise in all sectors of the India-China border. On 20th October 1962, China launched a pre-emptive offensive marking the start of India-China border war. During the month-long war, Chinese forces advanced deep into Indian territory in Ladakh and Arunachal Pradesh, before withdrawing back to their previous positions along the Line of Actual Control. The war ended with China's victory with ceasefire on 22nd November 1962. China voluntarily withdrew its army to position 20 km. behind the Line of Actual Control that had existed in 1959 and proposed that officials of the two sides hold meetings immediately. The Chinese made three proposals—to stop the border conflict, to reopen negotiations, and to settle the India-China boundary question. To create a good atmosphere for reconciliation between the two countries, China released more than 600 Indian personnel and returned the equipment that had been captured during the war.

India-China war proved Pt. Nehru's friendly policy towards China, such as granting recognition, the Bandung conference and accepting China's claim over Tibet, a failure. The Indians felt that they had been betrayed by the Chinese. On the other hand, the Chinese blamed India for the hostile developments. As a point of diplomatic history, it seems likely that the border war will be symbolic of the tortuous nature of India-China relations. All the euphoria about the India-China brotherhood dissipated. Both sides' inability to find a mutually acceptable proposal impeded the improvement of India-China relations. Haunted by the border war, India-China relations since 1962 have been characterized by mutual antagonism, rivalry, distrust, and hostility. Throughout the Cold War and in the post-Cold War era, the border dispute remained an indelible mark in India-China relations and China and India continued to hold each other responsible. The military clash is still deeply inscribed in the memory of strategic decision-makers and analyst, and has acted as an aggravating factor whenever India and China prepare to engage each other.

China tried to build up an image of being keen to settle the boundary problem by peaceful negotiation, the implication being that if the boundary negotiation between China and India failed, China should not be blamed. India's suspicion of China deepened in the wake of China's first nuclear test in October 1964, barely two years after the India-China border war. It placed great pressure on India and tensions continued as there were border skirmishes in 1965 and 1967. India's annexation of Sikkim during 1973-75 raised another diplomatic confrontation between the two countries.

After the war, the borders became quiet, but India still refused to negotiate with China on border issues, and India-China relations remained frozen until the late 1970s. In 1971, India renamed North East Frontier Agency (NEFA), the disputed eastern sector. NEFA became the Union Territory of Arunachal Pradesh, which was subsequently granted full statehood on 20th February 1987. However, Arunachal Pradesh was never recognized by China. Despite various constraints, both countries undertook efforts to normalize bilateral relations and restored ambassadorial relations in 1976. India was willing to resolve the border disputes through peaceful negotiations. In 1979, during India's foreign minister's visit to China, Deng Xiaoping put forward a package plan for both countries—advocating "mutual understanding and mutual accommodation" for the negotiation of the rival claims. But, India rejected the plan and insisted that the Chinese withdrew their troops from India's claimed territories as the precondition for mutual negotiations. Xiaoping also suggested that China and India could adopt a "one package deal" to solve the border dispute when Indian Foreign Minister Atal Bihari Vajpayee visited Beijing in 1979. He said that the package deal meant China would accept the border claimed by India in the eastern sector, namely, the McMahon Line, in return for Indian acceptance of the status quo in the western sector. Since then, the package deal has become one of China's basic principles to settle the longstanding border dispute between the two countries. On the other hand, India refused to accept the package deal and supported a separate negotiation of each sector's border, considering the specific aspects of each. The Indian side insisted on minor territorial adjustments in the eastern sector and China's unilateral concession in the western sector. India was more concerned with the effect of the border dispute on its security environment, insisted that a settlement of the border issue was a necessary precondition for improving bilateral relations, and rejected the package proposal of Deng Xiaoping.

India's border policy changed slightly under Rajiv Gandhi's leadership. Now, India no longer insisted that the Chinese withdraw their troops from India's claimed territories as the precondition for both countries to negotiate. In 1981, China's Vice Premier and Foreign Minister Huang Hua visited India, which led to both countries deciding to hold talks on border issues. Since each side merely reiterated its well-known position on the border problem and then dispersed, the eight rounds of border talks at the vice minister level between 1981 and 1987 did not lead to a breakthrough or even substantial progress being made in the solution of the border dispute. The only achievement was that both sides agreed to maintain stability and tranquility along the border and that the border dispute should be resolved through peaceful negotiations and friendly consultations. However, between 1986 and 1987, a severe military standoff occurred between India and China at the Sumdorong Chu Valley. Fortunately, this military conflict did not lead to another India-China war.

The visit by Prime Minister Rajiv Gandhi to China in December 1988 broke the impasse in India-China relations leading to the re-commencement of border negotiations and the ongoing border talk between the two countries was raised to a higher level. For resolving the boundary problem, the two countries decided to set up a Joint Working Group (JWG) on the boundary issue to work out a mutually acceptable resolution.

With frequent visits from leaders of both countries, bilateral relations improved throughout the early 1990s. During June 1989 and August 2001, fourteen sessions of the JWG meetings were held. In September 1993, Prime Minister Narasimha Rao visited to China and an India-China Diplomatic and Military Expert Group was created as a subgroup of the JWG. The Expert Group, which was designed to deal with technical details at the deputy director-general/undersecretary level, met fourteen times between February 1994 and June 2002. However, these meetings made little progress in reaching a concrete solution on the border problems, but they were instrumental in establishing a mechanism for regular discussions. More importantly, unlike the previous border talks held between 1981 and 1987, the JWG and Expert Group meetings proved successful in maintaining peace and tranquility in troubled areas along the India-China border, *i.e.*, to some extent, the dialogue mechanism itself was a kind of confidence building measures (CBMs), which tied both sides to the negotiation table, to avoid the need to resort to extreme measures.

Since early 1990s, some CBMs were proposed and followed by India and China to secure the peace along the disputed boundary areas. After Chinese Premier Li Peng's visit to India in 1991, the two countries agreed to regularize the meetings between border personnel, which would be held at Bum La in the eastern sector and in the Spanggur Gap area in the western sector in June and October every year. They also agreed to establish telephone links to facilitate communication between border personnel. Transparency, communication, and constraint measures were on the agenda, and the discussions focused on the mutual transparency of the location of military positions, prior notification of military exercise, prevention of air intrusion, and redeployment of forces along the Line of Actual Control (LAC).

The visit of Prime Minister Narasimha Rao in September 1993, provided the setting for the codification of the work done by the JWG meetings. The two countries signed the Agreement on the Maintenance of Peace and Tranquility along the LAC in the India-China border areas. The issues included in this agreement were troop reduction, conflict avoidance measures, notification measures, and the establishment of the Expert Group comprising diplomatic and military representatives from both sides to assist the JWG. Being the first CBMs agreement between the two countries, the deal was described as a "positive breakthrough" in India-China relations. After Prime Minister Narasimha Rao's visit to China, the JWG and the Expert Group worked toward the 1993 CBMs Agreement's implementation. A further step in that direction was taken with the signing of the Agreement on the Confidence Building Measures in the military field along the LAC in the India-China border areas during Chinese President Jiang Zemin's four-day state visit to India in November 1996, the first by a Chinese head of state since the two countries had established diplomatic relations in 1950. In this agreement, both the countries advanced beyond agreeing on declaratory principles and proposed more detailed implementation measures. For example, they set a ceiling on the scale of any military exercises and created a "no-fly zone" along the border areas. However, despite agreeing to limit the respective military forces to "minimum levels compatible with the friendly and good neighbourly relations between the two countries", India and China still could not reach an accord on the method of troop reductions. Furthermore, the 1996 CBMs Agreement was held up by a discussion over provisions for communication and constraint measures, and the lack of any means to verify and monitor. Like the 1993 CBMs Agreement, the 1996 CBMs Agreement functioned more as a conflict avoidance measure. However, it cannot be denied that the signing of the agreement was another new political initiative to help ease tensions along the India-China border. Even if the two countries were still unable to narrow their differences on troop reductions along the border, yet both sides expressed satisfaction with the results of the two CBMs agreements, and the border has since remained peaceful. Furthermore, both countries tried to marginalize the boundary dispute to make sure that the overall development of India-China friendship and cooperation would not be hijacked by the boundary issue.

The JWG mechanism has helped to build a CBMs regime along the disputed India-China border and to stabilize the LAC, but the difficulty of delineating the LAC made India believe that the boundary problem should be solved from a political perspective, rather than in a historical, technical, or legal manner. Again, it was India that proposed the new initiative to find a concrete solution of India-China border problem. During the visit of Prime Minister Vajpayee to China from 22nd to 27th June 2003, a new mechanism for border talks was set up. India and China agreed to raise the level of negotiators to a higher political status by appointing their respective Special Representatives as the key negotiators to explore the framework of a boundary settlement from the political perspective of the overall bilateral relationship. To show its seriousness on the initiative, India appointed its National Security Adviser as the Special Representative for India-China boundary problem. As it was India that had taken the decision to upgrade the level of talks, however, China accepted the overture reluctantly. Initially, China desired to appoint a secretary level official as its special envoy, but India had no intention of making the special representative a sequel to the JWG meetings, and, therefore, favoured a more senior leader with sufficient political clout. Then China appointed its Executive Vice Foreign Minister, Dai Bingguo as Special Representative. Apparently, the political level of Vice Foreign Minister is below that of National Security Advisor, but India believed the change of formalities for the boundary talks would help resolve the problem.

The first meeting of the Special Representatives was held in Delhi on 23rd-24th October 2003. By August 2009, thirteen rounds of Special Representative meetings had taken place on the basis of their mandate to evolve a framework for a boundary settlement and address the problem from the political perspective of the overall bilateral relationship, *i.e.*, India and China decided to stop the process of focusing on technical problems and prioritized the identification of common principles as the first task for solving the boundary problem. In general, there were two stages for meetings. During the first phase, the aim of the meeting was to hammer out a methodology to resolve the boundary dispute. Whereas during the second phase, the focus was on devising a framework agreement for resolving the dispute based on the "political parameters and guiding principles". The special representative mechanism was compatible with China's strategy towards the boundary dispute. According to Chinese Premier Wen Jiabao, it was important that the two sides "bear in mind the large picture, expand exchanges and cooperation in all areas, and properly settle questions left over from history".

After five rounds of talks, the meetings of Special Representative led to the conclusion of the Agreement on Political Parameters and Guiding Principles for the Settlement of the India-China Boundary Questions, which was signed on 11th April 2005 during Chinese Premier Wen Jiabao's visit to India. The Guiding Principles Agreement reveals that the two sides have reduced the differences in perception on the approach to the boundary problem. For instance, India had earlier insisted on a sector-by-sector approach for solving the border dispute while China wanted a package deal. India has now agreed to discuss the problem on a sector-by-sector basis, but to announce the agreement once the differences on all the sectors are sorted out. Thus, the Guiding Principles Agreement was an achievement of meetings of the Special Representatives. However, this positive development did not imply that all obstacles had been cleared and that a mutually acceptable solution could be reached any sooner. The conception behind the Special Representative meetings was that both sides first identified the principles and terms of reference on the basis of which the settlement of the boundary issue could be established. Then, both sides would apply such principles to construct a framework, which would be used to delineate the actual boundary on the ground, *i.e.*, the conclusion of the agreement on Guiding Principles in fact marked the beginning of the second phase of negotiations under the mechanism of Special Representatives.

Achievements on Boundary Talks

For India, a symbolic achievement on the boundary talks in the post-Pokhran era was the Sikkim issue. Earlier, China had steadfastly questioned the legality of Sikkim's merger with

India in 1975. But, in July 1994, the Chinese Vice Premier and Foreign Minister, Qian Qichen, stated that China was dropping its opposition to Sikkim's accession to India. China's decision at the third Expert Group meeting in March 1995 to hold border personnel meetings with India at Nathu La in the Sikkim sector implied its acquiescence that Sikkim was under India's rule. The former Chinese ambassador to India, Cheng Ruisheng also revealed that China was considering recognizing Sikkim's merger with India. Despite these signals, China did not formally recognize Sikkim as a state of Indian Union. China's inflexibility on the Sikkim issue was due to fact that China saw the Sikkim issue as a bargaining chip to be used in the boundary problem. However, during Prime Minister Vajpayee's visit to China in 2003, India successfully persuaded China to change its position and to accept the reality that Sikkim is the part and parcel of India. Both the countries signed a bilateral agreement about opening a point in Sikkim for border trade. India had recognized China's take-over of Tibet by signing the 1954 agreement, so it was expected that China would recognize Sikkim by signing the border trade agreement. In return for recognition, India agreed to China's terms on the status of Tibet as being an equivalent concession.

China had rejected any suggestion that it had recognized India's sovereignty over Sikkim, without even waiting until Prime Minister Vajpayee and his party were in China. Chinese Foreign Ministry spokesperson said that the political status of Sikkim was historical baggage and would still require to be solved in a gradual manner. China's reluctance to recognize India's annexation of Sikkim was seen as a surprise and embarrassment to the Indian side. China saw the Sikkim issue as part of the broader border negotiations, and as a means to deny India the possibility of taking advantage of the Tibet issue. However, China was also worried that India might withdraw its endorsement of the new discourse on Tibet if China continued to reject India's claims over Sikkim. As a result, China assured India in a low-profile way that the Sikkim issue would cease to be an irritant in India-China relations and that China wanted to build a long standing, stable, and healthy relationship with

India amid the fast-changing global scenario. Then the Chinese Foreign Minister deleted a webpage from its official website, which had showed Sikkim as a separate country in Asia, ahead of Chinese Premier Wen Jiabao's meeting with his Indian counterpart, Prime Minister Vajpayee, on the sidelines of the ASEAN summit at Bali in Indonesia.

Later Chinese Consul General in Kolkata Mao Siwei admitted that China had already recognized Sikkim as part of India during Prime Minister Vajpayee's visit to Beijing in 2003. However, China was reluctant to openly assert that it had already recognized Sikkim as part of India. When Chinese Premier Wen Jiabao visited India in 2005, the Chinese side finally presented to India a newly printed official map that showed Sikkim as being part of India. The joint statement issued by two sides clearly speaks of Sikkim as a state of the Republic of India.

Following this positive development, in July 2006, the two countries reopened border trade across the 15000 feet Nathu La Pass in addition to the Shipki La Pass, opened in 1993 and the Lipulekh Pass, opened in 1992. Border trade between the two countries in fact did not contribute much to the overall volume of trade between the two countries, partly due to restrictions in tradable items, but in this instance, it was an indication of a broader rapprochement.

However, the Tibet-Sikkim border was to play a further role in the boundary controversy and became a new point of contention. During 2005-08 close to four hundred Chinese intrusions took place into Indian territory in Sikkim. This time, the Indians were tormented with anxiety by China's claims over the so-called 2.1 sq. km. "Finger Area" in northern Sikkim. China further threatened to demolish existing stone structure there. India strongly rebutted these claims, lodged an official protest, and barred the Chinese troops from entering the area. This was after China had protested against other troop deployments in Sikkim resulting from the relocation of Indian troops from the western border. Due to this diplomatic discord, road construction near the area was halted. During External Affairs Minister Pranab Mukherjee's visit to China in June

2008, the Chinese reportedly tried to corner India by raising the issue of the "Finger Area".

Repeated incursions into Sikkim along with other disputed areas by the Chinese have been a cause of concern for India. From India's point of view, China's act was provocative and irritating, and in some cases, the intrusions were extremely provocative. For example, in April 2008, 10 red Chinese troops came 12 km. inside Maja in Arunachal Pradesh. An incursion event along the LAC in the western sector of the India-China boundary at Demchok, northeast of Ladakh, nearly led to a major confrontation between the patrol teams of the two sides, but conflict was averted by the timely intervention of senior officers from Indian side. China has always used ill-defined LAC to disturb India. The absence of a mutually accepted LAC being physically demarcated on the ground and on military maps means China will continue to make use of these lacunae. In response, Indian officials were compelled to announce in public the plan to upgrade the strategically located helipads in Arunachal Pradesh, including the eight of these located in the Tawang district. India had also to reinforce its positions and construct pathways in the area. With no demarcation of the border, India has to station over three lakhs of soldiers in the disputed India-China border areas.

Tawang Problem

Till now, not much headway has been made in the talks over China's claim to Tawang in Arunachal Pradesh. Obtaining Tawang forms part of China's package proposal, although Tawang is situated well to the south of the Indian side of the LAC. It is assumed that China would recognize India's sovereignty over Arunachal Pradesh while it would insist on taking over Tawang. This proposal is strategically unacceptable to India because Tawang is close to the northeastern states and Bhutan.

Chinese claim on Tawang is based on the fact that Tibet had traditionally exercised administrative control over the region and, moreover, Tawang was the capital of the Monyul district, which is the birthplace of the Sixth Dalai Lama. The

Chinese argued that ceding the area to foreigners would hurt the feelings of the Tibetans. China believed that it would fail to conciliate Tibetans if it were not able to repossess Tawang. The other reason behind China's intention to take over Tawang is that it wants to negate the McMahon Line. China's claim over the Tawang region of Arunachal Pradesh is an irritant to India. China has also indicated that India should be prepared for substantial adjustments on the LAC, which refers to China's claim on Tawang as well as other adjustments in the disputed areas. To deal with these issues, in the Guiding Principles Agreement, India successfully secured the following significant clauses, "In reaching a boundary settlement, the two sides shall safeguard the due interests of their settled populations in the border areas". For India, this clause implied that the status quo of the disputed populated areas, like Tawang or even the whole of Arunachal Pradesh, would be maintained. However, China showed little interest in sharing the same idea. Just before Chinese President Hu Jintao's visit to India in November 2006, the Chinese Ambassador to India, Sun Yuxi, declared that the whole Arunachal Pradesh, including Tawang, is China's territory. India reacted to this promptly and External Affairs Minister Pranab Mukherjee asserted that Arunachal Pradesh is an integral part of India and it was made clear that there could be no discussion on the issue.

Doklam—Interpreting India-China Relations

The recent standoff between India and China on the Doklam plateau which lies at a tri-junction between the India, China, and Bhutan, is the latest in an increasingly long history of conflicts along the border. It has turned into the biggest military standoff between the two armies in years. Although, the latest incursion by Chinese forces occurred in the Doklam region along Bhutan's border with China, and not the India-China border, Indian personnel responded in kind to back up their Bhutanese neighbours.

The relationship between India and Bhutan, in many ways, is a model relationship and they enjoy strong political, development, economic, and military relations. Following

China's adoption of communism and its incorporation of Tibet, Bhutan distanced itself from its northern neighbour China. India encouraged Bhutan to join the United Nations and establish diplomatic relations with other countries. Militarily, without an air force, Bhutan depends on Indian air support. It opts not to maintain official relations with China, although there are ongoing border talks between the two countries. Since 1984, twenty-four rounds of talks have occurred between Bhutan and China over their disputed border without a clear solution.

The standoff in Bhutan's disputed Doklam region occurred near the tri-junction of India-China-Bhutan, and just east of the Sikkim border. Doklam also lies close to the Indian Siliguri Pass, which is also known as "Chicken's Neck" in the Northeast region of India. This narrow region, flanked on two sides by Bangladesh and Nepal, is the only land access to the Northeast. Therefore, Chinese incursions so close to this area provoke a strategic threat to India as well as Bhutan. The incursion began in mid-June of 2017 when People's Liberation Army (PLA) personnel entered the disputed territory and began construction of a road. Bhutanese security forces requested their withdrawal from the disputed land, and India subsequently responded by sending troops to backup Bhutan's position. Later, China accused Indian troops of entering in its territory and India accused the Chinese of destroying its bunker (PLA bulldozed an old bunker of the Indian army stationed in Doklam). Thereafter, China stopped the passage of pilgrims heading toward Kailash-Manasarovar through the Nathu La Pass in Sikkim. However, no loss of life occurred, but there could have been a more intense military flare-up.

The recent incursion in Doklam appeared more brazen than other recent actions. Chinese mass media served up fiery rhetoric around the dispute and were dismissive of Indian complaints. Tensions were partly diffused when disengagement took place towards the end of August and preceding the 9th BRICS summit held in Xiamen, China. Although the situation has cooled down, the India-China border faces constant tension and the seventy-one-day engagement in Doklam is proof of the need for concerted diplomatic communication to prevent such instances.

Strategic Importance of Doklam: By virtue of following three key features of its geography, Bhutan is of vital strategic importance to both India and China.

1. Bhutan has no access to either the sea or another third country without passing through either Indian or Chinese land or airspace.
2. Bhutan controls a number of Himalayan passes that serve as overland routes for the two great powers.
3. Bhutan is a strategic buffer for the Siliguri corridor which is the narrow tract of land, between 20 km. to 60 km. wide, that connects India's Northeastern states with the rest of the country.

Bhutan and China share a 470 km. long border. Since 1984, annual border dialogues between Bhutan and China have reduced the size of the disputed territory from 1128 sq. km. to just 269 sq. km. in three small areas in Northwest part of Bhutan. However, notwithstanding this achievement and the 1988 signing of "The Five Principles of Peaceful Coexistence" by Bhutan and China, final settlement remains a distant prospect. The reason for the stalemate is essentially the strategic implications for India and Bhutan of accepting China's 'package deal' settlement, which consists of a territorial exchange rather than a traditional sectoral approach to border resolution. The exchange would involve China trading 495 sq. km. of territory in the central Bhutan border area in return for 249 sq. km. of territory in Northwestern Bhutan, where the territories of India, Bhutan, and China intersect in an area called the Doklam Plateau, adjacent to the Chumbi Valley. If this deal is materialized, it would bring the Chinese to within 500 km. of the Siliguri corridor and offer China a 'commanding view' of Indian border defences and provide a launch pad to progress operations into the Siliguri corridor. As a result, there are fears that the underlying motive for China's quest to resolve the disputed border seems not to be based on traditional usage or history but owing to the strategic nature of the Western border.

Moreover, the China-Bhutan border negotiations appear to be part of a larger Chinese strategy in South Asia, whereby China wants to gain as much as possible in the Western sector of the dispute with Bhutan.

Bhutan's urgency to demarcate its boundary with China reflects its desire to be an independent actor positively engaged in the region. However, acceptance of the Chinese deal would have profound implications for the Himalayan Kingdom. For the Bhutanese people, the deal would mean giving away rich pastoral land which is important to the livelihoods of people dependent on the area. Acceptance of China's deal would also, in all likelihood, breach Bhutan's "Friendship Treaty" obligations with India. In this treaty, both nations agreed to a provision that neither country would allow its territories to be used for activities inimical to the other.

India and Bhutan also share intimate bonds in the areas of foreign affairs, economy, trade, education and technology, as well as national defence and security. So, it is unlikely that Bhutan would agree to terms which could have such far reaching negative implications for India. Indian investment and strategic culture permeate all aspects of Bhutan's development, hence the catch-cry that India is Bhutan's 'most dependable and generous development partner'. This dependence means that any detrimental changes to India's strategic settings would invariably translate negatively for Bhutan.

Due to above-mentioned complex dynamics, Bhutan finds itself caught between the rivalries of two regional giants. From time to time, this rivalry plays out in favour of Bhutan. For example, India has stepped up its economic assistance programs in Bhutan in response to growing Chinese investment projects, such as the planned extension of the Tibet rail network into Bhutan. At other times, Bhutan has had to contend with the Chinese pressure tactic of border incursions to bring it to the negotiation table. This tactic of China can be described as a pattern of "military intimidation followed by diplomatic seduction".

Bhutan's border problem remains its biggest security challenge and, more broadly, an issue that is set to define its future as a nation state. However, as mutual suspicion is a hallmark of India-China relations, it is difficult to argue how Bhutan would agree to the Chinese deal given its critical security implications for India. Due to these reasons, the remaining 269 sq. km. of disputed territory is likely to remain unresolved for the foreseeable future.

Beyond the dynamics of India-China rivalry and the problems bestowed by geography for strategically-important buffer states like Bhutan, the Bhutan-China border dispute also points to a far more complex aspect of Himalayan geo-strategic politics, namely the role of Tibet. Bhutan and Tibet have a long and complex history and continue to share common cultural and religious bonds based on Tibetan Buddhist ideology. And for China, the Tibetan link with Bhutan is a powerful force in the dispute, as settlement of the border and the cross-border movement of people could help to legitimize China's rule in Tibet and vindicate its Tibetan policies. On the other hand, for Bhutan, in the absence of settlement progress, its continued cautious policy of non-advocacy of Tibetan causes could also aid in the normalization of Bhutan-China relations and lead to economic benefits from China's Western Development Strategy.

Border Disputes in the Larger Context of India-China Relations

Neither India nor China has allowed the bilateral ties to be hijacked by the border disputes alone. In the post-Cold War world, political leaders in both countries have realized that India and China share many common interests at the bilateral, regional, and global levels. Both countries have understood that they have a similar, if not completely identical task of sustaining strong economic growth and development in order to reduce poverty and improve the living standards of their respective growing populations. The prerequisite for either party to focus on its internal socio-economic advancement is to have a stable and peaceful border region. This is the reason why both countries have managed to set up various stabilization measures to handle their border disputes through negotiations. They have even initiated regular defence consultation meetings and joint military exercises, even though the exercises are small in scale and limited to low sensitivity areas. Due to both sides' strategic thinking that prioritizes overall stability, trade has over recent years grown at a phenomenal rate, significantly benefitting bilateral ties in trade and other economic aspects.

On the other hand, at the regional level, India and China are involved in a complex strategic rivalry—both sides have avoided actions that jeopardise the fundamental strategic interests of the other party. Since late 1990s, China has attempted to adopt a more balanced policy towards India and Pakistan—the two South Asian countries that have been embroiled in hostility for decades. China's growing presence in the Indian Ocean, also termed as string of pearls strategy, was aimed at protecting China's trade and energy interests in the region. On the other hand, because of its long tradition of non-alignment and the desire to sustain national autonomy in its relations with other major powers of the world, India has decided not to strategically align itself with the US in what China's fear is a US-driven containment policy against China. India has also not actively responded to the invitations from Japan to form an "arch of democracies" or a "diamond of democracies" among Japan, India, and Australia, which China argues is part of a policy of 'encirclement' against itself. To be sure, China will continue to be wary of India's strategic dominance in South Asia, and India will continue to seek to undermine any Chinese effort towards a China-centric regional order in East Asia. However, there are currently no indications that the two Asian giants are heading towards a strategic contest that will dampen bilateral ties. On the contrary, both China and India have expressed interest in the Regional Comprehensive Economic Partnership (RCEP) initiative spearheaded by ASEAN. It means that both the countries seem to be interested in participating in regional integration in East Asia.

At the global level, India and China have numerous very tangible and long-term common interests. Both the countries believe that the world should become multi-polar and emerging powers should play a more important role in international affairs. They also have very similar views on global policy responses on issues such as climate change, international trade and finance, and non-intervention in the domestic affairs of other countries. They have strengthened their cooperation in the context of the G20 and the BRICS, and other newly emerging multilateral institutions, in order to contend with Global Super Powers for global influence and decision-making power. However, India-China relations at the global level are not without problems. For example, China has always opposed India's bid for a permanent membership in the UN Security Council.

CHAPTER 5

The Tibet Issue

Historically India and Tibet were very close to each other. It was easier and convenient to go to Beijing from Lhasa via India and sea route than by land route. The Anglo-Tibetan agreement of 1904 had granted India military, communication, postal, trading and other rights in Tibet and at the same time recognized the Chinese suzerainty over Tibet. However, the changes in the geopolitical situation due to Chinese occupation of Tibet in 1950 made India to redefine its relationship with the China. India protested the use of force by China in dealing with Tibet and hoped that Tibet would be granted genuine autonomy. India recognized Tibet as a region of China and signed the first agreement in 1954 with the China after protracted negotiations. This agreement aimed at developing a good neighbourly relationship between the two countries and conduct border trade between India and Tibet. Trusting China's friendly gestures, India surrendered the special rights it had inherited from the British Government according to the 1904 agreement. The agreement of 1954, in addition to recognizing Tibet as a part of China, can be considered as the first confidence building measure between the two countries as it had for the first time laid Five Principles of Peaceful Coexistence that could still be considered a model for conducting relationship between any two sovereign countries. Besides establishing trade agencies in India and Tibet, specifying markets for trade, designation of traditional passes and routes, the 1954 agreement also accredited traditions and customs for pilgrimages from India and Tibet to each other's places. However, this agreement did not last for more than eight years due to strained relationship between India and China caused by the subsequent events in 1950s like Khampa rebellion, riots in Tibet and the Dalai Lama's exiled to India along with his followers, and border clashes.

China's Tibet policy has been influenced either by hardliners or moderates at different times over the years. China's domestic policies and its external environment have equal impact on its Tibet policy. Its Tibet policy has five discernible phases of different approaches.

Phase-1 (1951–1959): The 1951 agreement granted full autonomy to Tibet in the matters of governance, religion, language and culture, and preserving the traditional religious and administrative institutions like the institutions of the Dalai Lama and Panchen Lama within the geographical boundaries of Tibet and vesting the foreign and defence matters with the Chinese central government. However, as a young communist nation, China was in great hurry to introduce communist reforms in Tibet. It was a sudden and painful experience for the people of Tibet who had been leading an almost isolated different system for several centuries, away from external interference. Tibet was a neutral during the World War-II, which alienated the Tibetan people and their leadership. Due to this, riots and rebellion broke out in Tibet many times between 1952 and 1957, with certain external support. In February 1957, Mao had said that conditions in Tibet were not ripe for reforms and, therefore, the implementation of reforms be postponed till 1962; and offered to reduce the Han cadres in Tibet. Mao's policy of moderation and gradualism had the support of Dalai Lama and the elite Tibetans, but it was not implemented in practice. This phase was ended with the exodus of Dalai Lama and his supporters to India in 1959.

Phase-2 (1959–1976): This phase was dominated by the hardline policies and internal power struggle in China. The 'Great Leap Forward' and 'Great Proletarian Cultural Revolution' brought unparallel turmoil within China. The involvement of Communist Party of China (CPC) members in Tibet like attack on religious institutions, culture and language, and increasingly strained relationship with India only further alienated the people of Tibet. China reorganized Tibet by making U-tsang as Tibet Autonomous Region and merging Kham and Amdo regions with Yunnan, Sichuan, Gansu, and Qinghai provinces.

Phase-3 (1978–1986): In this phase, Deng Xiaoping adopted soft policy to handle Tibet issue and proposed to talk with Dalai Lama. However, this step also ended in failure, but a communication line was set up for the first time between Dalai Lama and the Chinese leadership.

Phase-4 (1987–2001): After failure of Deng's soft policy, China adopted a different approach to solve Tibet issue through economic development instead of focusing on political solution alone. This policy had some success as Dalai Lama diluted his demand from independence to autonomy, but Chinese leadership had not taken much interest in carrying any negotiations with the Tibetan leadership.

Phase-5 (2002– ...): Current phase is marked by realistic handling of Tibetan issue, which combines winning Tibetans through economic development and conducting dialogue with the Tibetan leadership in exile in India. China has proposed that since Tibet has already been liberated and integrated into the big Chinese family, Dalai Lama and other Tibetans who had left Tibet should come back and take part in the development of Tibet.

China considers Tibet issue its internal matter in which no foreign countries have any right to interfere. Since India has officially recognized Chinese claims over Tibet since 1954 when the two countries signed an agreement regarding trade and intercourse between the Tibet region and India, China believes that India should adhere to the Five Principle of Peaceful Coexistence and the Tibet issue will not come up in the agenda of India-China relations. However, the interactions over the last decade seemed to be against such an expectation as India's sincerity in honouring its commitment is frequently questioned by China, which has repeatedly expressed concerns about the anti-China activities of exiled Tibetans in India.

India cannot always conform to China's demand to stand away from the Tibet issue as, more significantly, it is identified as strategic leverage against China. Since India has security threat from China, the Tibet issue is one of the bargaining chips India can use when dealing with China. India's particular role in the

Tibet issue, especially India's hosting of the Tibetan leader, Dalai Lama, and thousands of his followers, gives India a say in the matter. Therefore, China is not satisfied with India's dealing on and attitude to the Tibetan question, but it expects to marginalize the Tibet issue in India-China relations in order to avoid India's involvement. China's continued suspicion about India's sincerity and interactions on the Tibetan question has contributed to the formation of a culture of distrust between the countries, which is also one of the features of India-China relations. Unless China and Tibet reach a final agreement on Tibet's relations with China, India's role and involvement in the Tibetan question will still be seen as a thorn by China, and a source of mistrust.

China's liberation of Tibet in the early 1950s appeared the only issue that might worsen India-China relations. In October 1950, China dispatched troops into Tibet to liberate the region. Then the Tibetan authority was compelled to send representatives to Beijing to negotiate its status and relationship with the new China. On 23rd May 1951, the Chinese and Tibetan deputations signed the Seventeen-Point Agreement for the Peaceful Liberation of Tibet. The agreement stated that the Tibetan people would return to "the big family of the Motherland", and Beijing would not alter the existing political system in Tibet and promised that the Tibetan people would have the right to exercise national regional autonomy under the leadership of China's Central Government. However, China's military action against Tibet came as a shock to the Indians. When India became independent in 1947, it inherited, the existing treaty rights and obligations of British India regarding Tibet. It also wanted to continue British policy towards Tibet, namely, treating Tibet as an autonomous buffer region between India and China, while recognizing Chinese suzerainty, but not sovereignty over Tibet. Therefore, India soon branded China's military actions against Tibet as an "invasion" and sent several notes to the Chinese Government to lodge protest. However, despite these diplomatic gestures, India was not willing to confront China over the issue. On 12th February 1951, Prime Minister Pt. Nehru said in Parliament that he would not allow the event to affect India's policy or desire to maintain friendly relations with China. Even he had no intention of letting the development affect India's China policy in general and the policy regarding the entry of China into the United Nations in particular.

India's policy of non-intervention in the Tibet issue was strengthened when China's takeover of Tibet was legalized by the conclusion of the Seventeen-Point Agreement. India accepted China's claim over Tibet by refusing to sponsor the Tibetan appeal to the United Nations against the People's Liberation Army's invasion. In order to solve India's inherited historical rights regarding Tibet, such as the deployment of military guards, India and China began negotiations in December 1953. Finally, the two countries signed the agreement regarding trade and intercourse between India and Tibet in April 1954, setting up the legal framework for India's relations with the post-liberated Tibet; and India accepted China's sovereignty over Tibet while using the term the "Tibet region of China".

India's reluctant attitude and caution could not prevent Tibet becoming a controversial issue between India and China, and the Tibet issue continued to test India-China friendship. In May 1959, the People's Liberation Army moved into Lhasa to quell the most serious revolt since the peaceful liberation, and there were rumours among the Tibetans that the Army would harm Dalai Lama. As a result, Dalai Lama and his associates decided to escape from Tibet. Dalai Lama with his associates fled to India and asked for political asylum. India soon granted asylum to the Dalai Lama and his followers. Indira Gandhi was given the task of setting up an all-party Central Relief Committee for the Tibetan refugees. However, India was still not willing to challenge China over Tibet issue, therefore, India abstained from voting on the United Nations General Assembly resolution that criticized the Chinese, of violating of human rights in Tibet. India hoped that such an abstention would facilitate eventual conciliatory efforts towards a peaceful solution of the Tibetan problem.

To solve Tibet issue, Pt. Nehru tried to play the role of mediator and requested China to send Panchen Lama, the second highest ranking leader in Tibet, or any other Chinese representatives to come to India to discuss the situation of Tibet with Dalai Lama. However, China rejected the proposal by saying that Tibet issue was entirely an internal issue, and China was not prepared to allow a third party to become involved. As China saw India's sheltering Dalai Lama as a breach of the spirit of the Five Principles of Peaceful Coexistence to interfere in China's internal affairs, Tibet issue began to shatter the mutual trust between China and India. In retaliation to India's Tibet policy, China encouraged the Naga and Mizo rebellions in northeast India.

Although, India remains very concerned about China's takeover of Tibet, from Pt. Nehru's administration onward, the Indian Government has clearly acknowledged the fact that Tibet is under China's control and it is very difficult for India alone to help Tibet split from China. In addition, India needs to take account of its own domestic situation if it wants to accommodate Tibet's independence. Like China's far-flung communities of Tibet and Xinjiang, India's Northeast and Kashmir are its weak spots. China was sponsoring Naga and Mizo insurgencies in India's Northeast by the late 1970s. It also backed Pakistan's stand on the Kashmir issue. Any Indian public support for Tibetan independence would possibly result in China taking revenge by interfering in India's domestic discord, especially the agitation in Kashmir and the Northeast region. In any way, China will not allow the secessionist movement of the Tibetans to succeed and weaken its hold on Tibet. Even if making Tibet a security buffer would serve India's interests, India has to be very cautious about any mention of Tibet's independence. Therefore, although India has a particular role and special relationship with Tibet, the Indian Government has had no intention of supporting Tibetan independence in public.

China's cautious treatment of the Tibet issue in India-China relations signals that it would like to develop relations in other fields while shelving the differences between India and China. On the other hand, it also hopes to encourage India to extricate itself from the Tibet embroilment while stressing that common interests outweigh the differences. For China, overemphasis on India's role in the Tibet issue would only give India greater leverage against China and contribute to the internationalization of the

Tibet issue. The continuous effort to reduce the significance of the Tibet issue in India-China relations were found during Prime Minister Narasimha Rao's visit to China in 1993. The Tibet issue received a relatively perfunctory treatment in the talks of Prime Minister Narasimha Rao and the Chinese leaders as they focused on the border talks. Similarly, in 1996 when Chinese President Jiang Zemin visited India, Tibet issue was raised only during the meeting between Chinese Foreign Minister Qian Qichen and his Indian counterpart Inder Kumar Gujral. These developments reflected that India and China shared the common aspiration to marginalize the Tibet issues while improving relations in other fields.

Tibet—A Source of Great Power Rivalry

Tibet lies at the heart of India-China relations and is the key to understanding China's stance on the India-China territorial dispute. China's territorial dispute with India is inextricably linked with the past, present and future status of Tibet, which has shaped the informal and invisible dynamics of India-China relations and politics from the 1950s onwards. Tibet is the legal foundation on which both India's and China's border claims rest. If the Chinese power elite consider Tibet to be strategically important to China, the Indian counterparts think that it is equally vital to Indian national security.

The history of Tibet is dominated by relationships with India and China, and Indian influence permeates Tibetan history, culture, and religion. Therefore, an orientation towards India is woven into the fabric of Tibetan society. On the other hand, Chinese influence stems from around 640 AD and is characterized by bitter territorial conquests between competing Tibetan and Chinese dynasties and the ritual obeisance of the imperial Chinese tributary system. Thus, both India and China see Tibet as within their historic sphere of influence, which invariably leads to a clashing of nationalist narratives between the two great powers.

The salience of Tibet to India and China is also rooted in Tibet's geo-strategic setting. Tibet was invaded by China not just on historical pretext but primarily on strategic grounds as it constituted an "open backdoor to China" for India. China's concerns over the ease with which Tibet could be used by India can be explained as, "Once Tibet became independent and was forced to ally itself with India, India would be able to advance thousands of kilometers into central China, and its missiles would be able to hit whole China from the Tibetan plateau. So, it is obvious that for China to lose such a vast barrier would be unacceptable from a national security perspective. Preparing for a possible future conflict with India, is the bottom line as to why China cannot allow Tibetan independence." Thus, China's dominant fear when it comes to Tibetan autonomy or independence is that in the case of a India-China war, Tibet would ally with India as a 'natural choice', which could bring Indian forces to within 100 kilometers from central China and Sichuan province. However, India also harbours fears founded on Tibet's geo-strategic setting. China's annexation of Tibet 60 years ago removed India's political buffer. And because of China's Western Development Strategy, India now sees the network of airstrips and airbases that China has built through the Tibetan plateau, along with other widespread infrastructure development projects as providing the logistical wherewithal for Chinese invasion across the border. Thus, Tibet's geo-strategic setting is effectively the source of the mutual threat perception and alignment patterns that dominate the India-China relationship.

Beyond its buffer-zone geography, economic factors also shape the Tibet's strategic value. Tibet literally means "Western Treasure House". It is estimated to hold approximately 40 percent of China's mineral resources, including coal, gold, lithium and copper. It is also the world's third largest fresh water repository, after the polar icecaps, and is the source of most of Asia's major river systems, including the Yellow, Salween, Irrawaddy, Yangtze, Mekong, Brahmaputra and Indus rivers. The value of these resources has two key aspects that shape the Himalayan security environment.

(a) As a country of scarce resources that sustains a "water-stressed economy", China views Tibet as a vast area of potential economic wealth to be exploited in support of its national development goals. In other words, China's objective for Tibet is to transform it into China's resource colony, as China cannot afford to loosen its grip over its Western Treasure House.

(b) The issue of water management for projects such as flood control, irrigation and hydroelectric power offers China the potential for enormous influence and leverage over downstream riparian nations, such as India, Bangladesh, Nepal, Bhutan, Pakistan, Vietnam, Burma, Cambodia, Laos and Thailand.

Moreover, China's plan to dam the Brahmaputra river in Tibet features heavily in Indian security calculations given that the consequences of China "turning off the tap" upstream could be famine in Northeast India. Overall, by virtue of its resource potential, Tibet is a potent source of both direct and latest Chinese power and influence throughout South Asia.

Some of the reasons for the India-China rivalry and border disputes are historical, geographical and resource factors that underscore Tibet's strategic value. The legacy of Chinese actions over 60 years ago also plays a major role in perpetuating the stalemate. In 1951, according to China, the People's Liberation Army (PLA) liberated Tibet from the British imperialists and their Indian heirs and pupils. On the other hand, according to the Tibetan Government in exile, 1951 marked Tibet's invasion by China, an action which changed Tibet's status from an independent nation to an occupied country, without United Nations representation. While India recognized Tibet as part of China as far back as 1954, its recognition was conditional upon Tibet's enjoyment of autonomy. Yet it is precisely the absence of autonomy that has led India to not give the Chinese the clear and unambiguous statements regarding their sovereignty over Tibet that Chinese interests so desire. Furthermore, India also plays host to the Tibetan Government in exile, including its leader Dalai Lama, and offers sanctuary to over 100000 Tibetan refugees. This remains a sore point for China and is seen as direct interference in China's international affairs. China perceives a strong exiled Tibetan community in India as the root cause of Tibetan separatism and, therefore, India, as the host nation for the government in exile, is seen as a 'hub of Tibetan separatism'.

In order to contain these forces, China wants to keep the dispute alive so as to pressure India not to allow the exiled Tibetans to create instability inside China. Its logic is that if the territorial dispute was settled and no longer weighted heavily on Indian calculations, then India may be impelled to take reckless action regarding Tibet. Thus, the active border dispute is actually a lever, which China can use against India to deter any aggressive Indian actions towards Tibet.

From India's perspective, it is the status quo of the Tibetan Government in exile that provides India with leverage over China in the border dispute. It is speculated that if Dalai Lama returned to Tibet, he would come under China's pressure to support its boundary claims, resulting in China's border claims gaining more legitimacy. Thus, for India, nurturing the China-Tibet deadlock is fundamentally in its national interest, as Dalai Lama and his government in exile effectively support India's border claims. To the greater point of view, Tibet can be seen as the source of the mutually-deterrent conditions that feed the border stalemate and restrain the dispute from escalating. In India's case, China appears to have the logistical upper-hand because of its Tibetan bases, airfields, roads and rail infrastructure which could serve as a ready network of forward operating points for any conflict. This perception of relative Chinese military advantage when compared to the infrastructure of India's border territories acts as a restraining factor against any Indian adventurism. Furthermore, a hostile local Tibetan population performs the same function in the case of Chinese adventurism. It is believed that as long as the Tibetan people are not reconciled with the Chinese rule in Tibet and continue to remain resentful of Chinese presence on the plateau, it is not prudent for China to get involved in a border war with India because such a war in the context of a resentful Tibetan population might prove like fighting a war on two fronts.

For China, a border war with India is inextricably linked to the security of Tibet. China prefers an undefined border as a bargaining chip because of its suspicions that India prefers an independent Tibet and aids Tibetan separatists. This position is set to endure given that from China's perspective, any weakening of the Chinese stand on Tibet could mark the beginning of their losing control over China's restive periphery consisting of Tibet, Xinjiang and Inner Mongolia. Therefore, net effect of China's enduring stance on its territorial integrity is to constrain and deter any military action against India along the disputed border.

India's Security Concern

India's security concern about the threat from Tibet can be understood from the fact that China has built up a military arsenal in Tibet. Once a militarily weak buffer zone between empires, Tibet has now been militarized to the point of containing at least 120000 Chinese troops and ten military airfields. China's military modernization and improvement of the infrastructure in Tibet could affect India's security in the long term. Although India has strategic interests while negotiating the Confidence Building Measures (CBMs) with China in raising concerns regarding the Chinese military build-up, China has maintained that its military deployments in Tibet are not open to discussion.

Another factor of serious concern to India about Tibet is the emplacement of Chinese nuclear-tipped missiles in Tibet. These missiles can target all Indian cities. The same strategic considerations over Tibet's geostrategic value made the Indian side watchful of China's Grand Western Development project. However, China has attempted to give an economic colour to the infrastructure development in this region. But India took China's mega-infrastructure build-up in the Tibet region as tentacles that not only strengthen China's grip on these restive regions and enable China to further exploit natural resources, but also advance China's capability to move troops and weapons stockpiled in its other neighbouring military regions. These strategic links, including the rebuilding of the Lhasa-Beijing Highway, would double China's military deployment and multiply the missile deployment in Tibet. Thus, China's Tibet-related western development would affect India's strategic environment and increase India's vulnerability.

Like China's Tibet and Xinjiang regions, India's Northeast and Kashmir are India's weak spots. In the late 1970s, China was instrumental in sponsoring Naga and Mizo insurgencies in

India's Northeast region. It is also backing Pakistan's stand on the Kashmir issue. Any Indian support for Tibetan independence would possibly result in China's taking revenge by interfering in India's domestic discord, especially the agitation in Kashmir and the Northeast region. Therefore, even if India has a particular role and special relationship with Tibet, the Indian Government has had no intention of supporting Tibetan independence.

CHAPTER 6

The Nuclear Dimension

The sunshine period in India-China relations once again disappeared behind a dark cloud after Pokhran-II, which was the series of five nuclear bomb test explosions conducted by India at the Indian Army's Pokhran Test Range in May 1998. It was the second nuclear test conducted by India—the first test, code-named Smiling Buddha, was conducted in May 1974. In May 1998, Defense Minister George Fernandes made a remark that China was India's main threat, which caused once again, after the Sumdorong Chu incident in 1987 in Arunachal Pradesh, a setback to India-China relations. The atmosphere became tenser after the nuclear test. The Chinese saw the test as causing serious damage to the bilateral relations and took stronger objection to Prime Minister Vajpayee's letter to US President Clinton, justifying India's decision to test nuclear weapon by pointing to the threat from China, and asked for an Indian explanation for considering China as a threat. Beijing also joined the other UN Security Council members in passing Resolution No. 1172, which condemned the nuclear test by India and Pakistan. China cancelled its decision to participate in the pre-scheduled 1998 meeting of the JWG (Joint Working Groups) alternately held in each country to discuss CBMs (Confidence Building Measures).

China successfully exploded its first atomic bomb on October 1964, which opened up a new dimension in India-China relations—the nuclear dimension. In such a scenario, the Indian leaderships had to consider in the light of the latest development whether India should continue to be a non-nuclear weapons state. India had tried to appeal to the US and the UK for some form of protection from China's nuclear threat, but had failed to achieve any reassurance. Therefore, the threat of

China's nuclear capability has continued to be an important driving force behind India's nuclear weapons programme to the present day. However, India remained in an ambiguous nuclear limbo, and had to choose between being a nuclear power and being a non-nuclear state. Although, India detonated its own nuclear device under Indira Gandhi's administration on May 1974, it maintained that the test was merely for peaceful purposes and it was reluctant to manufacture nuclear weapons. India's ambiguity towards developing nuclear weapons may have been seen as one strategic option for the Indian leaders, but it failed to come to terms with India's perceived threat arising from China's nuclear capability. By May 1998, India's deep-seated suspicions were reinforced by the possibility of China's nuclear coercion, China's clandestine support for Pakistan's nuclear weapons programme, and the enhanced international status China derived from nuclear weapons. The failure to achieve a satisfactory solution to its security concerns clearly spurred India's decision to move more surely down the road to nuclear weaponization. On May 1998, India finally discarded its traditional stance and proclaimed itself a nuclear weapons state after conducting a series of five rounds of nuclear tests. Unlike the 1974 tests, its rationale for exploding nuclear devices brought a new and more significant nuclear dimension to India-China relations.

India equipped with nuclear weapons presented a totally different challenge for China. India's possession of nuclear weapons altered the hard power structure and played a decisive role in building up a new military balance between India and China. Moreover, India's new identity as a nuclear power reshaped the ideational structure between India and China. Chinese leaders not only needed to reassess the implications of nuclear India's challenges to its security environment, but also needed to take account of India's enhanced international status derived from its possession of nuclear weapons. Meanwhile, China also had to deal with the "China threat" theory used by Indian strategic planners and to justify India's move against the international nuclear non-proliferation regime.

Before 1998, for China, the main concerns about a nuclear threat came first from the US and then the Soviet Union. Although, the hostile relationship meant that China became a potential nuclear threat to India, Chinese leaders did not feel it necessary to launch a nuclear attack against India, *i.e.*, China's nuclear deterrent was not directed towards India. On the other hand, India has perceived a clear nuclear threat from China since 1964. There were three sources of concerns that had contributed to the construction of this perception.

(a) The scenario that China could use its nuclear capability to blackmail or coerce India.

(b) China's stance towards nuclear proliferation due to China's assistance to Pakistan.

(c) China's political and diplomatic status as a nuclear power.

Partly due to its possession of nuclear weapons, China edged out India and secured a higher international status. This undermined India's prestige and leadership among the Asian and developing countries. These concerns related to China's nuclear power motivated India to consider the nuclear option.

China's nuclear capability, its nuclear connection with Pakistan, and the nuclear-state status constituted an imperative incentive for India to develop its own nuclear weapons. However, India's nuclear weapons programme remained dormant between 1974 and 1998. The next two decades after the 1974 test saw India continue its efforts to keep disarmament in focus in international fora. India maintained an ambiguous stance, showing its nuclear capability and keeping the nuclear option without building a nuclear arsenal. The most controversial aspect of China's nuclear policy was its position towards non-proliferation. Only since the late 1980s has China adjusted its foreign policy operation to actively take part in the nuclear non-proliferation regime. China joined the International Atomic Energy Agency (IAEA) in 1985, more than two decades after going nuclear, and agreed to place its civilian nuclear facilities under IAEA safeguards in 1988. In 1992, it acceded to the Treaty on the Non-Proliferation of Nuclear Weapons (NPT).

In addition, it joined the Zangger Committee in October 1997 and joined the Nuclear Suppliers Group (NSG) in June 2004. In September 2004, it officially submitted its application for membership of the Missile Technology Control Regime (MTCR). It was also among the first countries to sign the Comprehensive Test Ban Treaty (CTBT) in 1996.

As far as India-China nuclear relations are concerned, China's assistance to Pakistan's weapon programme has been a cause of grave concern for India's security. In the late 1970s, the media published evidence of China's aid for Pakistan's nuclear programme. Since then, apart from the conventional military equipment, China had been assisting Pakistan in developing its missile and nuclear capabilities to compensate for its deficit in weaponry vis-à-vis India. In 1983, China had transferred a complete nuclear weapon design and sufficient uranium to build a nuclear weapon in Pakistan. China also supplied nuclear-capable M-II missiles to Pakistan between 1992 and 1994. With Chinese assistance, Pakistan was believed to have moved towards serial production of solid-propellant Short-Range Ballistic Missiles (SRBMs), such as the Shaheen-I and Haider-I. China is also the 'mother' of Ghauri, Pakistan's Intermediate Range Ballistic Missile (IRBM).

Successive Indian governments had, over time, tried to restore the nuclear tests. According to former Indian Defence Minister (and later President), R. Venkataraman, India was ready with full preparations for an underground nuclear test in 1983, but was dissuaded from going ahead by external pressure. A similar attempt to carry out new nuclear tests was made in 1995, but the then American Ambassador to India, Frank Wisner, showed satellite photographs to Indian officials of India's preparations for nuclear tests and asked the Indian side to halt the programme. It was BJP, which won the general elections in 1998, that decided to end the long-standing ambiguity over the nuclear options. The reasons for the BJP Government to go nuclear were mixed. To put it simply, three main factors were behind the decision—India's perception of its security needs, domestic political considerations, and the ambition to make India a world-recognised great power.

China might not have played a part in the domestic factor behind India's decision to develop nuclear weapons, but played a major part in shaping India's security perception, and found itself relevant in India's pursuit of becoming a major world power. This reflected India's perception and assessment of the post-cold war security environment—the end of the Cold War had done little to ameliorate India's security concerns, and China was seen as the major contributor in destabilizing India's security environment. Defence Minister George Fernandes termed China as India's "potential threat number one", stressing that the potential threat from China was greater than that from Pakistan because India was encircled by Chinese military and naval activity—China had extended eleven airfields in Tibet, which posed a threat to India's security, and had set up electronic surveillance installations on the Coco islands, 40 km off the northern tip of the Andaman and Nicobar islands, to observe Indian missile trials and other exercises. Fernandes' comments on China had evoked sharp criticism from China, which had officially protested to India twice in less than a month. China's Foreign Ministry spokesman described Indian defence minister's utterances as "ridiculous and not worthy of refutation", but his statements had seriously sabotaged the atmosphere for improving relations.

Despite the furor created in China by India's nuclear test, a thaw between the two sides eventually emerged. The nuclear issue featured as an irritant in India-China relations for some time, which really put the bilateral relationship in a limbo. In order to mend relations, the Indian side took several initiatives to placate the Chinese. First was the statement by Brajesh Mishra, the Principal Secretary to the Prime Minister, who said that India wanted to have the best of relations with China and urged China to return to dialogue. This was followed by Vajpayee's statement that some misunderstanding between China and India had been created only by the distorted version of statements appearing in the media. However, China expected a more credible commitment from India. In February 1999, Indian officials were sent to Beijing in an attempt to urge their counterparts to restart the dialogue on the boundary question. The official visit brought about a positive result with an announcement by the Chinese Foreign Minister Tang Jiaxuan just a few weeks later that the Chinese side had recently acknowledged the statements issued by Indian leaders that China posed no threat to India. Tang's announcement came as the first positive signal of China's desire to put behind the bitterness that had arisen in the wake of India's nuclear tests. Finally, both countries were able to resume talks once again after a span of nine months when, in June 1999, the Minister of External Affairs Jaswant Singh visited China. Both the sides reached a consensus that the prerequisite for restoring and developing India-China relations, and it was assured that neither side will regard the other as a threat. President K.R. Narayanan visited China on May 2000, when his Chinese counterpart, Jiang Zemin, proposed a four-point proposal concerning the development of bilateral relations in the 21st century. After all these initiatives, the two neighbouring giants enhanced the level of bilateral personnel visits to increase mutual understanding and trust; expanded trade and economic cooperation; strengthened coordination and cooperation in international affairs; and properly handled issues left over from the past in the spirit of seeking common ground while reserving differences.

Following the trend to restore the pre-Pokhran-II relationship, at the twelfth Joint Working Group (JWG) meeting on the boundary problem in April 2000, India and China agreed to resume high-level military interactions, which had been suspended after India's nuclear tests. Chinese Foreign Minister Tang Jiaxuan visited India in July 2000, followed by Lt. General Tian Shugen, Vice-President of the Academy of Military Science, in August 2000. It was the first exchange between the two armies after the People's Liberation Army Chief of General Staff Fu Quanyou had visited India during April to May 1998. Subsequently, two Indian naval ships paid a goodwill visit to China in September 2000. Thus, there was a positive shift in the tone and content of the bilateral relationship between India and China. A comprehensive dialogue mechanism was formed with the aim of promoting an improvement of and a development in bilateral relations through dialogue. Despite the existing negotiation mechanism on boundary problem, a security dialogue was established in June 1999 during External Affairs Minister Jaswant Singh's visit to China. Three rounds of the dialogue were held between March 2000 and September 2002. An India-China Eminent Persons Group was constituted during President K.R. Narayanan's state visit to China during May-June 2000, and the first meeting of this group took place in New Delhi on 17th-18th September 2001. The group was expected to serve as an important advisory agency for the two governments. The India-China dialogue mechanism on counter terrorism was established during Chinese Premier Zhu Rongji's visit to India in January 2002 to address concerns in the wake of the September 11 events. The first meeting was held in New Delhi on 23rd April 2002.

The dialogue mechanism appeared to be a new feature of India-China relations in the post-Pokhran era, but there was still doubt whether both sides could make use of it to enhance mutual understanding and further strengthen bilateral relations. During Prime Minister Atal Bihari Vajpayee's visit to China from 22nd to 27th June 2003, both sides issued a declaration on Principles for Relations and Comprehensive Cooperation, which stated, "The two countries are not a threat to each other. Neither side shall use or threaten to use force against the other." However, the so-called "constructive partnership of cooperation oriented towards the twenty-first century" had not worked out as satisfactorily as hoped since its proclamation.

India and China showed a willingness and a capability to manage the diplomatic aftershock of India's nuclear tests, however, suspicions and distrust still remained. With India's emergence as a nuclear power in its neighbourhood, for the Chinese, a more significant question that needed to be answered was whether a nuclear India would undermine China's security. In fact, China had not ignored India's military power in assessment of India-China relations. In assessing India's nuclear weapons programme, the major concern for China was that China lost most of its nuclear superiority against India. No matter how credible India's nuclear weapons were, China perceived India's nuclear weapons as an unpleasant factor in its security environment. The quantitative and qualitative improvement of India's nuclear forces has led to an increased perception of threat in China. As a result, China is still very reluctant to recognize India's status as a nuclear state and tries to underline the illegitimacy of India's nuclear weapons programme.

Since India had taken China's and Pakistan's nuclear capability as the main security imperative in the development of a nuclear weapons programme, the implication was that India intended to use its nuclear weapons to counterbalance China's strength. In other words, India's possession of nuclear weapons had made an impact on China's strategic environment. China had become a member of the nuclear club decades before India and its nuclear weapons programme remained many years in advance of India's. However, India's decision to go down the route of developing nuclear weapons has neutralized China's perceived superiority in terms of military strength. Now, China will no longer be able to use nuclear blackmail and coercion against India, because India is also equipped with nuclear strike ability, *i.e.*, with India being a nuclear power, China would not like to antagonize India beyond a certain point.

One element of India's nuclear doctrine is that it unequivocally renounces the first use of nuclear weapons. The commitment to no-first-use has explicitly underscored India's lack of any intention to use nuclear weapons as a tool of pre-emptive policy and its intention to use them instead simply to dissuade attempts by any state at nuclear blackmail. Though it is tempting to dismiss the no-first-use commitment as a mere boilerplate, and although the efficiency of the no-first-use policy is also questioned by some analysts, the deterrent nature of India's nuclear doctrine appears clear. The primary role of India's nuclear force is to protect the nation from the prospect of nuclear blackmail and coercion at the hands of nuclear powered countries such as China and Pakistan. Since, China also claims that it will not be the first to use nuclear weapons, the no-first-use principle has become a set of double safety valves between India and China to avoid a nuclear clash. Therefore, even though the two countries are equipped with nuclear weapons, a nuclear war between India and China remains less likely.

The Deterrent Effects of India's Nuclear Programme on China

India developed its nuclear weapons to counterbalance China's and Pakistan's nuclear capability. Its possession of nuclear weapons had made an impact on China's and Pakistan's strategic environment. India had previously enjoyed massive superiority over Pakistan in conventional military strength. However, Pakistan had taken the same step to conduct tests and to declare itself a nuclear-weapons state on the heels of India's nuclear blasts. As a result, the option of joining the nuclear club had to some extent neutralized India's conventional military strength against Pakistan, since Pakistan was also armed with a nuclear deterrent.

The conflict between India and Pakistan in fact did not serve China's interests either. China had always been reluctant to be dragged into an India-Pakistan military stand-off and had concerns about the possibility of a Pakistan-India nuclear holocaust. Besides, it is also worried about the impact of a nuclear confrontation in its neighbourhood. This was one of the reasons why, instead of supporting Pakistan's adventure, China asked both India and Pakistan to show restraint during the Kargil war. In addition to the possible India-Pakistan nuclear conflict, for China, a more critical question was whether a nuclear-armed India posted a threat or a serious challenge to China's security. China joined the nuclear club decades before India and its nuclear weapons programme remained many years in advance of India's. However, India's decision to go down the route of developing nuclear weapons has neutralized China's perceived superiority in terms of military strength. Now, China will no longer be able to use nuclear blackmail and coercion against India, because the latter is also equipped with nuclear strike ability. Therefore, it is believed that, with India being a nuclear power, China would not like to antagonize India beyond a certain point.

China did not consider India a serious threat for itself. Even so, it has kept an eye on India's nuclear build-up and has tried to interpret India's real intentions towards China in the context of nuclear issue. Before India's nuclear tests, Chinese analysts deemed that China's western frontier was stable and peaceful. However, India's nuclear tests changed that opposite view. After the nuclear tests, the Chinese side suddenly found that India had developed unknown facets. Despite lacking a detailed analysis about how India's nuclear weapons programme would affect China's security environment, China has taken India's nuclear weapons as a negative factor. Therefore, it is believed that South Asia is no longer a region that poses only a minimum threat to China's security, instead it might become the region with the greatest potential threat. As a result, China has become more cautious, seeing India-China relations as an unstable factor in China's security environment.

Conducting nuclear tests indicates that a country is willing to take the step to cross the nuclear threshold, but is not necessarily proof of a country's capacity for mass destruction and a nuclear deterrent. The effectiveness and the credibility of the nuclear deterrent hinge on guidance over the conditions and possible scenarios under which the nuclear weapons will be used. Another significant factor contributing to the nuclear deterrent is the delivery system. In the case of China and India, in order to examine its implications for China-India relations, it is imperative to contemplate India's nuclear strategy and its development. The fundamental purpose of Indian nuclear programme is to deter the use and threat of use of nuclear weapons by any state or entity against India and its forces. India forswears first use of nuclear weapons and maintains a minimum credible deterrent. It also promises not to be the first to initiate a nuclear strike, although it will respond with punitive retaliation if the deterrent fails. It will not resort to the use of or threat to use nuclear weapons against states that do not possess nuclear weapons, or are not aligned with nuclear capable powers.

However, India and China have begun to include civil nuclear cooperation on the agenda, currently, China has no intention of discussing the nuclear CBMs (Confidence Building Measures), such as de-targeting committee members to avoid any endorsement. The Chinese leaders also avoid making any reference to India's *de facto* status as a nuclear-weapon state. A part of India's nuclear doctrine, *i.e.*, the no-first-use principle, underlined the value of reducing the risk of a nuclear war with China. But, at the same time, a part of the doctrine also emphasizes the need to maintain a credible minimum nuclear deterrent against China. Therefore, India needs to develop an effective deterrent against a potential adversary and ensure that it can and will retaliate with sufficient nuclear weapons to inflict destruction and punishment. India appears confident that a small nuclear force capable of surviving a first strike could meet this requirement, *i.e.*, its strategy is a kind of mutual assured destruction. Since a nuclear deterrent cannot be effective without an appropriate delivery system, the doctrine also recommends that India should develop a strategic defence system in which nuclear weapons could be delivered by land-based missiles, aircraft and submarines.

India needs more time to counter the stark strategic imbalance with China in terms of nuclear and missile arsenals, but narrowing of the military asymmetry with China provided a significant boost for India, even if its strike range is much less than those of China's missiles. As India moves closer towards building a credible nuclear deterrent against China, it gains more faith in its ability to deal with China without making humiliating concessions. Although India is still in the process of building and deploying a nuclear arsenal capable of threatening China, India's perception of a "China threat" seems to have abated. However, an India empowered with a nuclear military force may not be disadvantages to the development of India-China relations. Although all major cities in India are under Chinese missiles target, the Indian side has deemed that it is sufficiently empowered to dissuade China from any aggression. Thus, the development of missiles reflects a strategic mindset that seeks to augment military capability as a way of keeping the peace.

All the activities related to nuclear and missile front have not adversely affected the overtures of efforts to reduce sources of tension between India and China. However, it has not assuaged the apprehensions either in the region or globally. As India is determined to develop and deploy a credible minimum nuclear deterrent, it has established the ability to strike well beyond its immediate border zone. As a result, India's nuclear capability constitutes a negative factor in China's security environment. In the long run, as India's nuclear strike capability becomes more credible, China will find it imperative to take India's nuclear and missile capabilities more seriously.

China's condemnation of and concern over India's nuclear programme have not much credibility due to its controversial role in building the nuclear and missile capabilities of Pakistan. But, it was easy for China to gather international support to halt India's nuclear programme, as India's and Pakistan's nuclear tests had delivered a blow to the regime. The United Nations Security Council had passed Resolution 1172 on 6th June 1998 calling on India to cease the development of ballistic missiles capable of delivering nuclear weapons. Under the cloak of the Resolution, China toughened its opposition to India's nuclear programme, asking India to fulfil all the requirements of the Resolution 1172 and to renounce its nuclear weapons programmes. China was also opposed to any deal that would allow India to maintain a minimum nuclear deterrent in return for joining the Comprehensive Nuclear-Test-Ban Treaty (CTBT). It has adopted the view that it would be a direct violation of the Security Council Resolution 1172 to negotiate, or even discuss, with India its insistence on maintaining a minimum nuclear deterrence capability. Signing of the CTBT by India was seen as a factor in China's security and, therefore, China wanted India to sign and ratify the CTBT and adhere to the Treaty on the Non-Proliferation of Nuclear Weapons (NPT) unconditionally. As a result, among the five nuclear powers, China was the only country that had adopted the toughest line against India in the wake of the Pokhran nuclear tests.

To demonstrate that India is a responsible nuclear state, it has taken a number of moves, such as a voluntary moratorium on testing and offers to convert this moratorium into a formal obligation through negotiations, to abide by some of the provisions of the CTBT, to tighten government control over the export of sensitive materials and technologies, and to participate seriously in the Fissile Material Cut-off Treaty (FMCT) negotiation, which is a proposed international agreement that would prohibit the production of the two main components of nuclear weapons—highly-enriched uranium (HEU) and plutonium. India has also announced that it will never be a proliferator of weapons of mass destruction even though it is not a signatory to the NPT. Thus, India has tried to convince the international community that it is a responsible nuclear state, and hopes the international community will not use the nuclear non-proliferation concerns as the reason to undermine India's *de jure* status as a nuclear weapon state.

India's Relation with Nuclear Suppliers Group (NSG)

In response to India's nuclear test in 1974, the United States terminated nuclear cooperation with India and proposed the formation of the Nuclear Suppliers Group (NSG) as a mechanism to control the transfer of nuclear technology. Then, the NSG had prohibited the transfer of nuclear technology to India and, in this way, the United States thwarted India's plan to conduct nuclear tests in the mid-1990s. In reaction to the Pokhran II nuclear tests, the United States and a number of partners of NSG imposed economic sanctions against India, which lasted till 22nd September 2001 and was lifted due to the needs of the post-September 11 cooperation on anti-terrorism. However, at the same time, the United States realized that it had to engage the new *de facto* nuclear power in dialogue. Fourteen rounds of talks on the nuclear issue were held between the United States' Deputy Secretary Strobe Talbott and Indian External Affairs Minister Jaswant Singh between June 1998 to September 2000. Although differences on proliferation issues were not fully resolved, these engagements allowed the United States to gradually recognize India's status as a nuclear state.

Over the years, India-US relations continued to witness intensive engagement towards a qualitative transformation, which was well reflected in their efforts to normalize the nuclear issues between them. Indian Prime Minister Vajpayee and the United States' President George W. Bush declared in January 2004 the joint statement "Next Steps in the Strategic Partnership" (NSSP) that described the vision for the Indo-US strategic relationship, including an expansion of cooperation or dialogue on civilian nuclear activities. This move was termed as an important "milestone" or "manifestation of the qualitative change" in the India-US relations. NSSP marked an important shift in the nuclear dialogue between India and the United States.

In July 2005, Indian Prime Minister Manmohan Singh and the United States' President George W. Bush ended the long-standing nuclear dispute between the two nations, which had lasted since May 1998, by agreeing to cooperate in the area of civilian nuclear energy. In the Joint Statement, the Bush administration acknowledged India as a responsible state with advanced nuclear technology and committed itself to seeking agreement from the US Congress to adjust US laws and policies, and working to adjust international regimes to allow full civil nuclear energy cooperation and trade with India. In return, India agreed to segregate civilian and military nuclear facilities and programmes, and voluntarily place its civilian nuclear facilities under International Atomic Energy Agency (IAEA) safeguards. India also agreed to take the same responsibilities and practices as other nuclear-weapon states, continuing India's unilateral moratorium on nuclear testing and adopting nuclear non-proliferation measures. During President George W. Bush's three-day visit to India in May 2006, the two countries agreed on India's plan to separate its civilian and military nuclear reactors, and to put fourteen of the twenty-two existing nuclear reactors under IAEA safeguards. In exchange, the United States and other countries agreed to relax measures restricting the export of advanced nuclear technology and materials to India. The Bush administration had amended the United States' domestic laws to accommodate the policy change. In December 2006, the United States' Congress passed the Hyde Act, allowing, in principle, nuclear commerce with India. In July 2007, the two countries signed a bilateral pact, called the 123 Agreement. This deal helped to bring India out of international nuclear isolation. The separation of civilian and military reactors acknowledged that part of India's nuclear facility was for military use, thus implicitly recognizing India as a nuclear-weapon power, but without conferring *de jure* status given the constraints of the NPT.

In order to implement the Indo-US nuclear deal, the United States also helped India to secure approval from the 35-member Board of Governors of the International Atomic Energy Agency (IAEA), which agreed with the India-specific safeguards agreement in August 2008. Fourteen of India's twenty-two existing and future nuclear reactors would be under the IAEA's inspection. In September 2008, the 45-members of NSG granted India a waiver from the existing rules forbidding nuclear trade with a country that had not signed the NPT. After that India not only could obtain nuclear fuel and technology from the United States, but also could access to the global market for nuclear fuel and technology. Thus, under the deal with the United States, India's military nuclear facility would remain outside of international purview, *i.e.*, both India's economy and military will benefit from the ending of nuclear isolation.

As negotiations with NSG progressed, China continued to argue that there should be no country-specific exemption in a global nuclear regime. Even though international society is going to recognize India's nuclear status, the Chinese argued, it should not adopt "double standards" in dealing with India's nuclear issues. China expressed its concern that the Indo-US deal would help India expand its nuclear arsenal. India would fuel its civilian reactors with imported uranium while conserving native uranium fuel for weapon-grade plutonium production. The transfer of advanced technology by the United States would also help India advance its missile programme. China also suspected Washington's strategic intention of pushing an Indo-American nuclear deal to cultivate India as a nuclear power against China. However, India also needed China's support at the NSG and IAEA, as China is a key member of the two groups. Indian Prime Minister Manmohan Singh had tried to secure China's support while meeting Chinese President Hu Jintao on the sidelines of the G-8 summit in Sapporo, Japan. China expressed its willingness to cooperate with India on civilian nuclear use, but it was reluctant to give India a firm assurance in this regard. However, contrary to India's expectation, China made a last-minute objection to India's case at the NSG meeting in September 2008, trying to boycott the resolution of lifting the nuclear embargo on India.

A majority of the 48-member group backed India's membership, but China along with New Zealand, Ireland, Turkey, South Africa and Austria were opposed to India's entry into the NSG. China insisted that India should sign NPT for the NSG membership. It wants a non-discriminatory criterion for the admission of countries who have not signed NPT. China's resistance is to facilitate the entry of its close ally Pakistan. But Pakistan's credentials for the NSG membership are highly flawed and inadequate. On the other hand, over the years India has shown adherence to IAEA safeguards and has taken voluntary measures to abide by NPT and NSG guidelines while Pakistan has not taken any such initiatives. However, the issue of India-specific waiver in the NSG led to a split among the member countries into three distinct groups.

(a) The first group, which included major nuclear exporters such as Russia, France, and the UK, strongly supported the waiver for India.

(b) The second group, which included countries such as Germany, Japan, and Canada, supported the process of India's accommodation in the global non-proliferation regime but required some more persuasion.

(c) The third group, which included countries such as Austria, China. Ireland, New Zealand, and Switzerland, was highly reluctant to grant the waiver and sought to keep the non-proliferation principle intact.

Those in the last group raised broad questions as to the effects of the India-specific waiver on the nuclear non-proliferation regime, which invariably invited fundamental and technical questions regarding the sustainability of the NPT regime in respect to India's entry in the NSG. They demanded that India should have a legally moratorium on nuclear tests, to establish an individual monitoring system in order to be vigilant about India's commitment and to incorporate a clause reaffirming NSG's strong support for NPT. However, India received strong support from Russia, France, and especially the United States. This generated intense pressure on the holdout countries, eventually leading to a unanimous consensus for an

India-specific NSG waiver. Finally, India gained a NSG waiver in 2008, which allowed India to trade in all nuclear or dual-use items on the NSG Trigger List. The waiver granted to India was not absolute as India was prohibited from accessing Enrichment and Reprocessing (ENR) technology and the NSG members would consider India's non-proliferation commitment before any nuclear trade. The resulting NSG waiver took immediate effect, granting India a unique status. India is the only non-NPT nuclear weapon state to possess a legal sanction for both a military and a civilian nuclear program.

During the United States' President Barack Obama's visit to India in November 2010, the India-US Joint Statement clearly indicated the United States' support for India to join four multilateral export control regimes—the NSG, the Missile Export Control Regime, the Australia Group, and the Wassenaar Arrangement. The United States' support for India's entry into the NSG was apparent when the former submitted a 'Food for Thought' paper on India's NSG membership in 2011. The aim of this paper was to provoke a discussion about the NSG membership guidelines concerning new applicants. The paper identified the NSG as the consensus-based decision-making body and thus argued that new members could be accommodated in reference to the NSG guidelines. Membership application required the new applicants to be compliant with the NSG's control lists; to follow and act in respect to the NSG guidelines; to have a legal domestic export control system in effect; to support international efforts to prevent the proliferation of weapons of mass destruction; and to be party to the NPT or any equivalent international non-proliferation treaty. The United States set out to ensure that India met some of these conditions, especially being supportive of international efforts toward the non-proliferation of weapons of mass destruction and in force a legally-based domestic export control system in accordance with its commitment under the conditions of the NSG waiver. India enacted new laws to ensure strict export controls, which was codified in the Weapons of Mass Destruction and Their Delivery System Act of 2005. Indian laws are even more stringent than the requirements under the NSG guidelines.

Prior to the NSG Plenary meeting in Seoul on June 2016, India made an intensive push for the membership based on a political calculation that at least 24 out of the 48 members were strongly in favour of its membership bid. India also believed that several of the hold-out countries may shift their position in favour of India, given it makes a firm diplomatic push to convince them. From April to June 2016, Prime Minister Narendra Modi visited Ireland, Mexico, and Switzerland, while President Pranab Mukherjee flew to China and New Zealand. The Minister of External Affairs, Sushma Swaraj, also contacted 26 NSG member countries. Believing Switzerland's stance had swung from opposition to support, India expected a domino effect on opposing NSG members that would leave China isolated. However, Switzerland ultimately remained unconvinced, joining eight other NSG members—Austria, Brazil, China, Ireland, New Zealand, Norway, South Africa and Turkey—in opposition. Although China was not the only member opposed to India's entry in the NSG, its opposition combined with Pakistan's application for NSG membership complicated the process of entry for India. Pakistan raised two specific demands—first, that all non-NPT membership applications should be considered together (based on the all-or-none principle), and second, that the membership process should not be discriminatory. According to Pakistan, the Indo-US deal was a breach of promise as stated in the 1992 NSG Plenary meeting at Warsaw, which stated, "there was a recognition by all participants of the need to ensure that supplier cooperation does not contribute directly or indirectly to nuclear proliferation, as well as the need to ensure that commercial competition does not compromise their mutually shared non-proliferation objectives". For China and Pakistan, it was more of a strategy to complicate India's application. However, India held direct negotiations with China to resolve these differences. India was persistent in holding official and unofficial bilateral talks uninterruptedly with China until the November NSG meeting in Vienna. In spite of all these, India failed to accomplish its bid at the Seoul and Vienna NSG meetings in 2016, but India's bidding process for NSG membership reflects upon the expanding scope of its participation in the NSG process and discussions with other member states.

On 15th November 2016, India and Japan signed the nuclear agreement which demonstrates a positive change in Japan's position on the issue of nuclear trade with India. Such nuclear agreements create more legitimacy for India's unique nuclear status and further expand its influence on the NSG. Beginning with the Indo-US nuclear deal, bilateral nuclear agreements that India has been able to sign with countries such as Australia, Britain, France, Japan and Russia demonstrate the fact that India has been quite successful in selling its normative agenda of being a responsible nuclear power.

सत्यमेव जयते

CHAPTER 7

The Water Diplomacy

Tibetan plateau, known as Water Tower of Asia, is the origin of ten major river systems of Asia, including the Indus, Brahmaputra, Sutlej, Yellow, Yangtze, Mekong, and Salween. These rivers traverse eleven countries and support two billion people stretching from Afghanistan to India in South Asia, and to Vietnam in Southeast Asia. Both the Indus and Brahmaputra rivers flow downstream from China into India. China is the source of more transnational water flows than any other upstream power in the world. However, despite the wealth of water in Tibet, China faces an emerging water crisis further aggravated by overuse and pollution. In 2004, China's available water per capita was one of the lowest in the world for a populous country, just one-third of the average for developing countries, one-fourth of the world average, and one-fifth of the US average. The comparison indicates a 23 percent decrease in China's available water per capita over the past 20 years. But, the demand for water is growing more than 10 percent annually in Chinese cities and more than five percent annually for its industries. The decline in available water resources has worsened an already critical shortage in drinking water for China's huge population. More than 25 percent of Chinese population are without access to drinking water and almost half of China's 668 largest cities are short of water with 108 identified as serious and 60 as critical. According to Chinese Government, by 2030, China's annual freshwater shortage will reach 200 billion cubic meters. China's worsening water shortage is exacerbated by increased pollution on a historic scale. More than 90 percent of China's underground aquifers, which supply 70 percent of the country's drinking water, are polluted. More than

75 percent of surface water flowing along China's rivers is unsafe for drinking or fishing, and 30 percent is unsuitable for agriculture and industry. China's water problem has a stark regional dimension as well—the Southern part has the preponderance of water while the Northern part has the higher demand. This has created a significant regional disparity that is getting worse with time. While 45 percent of China's population and 60 percent of its agriculture are in the Northern part, the region has only 13.8 percent of the fresh water. In per capita terms, the amount of available water in the Northern part is about 25 percent of that available in the Southern part.

On the other hand, water resources are scarcer in India, yet the country does not have a water supply problem, but rather poor water management practices. India will suffer from water scarcity unless it acts to alleviate demand-side pressures and expand its water supply. It receives a large amount of rainfall during its monsoon season, but it lacks the infrastructure to store this water. Its poor water management stems from the agriculture sector that consumes the vast majority, about 90 percent, of its available water supply. Climate change threatens to affect monsoon intensity and frequency, which would prove detrimental to agricultural production and significantly affect Indian food security. Part of India's water scarcity can be attributed to poor surface water storage capacity which is one-eleventh of the size of China's. Rapid population growth, urban expansion and significant industrialization all compounded India's water scarcity. By 2030, India's demand for water is expected to surpass supply by 50 percent. By 2050, India's population is expected to reach 1.6 billion, therefore, the country must enhance its water storage capacity, particularly as rapid urbanization is proving detrimental to India's aquifers and surface waters.

Thus, due to multiple causes, both India and China are stressed for water, which has contributed to tensions between the two neighbouring countries. Climate change, depleting aquifers, rapid population growth and urbanization are placing pressure on scarce water resources within the two countries. Tibet has remained an underlying issue that has an impact on India-China relations. Coupled with on-going border disputes over Arunachal Pradesh, tension over water has continued to strengthen since China began constructing dams upstream.

India is the middle riparian country between China and Bangladesh on the Brahmaputra river, which is also known as the Yarlung Tsangpo in China and has its headwaters in Tibet, and flows 2900 kms from China, through India and Bangladesh where it meets the Ganga river before draining into the Bay of Bengal. The river's unruly, braided physical flow through the three countries parallels a tricky political configuration. The river originates in troubled Tibet, a recurring source of India-China discord since the Dalai Lama fled to India in 1959. It flows through land that is still contested by China and India following a 1962 border conflict and is the basis of an evolving competitive-cooperative relationship. The river serves as both a socio-economic resource and occasional threat to livelihoods in Northeast region of India. And finally, Brahmaputra becomes a critical lifeline for Bangladesh, whose Indian-centric historical origins and land, as well as riparian connections, create fraught relations. India's middle riparian position provides it with a whole-of-basin perspective. But its discrete, distinct interests and troubled relations with its upper riparian and lower riparian neighbours, combined with the domestic dynamics of center-state relations in Northeast India, pull India's concerns, drivers and cooperative and competitive activities in complex, inconsistent directions, shaping India's intense debate and mixed policies regarding the Brahmaputra river.

Strategic Interests along the Brahmaputra River

India and China are faced with increasing water demands from their rising middle-class population and urbanization. Irrigated framing, while attempting to ensure food security, uses large amounts of water along with the growth of water intensive industries. Climate change is also adding significant pressure to regional water and food security. Glacial melt in the Himalayas is threatening future water security not only for India and China, but for the majority of South and South-East Asia.

Now, the global competition for energy resources is driving the need for hydropower which is a clean alternative source of energy and will enhance the economic growth of the country. China is giving greater attention towards hydropower generation which will reduce the income gap between its eastern and western provinces. Also, hydropower technology is facilitating greater regional engagement with countries such as Thailand which purchases electricity from China.

China is exploring the possibility of the Grand Western Water Division plan at the Great Bend to divert water to its arid northern region. The proposed rerouting of the Brahmaputra at the Great Bend will significantly decrease the quantity and quality of water flowing into India. Salinity will increase, posing a threat to agriculture, aquatic life, and livelihoods downstream. The Brahmaputra makes up 30 percent of India's water supply. If China proceeds with its water diversion plan, water flow will be reduced by 60 percent, enough to create serious consequences downstream. However, China has dismissed its plans as economically and environmentally unfeasible, but great suspicion exists within India about the project. China has claimed that it does not want to antagonize India, but China's historical tendency to withhold hydrological information has created an air of mistrust between the two countries.

China can use water as a potential political tool. Chinese damming and potential hydro-diversion projects are an imminent threat to water security in India. In November 2014, the first unit of China's US$ 1.2 billion Zangmu Hydropower Station on Brahmaputra River at Gyaca, Tibet Autonomous Region of China, became operational. The dam is located in the middle reaches of the river and has the capacity to generate 2.5 billion kilowatt hours of electricity per year. Five other generating units of the project have been completed in 2015. China has assured that it will continue to liaise with its downstream riparian, following Indian concern that the dam could disrupt downstream water supply. If it is taken seriously by both countries, the potential for conflict would be reduced.

Water Scarcity and its Ties to Conflict: Water security is defined as the availability of an acceptable quantity and quality of water for health, livelihoods, ecosystems, and production, coupled with an acceptable amount of water-related risks to people, environment, and economies. This concept of water security includes the negative effects of having too little water or water scarcity, and damage from having too much water such as floods, contamination, erosion, and epidemics. We can survive diseases and natural catastrophes, but we cannot survive without water. Unfortunately, fresh water is an increasingly scarce and precious resource. Less than 2.5 percent of all water on earth is fresh water, and more than half of it is trapped in polar ice and high-altitude glaciers around the world. This precious-little amount is declining due to increasing consumption, pollution, and climate change. Global per capita freshwater availability is continuously declining for more than a century, plummeting more than 60 percent since 1950 alone. According to a study, approximately 66 percent of the world's population, or more than four billion people, live in areas under severe water scarcity. Of these four billion people, one billion live in India and 900 million live in China, the majority of their populations thus live in areas of sever water scarcity. In 2006, a World Bank Working Paper on water scarcity revealed that China will soon become the most water-stressed country in East and Southeast Asia.

The glaciers in Tibet region are melting at a faster rate and coupled with growing water scarcity and a widening North-South regional water gap, China is facing increasing pressure to implement a controversial upstream water diversion plan in its western provinces. This project will threaten India since the downstream portion of the Brahmaputra river flows through a disputed area with strong implications for national sovereignty. Then, both the countries will increase their security postures in an already heavily militarized border region. Thus, China's established and planned hydropower and water diversion projects along the Brahmaputra river are a security concern that has the potential to impact on India-China relations.

China is not a signatory to any multilateral treaties on water resources, nor did it sign the 1997 United Nations Watercourses Convention that set the legal framework for rules and cooperation between more than 100 nations and their relevant international watercourses. Given its control over the source of most of Asia's rivers, China is in a unique position to unilaterally secure its water supply and future needs. On the other hand, India's damming of the Ganga river has reduced river flow in Bangladesh, which has increased soil salinity and affected agriculture, forcing many Bangladeshis to relocate to Northeast India. The influx of Bangladeshis has initiated ethnic conflicts in Assam. If upstream damming were to have an effect on the flow of the Brahmaputra, the potential for ethnic tension in India and Bangladesh could increase. Chinese activity in upstream has the potential to exacerbate water scarcity downstream, which, in turn, could lead to mass migration that will affect the entire region in Bangladesh. As the upstream riparian of the Brahmaputra, China has an advantageous position. It can choose to withhold hydrological information and build infrastructure to intentionally prevent water from flowing downstream. However, China is one of India's primary trading partners and India exports raw materials and imports Chinese electronics and manufactured goods. Also, India and China are arguably the largest powers in the region, as well rising global powers. Therefore, given their interdependence, the potential for conflict could be seen as relatively low.

China's relatively higher position in the international order could encourage it to use water to gain leverage over India. China sees the strategic partnership between the United States and India as a threat to its power within the region. Chinese apprehension towards a deepening military connection between the United States and India may cause China to use its upstream advantage over India in the future. Given China's desire to be global power, the improving relationship between India and the United States could increase the likelihood of China engaging in destructive upstream activity. However, the potential for conflict remains low, because China is increasingly demonstrating a willingness to cooperate with downstream riparian. But, China's willingness to engage with transboundary water issues remains susceptible to its political climate and still has the potential to be used as a tool for negotiation. Many of the major rivers originating in Tibet are the sources of water needed for agriculture and livelihoods downstream in many Asian countries. Any attempt by China to redirect the flow of rivers would be provocative and risky; and would increase the geopolitical tension. Since, China is not party to any international agreement on water resources that it is obliged to comply with, it appears that lower riparian will be significantly affected by its hydro-activity and its dam-building activities may destabilize the region and will result in a zero-sum game.

India's Policies Regarding the Brahmaputra River

The poor state of India-China relations generally and the fact that the Brahmaputra runs through disputed territory drive India's anxieties. Three most important drivers that influence India's policies regarding the Brahmaputra are China's plans to dam and possibly divert the river; India's desire to uphold user rights on the river and consolidate its existing hold on territory; and India's need to manage flooding and soil erosion in its Northeastern states.

China's Damming and Possible Diversion of the Brahmaputra: India's most important concern is China's damming and possible diversion of the river to meet the needs of Northern and Western regions of China that are more populous, agricultural, industries, and/or urban than remote, under-populated Southern Tibet. Its anxiety over China's upper riparian activities increased in 2005 following publication of the book *Tibet's Water Will Save China*, by Li

Ling, an officer of the 2nd Artillery Corps. The book suggests various options for diversion of river water in the amount of 200.6 billion cubic meters, of which the Brahmaputra would account for the overwhelming share at 118.8 billion cubic meters. Soon after publication of the book, India began to undertake numerous cross-ministry and -agency studies to investigate and respond to Chinese activities. On the other hand, India continues to pursue incremental and limited riverine cooperation with China, but it is unable to influence China to cease dam construction.

India's User Rights and Consolidating its Hold on Disputed Territory: One of the most important priorities for India and China has been establishing their riparian rights. In 2008, India established a Technical Expert Group (TEG) headed by the joint secretary level in the Ministry of Power which includes representatives of the Ministry of Water Resources, Department of Road Transport and Highways, Ministry of Environment and Forests, Ministry of External Affairs, and Arunachal Pradesh state government, to draw up an Action Plan for establishing India's user rights on Brahmaputra and its tributaries coming from China. Technical Expert Group's first recommendation was that "in order to establish the First User Rights, the first priority would be to complete Lower Subansiri ... the Lower Siang ... and Demwe Lower ...". The second recommendation was for state government of Arunachal Pradesh to expeditiously allot at least one major project in these basins as close to the international border as possible, and get them implemented promptly, in order to quickly and more firmly establishing "Existing User" rights.

India's anxiety about asserting its riparian rights on the Brahmaputra has not steamed from a legal or political challenge to these rights by China as there is no evidence that China has ever challenged these rights. More likely, its anxiety comes from the objective of consolidating India's rights to the territory where the transboundary Brahmaputra flows rather than to the water of the river per se. India has taken it as a prudent course of action given the disputed territory through which the river flows and China's international efforts to challenge India's claims to the territory. In March 2009, China had opposed a nearly US$ 3 billion Asian Development Bank loan to India because it included funding for a US$ 60 million flood management and hydro program in Arunachal Pradesh.

In India, dam building is an extremely slow and limited process, largely due to political and civic opposition to dam construction but also because of financial and technical constraints. On the other hand, China is robustly building dam on its portion of the upper Brahmaputra river. India has plans to build several dams to consolidate its hold on territory and further establish riparian rights, control flood and soil erosion, develop hydro-electric power, and contribute to the overall development of the Northeast region.

Managing Flooding and Soil Erosion: Soil erosion is a major feature in the catchment area of Northeast India. According to the Brahmaputra Board of India's Ministry of Water Resources, "Due to heavy deposition of silt, the river has frequently changed its course. Excessive silt deposition has also given rise to braiding and meandering pattern in the alignment of the river system". High siltation arises from many factors, including landslides due to heavy rainfall in the area, earthquake shocks, and manmade actions such as changes in cultivation patterns and exploitation of forest resources in the hills above the valley through which the river runs. But flooding is the cause that directly initiated India's cooperative outreach to China, resulting in the current ongoing dialogue and limited hydrological data sharing agreements. India-China bilateral discussions on cooperation about the river began in the early 2000s as a result of the flooding concerns. Hydrological data sharing between China and India has gone hand in hand with a more unilateral Indian approach to controlling floods, *i.e.*, by building dams. However, the number of dams actually being built still appears to be extremely limited. Thus, the need to control flooding and soil erosion, along with the threat of China's dams and possible water diversion, and India's need to establish user rights and consolidate a hold on territory, appears to be a key driver of India's activities vis-à-vis China regarding the Brahmaputra.

Co-operation along the Brahmaputra—Steps to Avoid Conflict

A major flood in Northeast India took place in June 2000 when a natural dam that had formed due to a landslide on a tributary of the Brahmaputra in Tibet, broke. Due to this, 3-4 billion cubic meters of water poured into Arunachal Pradesh and Assam, killing 30 Indian nationals and leaving 50,000 homeless. It is believed that China withheld hydrological data that could have prevented the disaster—this led to friction in India-China relations.

Concerning floods in Northeast India, India and China have established a series of agreements to share hydrological data. In April 2002, China agreed to provide India with hydrological data from three monitoring stations on the Brahmaputra between 1st June and 15th October of each year, corresponding to the annual flood season. During visit of Chinese president Hu Jintao to India in November 2006, the two countries agreed to establish an expert-level group to discuss hydrological data and emergency response measures. Further, in 2013, India and China signed a Memorandum of Understanding, recognizing that transboundary rivers are an important asset to the development of all riparian. Both countries agreed to strengthen communication and strategic trust. China agreed to provide more hydrological information to India at the start of the flood season. It has also extended the data-sharing period from 15th May to 15th October.

India-China cooperation related to the Brahmaputra is likely to be limited by two factors—ongoing border dispute and mutual distrust. Contested ownership of Arunachal Pradesh means that China and India will probably be unable to reach a major accord on transboundary river rights and objects, such as a water-sharing treaty. There are no signs that this dispute is set to abate in the near to medium term. While mutual distrust may be a factor at the official level, it may be more pronounced within civil society in both countries. Nevertheless, there may still be opportunities for a modest expansion of India-China cooperation on Brahmaputra issues. This is most likely on narrow technical subjects that can be separated from the border dispute. Specifically, China may be receptive to cooperation in areas such as disaster management, environmental protection and river safety, or on scientific topics, such as the effects of climate change on long-term river flow. Some of these issues may be discussed at an official level, such as between the water resource ministries of both countries, while others may be more usefully deliberated initially at the Track 2 level, perhaps involving specialists from Indian and Chinese Government-funded research institutes. Following are some of drivers that could promote enhanced cooperation on these issues.

(a) A positive overall direction in India-China relations, symbolized by fruitful high-level exchanges and economic agreements, could remove obstacles and set the stage for cooperation on transboundary river issues.

(b) China may be able to draw on its own initiatives related to the Brahmaputra to portray itself as a responsible upper riparian. For China, modestly enhancing outreach on water security challenges could be a relatively low-cost way to foster diplomatic goodwill with India.

(c) Additional progress may be facilitated if initiatives are proposed and encouraged by India.

A conflict may arise and escalate if either India or China falsely believes it is under threat from the other. Fear has been created in India because of previous tendencies where China has been unwilling to provide details of its hydro-projects, and when it did, gave contradictory information. There is a need for both countries to develop mutual goodwill. Undertaking joint research projects in the region and sharing water data more extensively could foster stronger bilateral relations. Therefore, developing an understanding of shared water resource challenges will help limit the potential for conflict. Also, implementing efficient water management policies will reduce the severity of future food and water crises and reduce the risk of conflict. Poor water resources management and underdeveloped infrastructure undermine food and water security in India. Water should be conceptualized as a scarce and strategic resource. In case of China, pollution and unequal natural water allocations threatens its food and water security. Therefore, efficient water management is essential to food security, economic growth, population health and social stability; and managing water as a scarce resource with holistic ramifications is essential to reducing the potential for future wars on water.

China's role as a water hegemon should involve soft power as the primary use of negotiation and diplomatic actions. Its communication is essential to reassure riparian of its hydro-intentions and reduce the potential for conflict caused by mistrust. In the interest of regional stability, it is crucial that no country feel it is under threat of acute water insecurity as a result of upstream damming or diversion projects. Therefore, China should change its strategy from "responsive diplomacy" to "preventive diplomacy", where it should be responsible for proactively engaging with riparian to avoid disputes. Only a combination of bilateral cooperation and strong leadership with demand and supply side management can influence the future and reduce the potential for an India-China conflict on water.

Multilateral Cooperation in the Brahmaputra Basin: India, China and Bangladesh

China has concentrated its diplomatic outreach on Brahmaputra issues at a bilateral level and signed hydrological data sharing agreements with both India and Bangladesh separately, but has not engaged the two countries in a multilateral setting. This is consistent with a larger pattern of bilateralism in China's water diplomacy which has focused on achieving bilateral agreements with neighbouring states. Aside from its agreements with India and Bangladesh, China has signed accords on boundary and cross-border rivers with Russia, Kazakhstan, Kyrgyzstan, Mongolia, North Korea, and others. These agreements are diverse in scope, covering issues such as water navigation, hydrological projects, environmental protection, emergency notification, and data sharing.

China has avoided multilateral diplomacy as a way to solve shared water challenges. It was one of three states (others being Turkey and Burundi) that voted against the 1997 United Nations Watercourses Convention, which outlines principles for cooperation related to international waterways, such as transboundary rivers, and procedures for dispute resolution. The reasons given by China for the opposition to the treaty included inadequate protection of state sovereignty and an imbalance between the rights and duties of upper and lower riparians. China's preference for bilateral diplomacy on Brahmaputra issues is consistent with the larger pattern which may be underscored by two factors.

(a) The absence of existing institutions relevant to discussions among all three riparians. For example, the SAARC does not include China, while the Shanghai Cooperation Organization (SCO) does not include Bangladesh.

(b) The problem of mutual distrust, not only in India-China relations, but also in India-Bangladesh relations, which would undermine any plans to promote cooperation on a basin-wide scale.

Therefore, China thinks that it is more practical and effective to work with India and Bangladesh separately than to work with them together. However, there are several reasons why China may revisit its current preference for bilateralism on Brahmaputra issues.

(a) At broad level, China has participated in, and even shaped, multilateral regimes and institutions since the 1990s. It is evident in China's role in organizing the Six Party Talks on North Korea and in its participation in the Association of Southeast Asian Nations (ASEAN) Regional Forum. China has also sought to play a more prominent role in SAARC, which includes both India and Bangladesh. Thus, China's bilateral approach to water diplomacy is increasingly out of step with its confidence in other policy arenas that multilateralism can support China's interests.

(b) There is a precedent for Chinese participation in water diplomacy at a basin-wide level. Namely, China signed an agreement with the Mekong River Commission (MRC) in 2002 to supply hydrological data from June 15 to October 15 of each year, a period corresponding to the monsoon season. That agreement was expanded in 2008, and again in 2013.

(c) The barriers to basin-wide cooperation on the Brahmaputra are likely not insurmountable. For one thing, the lack of an existing mechanism does not necessarily rule out cooperation. In other contexts, China has established new bodies to address transnational challenges when one did not currently exist. For example, China helped establish the Shanghai Cooperation Organization (SCO) to address terrorism and other challenges in Central Asia. China may also be receptive to the possibility that existing bodies, such as the Bangladesh-China-India-Myanmar (BCIM) forum, could be expanded to address water issues.

(d) China has a number of incentives to cooperate with other Brahmaputra riparians in a multilateral context—(i) China's reputation would benefit if it takes a leading role in proposing basin-wide cooperation and it could argue that it is engaging proactively as a responsible regional stakeholder. (ii) Basin-wide cooperation could help reduce a source of friction on China's Western periphery at a time when it is facing increasing challenges in its Eastern maritime region and in its relations with the United States and others. (iii) At a practical level, a basin-wide approach could yield a more holistic understanding of the river system and insights into how to address flooding and other challenges.

Now, let us discuss India's perception on multilateral cooperation in the Brahmaputra basin. India takes a bilateral approach to the Brahmaputra River for the following reasons.

(a) India mostly favours bilateral diplomacy with its neighbours, especially on sensitive issues.

(b) India's main interlocutor and challenge on the Brahmaputra River, China, also emphasizes bilateral diplomacy.

(c) India, as a middle riparian country, has different concerns and interests vis-à-vis upper riparian China lower riparian Bangladesh that are likely better addressed bilaterally.

(d) A multilateral setting would allow Bangladesh to gain China's support for criticisms of India's river policies.

(e) India already has bilateral water sharing and hydrological information sharing agreements with South Asian riverine neighbours and with China.

However, India's current emphasis on bilateral approaches to Brahmaputra issues does not rule out future multilateral cooperation. This is evident from the following facts.

(a) India is a member of numerous organizations and arrangements that bring together countries with shared river waters, including the widest such organization relevant to the region, SAARC. Improved relations across South Asia over time could theoretically create a mechanism along the lines of the Mekong River Commission (MRC).

(b) In the absence of a Brahmaputra-specific arrangement, India and other riparians could create a trilateral, Brahmaputra River only Organization.

The closest organization in terms of membership and relevance to Brahmaputra River management is the Bangladesh-China-India-Myanmar (BCIM) forum. While Myanmar is not a Brahmaputra riparian, BCIM could theoretically address water issues. However, India remains quite cautious regarding BCIM and appears to want that organization to continue to focus on land transportation connections for now rather than expand its agenda.

China-Bangladesh Relations in the Background of the Brahmaputra River: China's interactions with Bangladesh related to the Brahmaputra have been relatively free of controversy. Its cooperation with Bangladesh has proceeded on several fronts. In 2008, China agreed to share hydrological data on the Brahmaputra with Bangladesh. In 2010, China and Bangladesh also agreed to improve cooperation on water resource management, hydrological data sharing, flood control, and disaster reduction. China also proposed to assist Bangladesh with riverbed dredging and personnel training. In March 2015, a memorandum of understanding (MOU) was signed on the sharing of rainfall data in the river's catchment area in China, which would help in flood forecasting in Bangladesh.

China-Bangladesh cooperation on Brahmaputra issues is consistent with a broader expansion of the bilateral relationship between the two countries. China is Bangladesh's largest trade partner, and Bangladesh plays an important role in China's vision of creating a "21st Century Maritime Silk Road" stretching from Asia to Europe. China also competes for influence in Bangladesh with India, which is also reaching out to Bangladesh with various agreements and incentives. In this scenario, China's willingness to share hydrological information and provide assistance in river dredging may simply be designed to cultivate diplomatic goodwill with Bangladesh.

India-Bangladesh Relations in the Background of the Brahmaputra River: The physical, historical, and political interdependence of India and Bangladesh shapes bilateral relations, including those regarding the Brahmaputra River. India's Northeastern states surround Bangladesh for approximately 4000 kms. broken only by a stretch of roughly 300 kms. along the Southeast corners where Bangladesh and Myanmar share a border. If Bangladesh is "encircled" by India, India is "separated" by Bangladesh. India's Northeastern states are essentially separated from peninsular India by Bangladesh—except for the narrow Siliguri Corridor.

Most of Bangladesh's 57 major rivers originate in or flow through India. Upon entering Bangladesh, the Brahmaputra, for example, becomes the Jamuna River, which joins with the Ganges River (called Padma in Bangladesh), which in turn joins the Meghna River to flow into the Bay of Bengal. India-Bangladesh relations concerning the Brahmaputra River focus on three elements—cooperation on the Ganges River, waiting for implementation of an agreement on the Teesta River, and implications of India's Rivers-Linking project for Bangladesh.

A 1996 India-Bangladesh water-sharing agreement on the Ganges River can be seen as an example of India's accommodative and cooperative behaviour on riverine issues. However, Bangladesh see India as less generous, after noting India's use of the Farakka Barrage to divert water from the Ganges to flush the silt-heavy Hooghly River in Kolkata. The Ganges River Treaty clearly does not solve all the difficulties faced by lower riparian Bangladesh, but it is one of just three water-sharing agreements on major rivers in South Asia.

The second India-Bangladesh water-sharing agreement on the Teesta River, awaits political approval for implementation since 2011. However, both in India and in Bangladesh, there is currently optimism that the Teesta Agreement will go forward in due course, though this might require further political alignment between New Delhi, Dhaka, and Kolkata. Such political alignments both between the center in New Delhi and the state in Kolkata, West Bengal, and between these two jurisdictions and Dhaka, Bangladesh, are unpredictable and not necessarily decisive. For example, while the Teesta Agreement could not move forward during either Prime Minister Manmohan Singh's or Prime Minister Narendra Modi's visits, final ratification and implementation of an India-Bangladesh land boundary agreement, whose negotiation has been complete for decades, occurred during Prime Minister Narendra Modi's June 2015 visit to Bangladesh in the absence of political alignments among the three key jurisdictions.

The third issue in India-Bangladesh relations regarding the Brahmaputra River relates to India's plans for a River-Linking Project (RLP). While the RLP overwhelmingly deals with inter-linking rivers within India, there are implications for trans-boundary flows. The precise impact on trans-boundary water flows appears to be a subject of significant debate and rests in part on the technical as well as political decisions that are made in any implementation of such a project. However, whatever the impacts might be, the prospect for implementing the RLP in the near term in a way that would affect Bangladesh is widely regarded, both in India and in Bangladesh, as unrealistic for a host of technical, financial, and political reasons. Concerns about the RLP in India-Bangladesh relations are trumped by differences over the existing Ganges water-sharing agreement and implementing the completed Teesta Agreement, as well as over managing overall India-Bangladesh riverine relations through the Joint Rivers Commission (JRC).

Beyond these three concerns, India-Bangladesh cooperation is limited. Each recognizes its dependence on the other. India knows that transit rights through Bangladesh will help boost development in India's Northeast, and Bangladesh appreciates India's upper riparian position. However, such mutual dependence has led to only limited cooperation beyond directly bilateral issues and approaches.

Bangladesh's Support of Multilateral Cooperation in the Brahmaputra Basin: Bangladesh is the most interested in pursuing basin-wide cooperation among the three stakeholders of the Brahmaputra basin. As one of the leaders in creating the SAARC, Bangladesh is a strong proponent of multilateral approaches and sees water cooperation as opening up greater possibilities for regional integration, such as through increased river navigation with India and hydroelectric power generation with India and China. Bangladesh's geographic location may be proved a key to achieving connectivity, meaning connecting mainland India with its landlocked Northeastern states as well as promoting interactions between China and South Asia and between South Asia and Southeast Asia.

Trade and transportation opportunities with Bangladesh can help improve Indian mainland connecting to the country's Northeast. Bangladesh and China have agreed to enhance transport links through road and rail transit which require navigation along the Brahmaputra. They also agreed to explore opportunities for cooperation on hydropower generation. For example, the two countries might draw on China's dam-building expertise to help Bangladesh address its need to store monsoon water for use in the dry season.

Given the openings for basin-wide cooperation that Bangladesh has with India and China separately, the Bangladesh-China-India-Myanmar (BCIM) Forum for Regional Cooperation offers an existing multilateral framework that Bangladesh could use to encourage the two upper riparians in the Brahmaputra basin to cooperate with each other. The interactions arising from Bangladesh's bilateral efforts to encourage India and China to work for basin-wide development and cooperation in the Brahmaputra could lay the foundation for a Brahmaputra Basin Organization, a Brahmaputra Commission, or a Brahmaputra River Basin Authority. This formal body would be the most ambitious means of managing and developing the Brahmaputra basin. It would involve all riparians as equal parties, require regular interaction and communication, and specify a dispute-settlement mechanism. Because two of the basin riparians, India and China, are nuclear armed and have a border dispute, the creation of a formal commission could be a confidence-building measure that preserves communication and insulates water interactions from political-military crises.

CHAPTER 8

सत्यमेव जयते

Pakistan as a Factor in India-China Relations

India has projected the China-Pakistan relationship as a strategic convergence against India, where Pakistan is acting as the proxy of China to counter Indian influence in the region. China has characterized its ties with Pakistan as an "all-weather friendship", implying that the two countries have developed a strong partnership that has indeed weathered the changes that have taken place in the domestic and international scenario. The China-Pakistan friendship reflects the saying that "an enemy's enemy is a friend". It implies that the China-Pakistan bonhomie is based upon their common bitter relationship with India.

China has acknowledged India's dominant role in South Asia, but at the same time it has ensured that Pakistan remains a strong military counterweight to India. The China-Pakistan "special relationship" is a part of China's grand strategy that moulds the Asian security environment. The China-Pakistan military alliance, in particular the nuclear and missile nexus, has ensured that the South Asian military balance of power is neither pro-India nor pro-Pakistan but is pro-China. China shares Pakistan's deep mistrust of India's strategic ambitions and sees India as a rising power that must be balanced. China believes that as long as Indian military is preoccupied with Pakistan on its western frontier, India cannot focus on China and East Asia. China thinks that if India cannot sway the subcontinent, its influence in the larger arena becomes moot.

Pakistan cannot be a threat to India without China's military support just as Taiwan cannot be a threat to China without United States support. China's nuclear assistance to Pakistan is considered as the root cause of "deficit of trust" between the two countries. However, China has made it clear that it will not improve ties with India at the cost of Pakistan. On a cost-benefit analysis, the combined strategic and political advantages that China receives from its alliance with Pakistan, and through Pakistan other Islamic countries, easily outweigh any advantages of a closer relationship with India. Pakistan is vitally important to China's energy security (by providing access to and naval bases in the Persian Gulf), military security (by keeping India's military engaged on its western frontiers), geopolitics (given its geostrategic location at the intersection of South Asia, Central Asia and the Middle East), national unity and territorial integrity (maintaining control over Tibet and Xinjiang), maritime strategy in the Indian Ocean, and as a staunch diplomatically (in international forums, including the Islamic world), a buyer and supplier of conventional and unconventional weaponry, and above all, as a powerful bargaining chip in China's relations with India and the United States. However, China has also advised Pakistan against embarking on military misadventures and flirting with terrorism and religious extremism to further its geopolitical interests in Afghanistan and Kashmir.

China's Balanced Policy Towards the India-Pakistan Conflicts

China's approach towards India-Pakistan conflicts in the post-Cold War era was determined by its motivation to launch economic development at home and supported by the change in the security environment in South Asia. It favours a stable peripheral environment conductive to its domestic economic development. In a shift from unequivocal support to Pakistan, it no longer thinks India-Pakistan conflicts are in its interest and is now reluctant to side with either country in any dispute between them. Under the good neighbourly policy, China is trying to establish a more balanced relationship with India and Pakistan than the complicated equation in the past. As a result, China has shifted from a focus on exploiting the India-Pakistan conflict to a policy designed to help stabilize the region. In an attempt to relieve India's concerns, China stresses that the China-Pakistan friendship has no animus against any third country. It has emphasized that its relationship with Pakistan is "normal" and not directed towards India. This more balanced policy also indicates that China seems to think it possible to develop a parallel close relationship with both India and Pakistan. In order not to irritate Pakistan, China stressed that the improvement of India-China relations would not be the detriment of a third party, nor would it affect China's existing friendly relations with other countries. China also wants to enhance the scope of a "constructive cooperative partnership" with India and, at the same time, it wants to remain engaged with Pakistan.

China's Shift on the Kashmir Dispute: China's stand towards the Kashmir issue probably best describes the change of its stance towards the India-Pakistan conflict. It has had a role to play in the Kashmir issue because of its alliance relationship with Pakistan, and also because it obtained a piece of Kashmir under the 1963 China-Pakistan border treaty. Being the close ally of Pakistan, it has openly backed Pakistan's claim to all of Kashmir after China-India relations deteriorated. However, contrary to the traditional impression, China has not always supported Pakistan's stance over Kashmir. Ever since the late 1980s, China has tried to approach the Kashmir issue on its own merits and appeared to avoid taking sides with Pakistan in tune with increasingly warm relations with India. After the end of the Cold War, in 1994, China even pressured Pakistan to withdraw a resolution, tabled at the United Nations Human Rights Commission in Geneva, condemning India for human rights violations in Kashmir.

China's altered attitude towards the Kashmir issue has also been contributed by serious nationalist unrest in Xinjiang. Since 1980, China has distanced itself from its support for Pakistan's position to hold a plebiscite to decide the future of Kashmir. China has also declined to intervene in the Kashmir issue by emphasizing the need for India and Pakistan to resolve the problem through dialogue. China thinks that an independent state of Kashmir would inspire Muslim separatists in Xinjiang to seek independence. According to China, Kashmir issue is a legacy from the British Empire and involves conflicting territorial claims, religion, ethnicity and other complex factors. China has supported Pakistan's stand that the sovereignty of Kashmir has not been defined and that it is the "core issue" in India-Pakistan relations, in contrast to the Indian position that Kashmir has always been a part of India. However, China has agreed that the dispute is steeped in history and India and Pakistan should seek an effective solution to the Kashmir conflict through peaceful dialogue, implying the issue should be decided by India and Pakistan bilaterally. This position of China is against Pakistan's hope to internationalise the Kashmir issue, and meets India's demands. The China referred to the United Nation Resolution on Kashmir in the context of solving the problem after India's nuclear tests of 1998, but then went back to insisting that a peaceful negotiated settlement between India and Pakistan should be made possible. Clearly, China is determined to insulate itself from the ups and downs of India-Pakistan ties, such as the Kashmir dispute, while improving its relations with both India and Pakistan.

However, dealing with India-Pakistan conflicts is a key question regarding China's western geo-political strategy and frontier security. The Kargil crisis of 1999 had put China's balanced approach to the test. Although Pakistan approached China for support, China appeared to have taken a position of cautious neutrality and did not give any special diplomatic favours to Pakistan. China repeatedly stated the need for restraint by both India and Pakistan, and the importance of resolving the problem through peaceful negotiations. This balanced posture was due to China's mounting concern about a major military conflict between India and Pakistan. Cheng Ruisheng, the former Chinese Ambassador to India, even claimed that China has a traditional friendship with Pakistan, but China's policy is not to side with Pakistan on the Kashmir issue. China refused to give Pakistan "carte blanche". Thus, China's position in the Kargil crisis confirmed the trend that China was determined to follow, specifically, a calibrated balanced policy in navigating the turbulence arising from India-Pakistan relations. China's moderate posture towards the India-Pakistan conflict altered the traditional impression of Chinese support for Pakistan and gave India some relief in its dealings with Pakistan. In addition to the demonstrated neutrality in the latest India-Pakistan confrontation, another significant development has been China's demonstration of its desire to play a more positive role to damp down the India-Pakistan conflict, rather than keeping the India-Pakistan tension at a distance. Even Pakistan has appealed to China to play an active role in South Asia to maintain a regional strategic balance and to settle the Kashmir issue, but during Chinese Premier Zhu Rongji's visit to India in January 2002, China assured India that it had neither any intention of mediating between India and Pakistan nor would it play any mediatory role between them.

China-Pakistan Military Ties

Although India acknowledges China's changing policy towards the India-Pakistan conflict, the Pakistan factor in the China-India interactions has not been erased completely as a result of China's even-handed approach to India-Pakistan conflicts. Therefore, India is still very concerned with China's intention of forging strategic ties with Pakistan and other South Asian states. For India, the China-Pakistan arms nexus is one of the main unresolved problems between India and Pakistan. Although, China has been trying to move forward relations with Pakistan in other fields, such as more cooperation in the economic field, the military tie remains an important element of China-Pakistan relations. China has clarified that China's military sales to Pakistan are based on the profit motive and are not a move against India. It is also ready to sell military equipment to India if India wants. In fact, even though China has offered Pakistan military assistance, India traditionally enjoys better access to conventional weaponry from Russia. The United States, since the Bush administration, has also given India access to America's military transfer, which was denied for most of the Cold War.

China has consciously sought to develop military links with countries in India's neighbourhood so as to deny India dominance in the subcontinent. Therefore, the most obvious rationale for China to arm Pakistan is to imbue Pakistan with strategic parity with India. Given the tension between India and Pakistan, India sees the military transfer as a serious concern and as having a direct and negative bearing on its national security environment. Particularly, China-Pakistan military cooperation in the fields of nuclear and conventional missiles have caused grave concern for India's security. For addressing these concerns, India has continuously raised the issue of missile transfers from China to Pakistan during its interactions with China. For example, Prime Minister Atal Bihari Vajpayee has expressed concern over the military nexus between China and Pakistan, arguing that "all weapons and missiles Pakistan receives are aimed at India". He added that "wherever our neighbour Pakistan gets its arms from, we keep telling those (supplier) nations that whatever be your intention, these weapons, experience has shown, have been used against us". He even urged China to reconsider its support for Pakistan's nuclear and missile programmes to reciprocate India's moves to back China's position on Taiwan or Tibet Issues.

But, China did not take India's anxiety seriously. Maintaining that the military supply programme and cooperation between China and Pakistan was routine in nature and well within international norms and international treaty obligations, China does not agree that its military transfer to Pakistan would break regional balances or undermine peace and tranquility in the region. Furthermore, China justified its arms transfer to Pakistan on the basis that military relations are part of the normal gamut of state-state relations and that, as far as the Chinese are concerned, every sovereign, independent country has the right to acquire those materials it deems necessary for its defence, and China as a sovereign country also has the right to sell such material. Defending China's stance on China-Pakistan military cooperation, the Chairman of the Standing Committee of the National People's Congress, Li Peng, said, "Normal military trade is undoubtedly part of the normal state-to-state relations. India enjoys similar cooperation with other countries as well." The then Chinese Foreign Minister, Tang Jiaxuan, also said that the China-Pakistan military cooperation was a normal military cooperation based on normal state-to-state relations and was not directed against any third party or country. Despite India's protests, China pledges its commitment to continuing military exchanges with Pakistan and argues that it is inappropriate and unnecessary to exaggerate or worry about China-Pakistan military relations. Therefore, while making efforts to improve relations with India, China did not scale down its military cooperation with Pakistan to meet India's demands. For example, within two years of the mould-breaking visit of Prime Minister Rajiv Gandhi to China in December 1988, China supplied short-range M-II missiles to Pakistan. Likewise, the Chinese moved ahead with the supply of medium-range M-9 missiles and ring magnets for Pakistan's nuclear weapons programme after Prime Minister Narasimha Rao's visit to China in 1993.

China's entity assistance has helped Pakistan to have moved toward serial production of solid-propellant short-range ballistic missile, such as the Shaheen-I and Haider-I, and has supported Pakistan's medium-range ballistic missile. In mid-January 2002, China transferred the first 10 of 40 China-made F-7 PG fighter aircraft to Pakistan during the period of the India-Pakistan military stand-off, though China diplomatically conducted a balanced policy towards India and Pakistan. While trying to improve relations with India, China is very reluctant to share India's apprehension regarding China-Pakistan relations and insists that there is nothing wrong with it consistently providing Pakistan with wide-ranging assistance regarding arms. But, for India, China's military cooperation with Pakistan is far more significant than the normal military cooperation among other countries. Despite China's protestations of innocence, China's transfer of arms and military expertise to Pakistan are being perceived as hostile by India and has forced India to revise its security agenda towards China leading to a difficulty in India-China relations.

Renewed China-Pakistan Strategic Relations

China does not consider India as an immediate enemy and has tried to broaden the bilateral cooperation resulting in Pakistan's losing some of its strategic value as a pawn to be used in the game of strategy against India. The present nature of China-Pakistan relations is not of the same strategic genre as it was in the Cold War Era. However, it does not imply that India and China are becoming friends and that China no longer needs Pakistan. Still China has more common interests with Pakistan than with India. Pakistan is a loyal friend of China in the region to counterbalance a potential Indian challenge to Chinese preponderance in Asia and, therefore, China will not neglect its traditional friendship with Pakistan while trying to improve relations with India.

The strategic bonhomie between China and Pakistan can be understood with the following examples. While India was trying hard to persuade international community to isolate General Pervez Musharraf's military regime after he took over the reins of power following a coup on 12th October 1999, China became the first non-Islamic county to roll out the red carpet for the controversial general and offered support to Pakistan on the grounds that "the internal affairs of a country should and must be handled by its own people, which is not only the core of the Five Principles of Coexistence, but also a basic policy China has steadfastly pursued and carried out in handling relations between different countries". Chinese Premier Li Peng visited Pakistan in November 1989, the first visit abroad by a senior Chinese leader after the 1989 Tiananmen incident. China has assured Pakistan that "no matter what changes occur internationally or domestically, it will continue to foster its comprehensive partnership with Pakistan".

Even though China might not need the China-Pakistan friendship as a bulwark against India as it did in the Cold War Era, China has other reasons to maintain its special relationship with Pakistan—a link that includes the transfer of arms. For example, a close relationship with Pakistan would give China more diplomatic and strategic angles to bring into play in South Asia. During Premier Zhu Rongji's visit to Pakistan in May 2001, China agreed to support Pakistan in its decision to build the strategically located Gwadar port and coastal highway projects leading to the Iranian border. As a deliberate gesture of support, China held the first ever joint marine exercise with Pakistan on 23rd October 2003, just three weeks before the first India-China marine exercise. The sequence of the joint exercises reflected China's desire to acknowledge friendship with Pakistan as a strategic priority instead of friendship with India, and to underscore China's strategic bonhomie with Pakistan on the South Asian scene. Pakistan also plays an important link for

China to the Islamic world and has influence on the Xinjiang problem. Relations with India cannot provide China the same benefits.

China has also to reassess its strategic proximity to Pakistan in the context of the United States' presence in the wake of the war against terrorism. The war against terrorism in Afghanistan has brought the United States' troops right to China's western doorstep. China appeared to be uncomfortable with the United States' military presence in Central Asian states and Pakistan and was reported to have threatened to pull out of the project to develop the Gwadar port as a fully fledged military base if Pakistan allowed the United States to access the airports at Jacobabad and Pasni and to set up some listening posts in the Northern areas to monitor any nuclear or military activities in the region. China fears that the United States might use Pakistan as a base for operations against Tibet and Xinjiang. Therefore, it does not want Pakistan becoming a pawn to be used against China. Feeling threatened by the emergence of closer strategic bonds between the United States and the region, China is attempting to avoid the formation of an anti-China stronghold in the region by the United States and its coalition partners. Hence, it is logical that China should embrace Pakistan even more tightly despite its relationship with India.

For India, even though China assures that the renewed China-Pakistan strategic relations are not directed against India, a close relationship between two unfriendly neighbours can only bring trouble. Therefore, for its own security, India has sensed the need to separate China and Pakistan to prevent a joint China-Pakistan attack and treats the issue of China-Pakistan military cooperation as the "litmus test" of China's sincerity towards India.

Kargil War and China-Pakistan Relations: China's behaviour during the Kargil war (May 1999–July 1999) showed that it now wanted the prosperity in the place of competition. During the war China did not give any anti-Indian statements. In spite of Pakistan being the major market for Chinese arms, during Kargil conflict, Chinese leadership did not show any hurriedness in making moral sympathy with Pakistan. In place of helping Pakistan, China advised Pakistan to observe the Line of Control and withdraw Pakistani intruders from Kargil. China was concerned over security and stability over its South-Western borders. Therefore, it avoided to take sides in India-Pakistan conflict. At global level, China also apprehended that conflict between its neighbours could enhance the United States' influence in the region. Therefore, China made a special effort to appear as even-handed as possible. Pakistan was not happy with this behaviour of China. When, despite the Kargil conflict, the Chinese persevered with their invitation to the Indian Foreign Minister, Jaswant Singh, to visit China, the Pakistani Foreign Minister, Sartaj Aziz, rushed out for a one day "working visit" to Beijing on 11th June 1999, on the eve of his visit to Delhi. Sartaj Aziz had hoped that he would be able to proceed to Delhi with his diplomatic hand strengthened by a more favourable Chinese position, but he has been disappointed. China was not willing to extend only public support to Pakistan or to criticize India even by insinuation or mention the United Nations or any other kind of international intervention.

Pakistan is disappointed by China's stance on Kashmir in general and Kargil conflict in particular. But the issue of Kashmir is only one of the driving forces of China-Pakistan relations. The fact that China is still committed to the "sovereignty and territorial integrity" of Pakistan is no mean achievement. Moreover, the close military relationship between the armed forces of both the countries continued apace. Pakistan sees China as a reliable friend that, unlike the United States, could be counted on in emergencies and Pakistan is confident that China will continue to support Pakistan against India. It understands China's need to mince words for the sake of placating India but is confident that when push comes to shove, China will be there. Therefore, China-Pakistan relations are still strong and serve national interest of both countries.

Terrorism, Pakistan and India-China Relations

After the 9/11 terror attack on the United States, the new phase of terrorism is flashed up. Now, it is believed that terrorists can acquire nuclear weapons and pose a threat to the world peace.

The impact of the 9/11 terrorist attack was tremendous, and the South Asia became an important site of the anti-terrorism war. Initially, China was comfortable with the prominence of Pakistan in the United States' war against terrorism. Moreover, China was concerned over the growing United States-India ties, in particular defence relations. In some ways, therefore, immediately after 9/11 China was comfortable with Pakistan's growing ties with the United States. China hoped that China-United States-Pakistan triangular cooperation in the aftermath of 9/11 will materialize as happened in 1970's and again in 1980's after the Soviet's intervention in Afghanistan. And the growing triangular cooperation to some extent would keep the United States away from India as the United States' sale of arms to India has enabled it to become the first country to have close military relations with the world's two big powers—the United States and Russia. China condemned terrorism on the one hand, but its condemnation of Pakistan sponsored terrorism was opaque.

India intended to use the opportunity of the international anti-terrorism struggle to press Pakistan to stop once and for all "cross-border terrorism". China condemned the Mumbai terror attack of 26th November 2008 and called it 'worst for humanity'. After the 26/11 terror attack, Pakistan was targeted as the main sanctuary for terrorists and the international community increased pressure on Pakistan to show genuine action against terrorist on its land. However, the attack and suspicious Pakistani hand in it did not irritate China to help Pakistan on this matter against India. The historical incidents witnessed the India-Pakistan tensions had been lessen cordiality in India-China relations, but 22/11 terror attack and Indian allegation on Pakistan as the center of terrorism did not frustrated India-China relations. Thus, it can be said that Pakistan's role as a determinant of India-China relations has been reduced by the changing Geopolitics and Economic order of the world. Both China and India know that the attempts to encircle each other in strategic forms by using other nations, is not a favourable thing. China is using the duel form of strategy. On the one hand, China declares that Pakistan is not an obstacle in India-China relations and on other hand China's objective is to constrain India by a threat on two fronts—by locking it within South Asia so that it cannot emerge as a rival to China on the wider regional and global stage. Therefore, when the future of China-India relation is speculated, it is found that China-Pakistan cooperation in defence postures perpetuated hostile image of China in India.

India, China, Pakistan and a Stable Regional Order

Three nations—India, China and Pakistan—hold the keys to the future of South Asia. As the Western countries withdraw from Afghanistan and the United States' influence in the region declines, this triangular strategic relationship will become more complicated unless India and China, the two major powers, define the parameters of a new regional order. Thus, the strategic landscape of the sub-region is defined by the complex interactions between three powers—China, a rising superpower with a commercially defined unilateral approach to the region's strategic fault lines; India, a reluctant emerging power unwilling to commit political or diplomatic resources to stabilize the region or even to preserve the status quo; and Pakistan, a deeply dissatisfied revisionist power intent on redrawing the regional order, with the not-so-explicit approval of the rising superpower.

China's involvement in the region serves as a good example for speculation on how its rise will change the international order. By reaching out to the Taliban, China has demonstrated that it is not averse to sponsoring conflict-resolution processes, though this may be mostly aimed at safeguarding its own commercial interests in mineral-rich Afghanistan. India's one of the major security concerns is also linked to Pakistan—the issue of post-NATO Afghanistan, where Pakistan is attempting to control the Kabul regime through proxies, and where the Taliban is gaining ground. For India, the near-certain return of the Taliban to Kabul, in one form or another, brings back memories of the 1999 hijacking of Indian Airlines flight IC-814 by a Pakistani Islamist group, when Indian Government was forced to release high-ranking terrorists in order to get its passengers released from Taliban-controlled Kandahar province.

One of the aspect of contemporary China-Pakistan ties that bothers India is the strengthened three-way partnership between

Pakistan, Afghanistan and China. China is steadily increasing its influence in the region with its innovative "New Silk Route" strategy, and by offering economic and development assistance to Pakistan. China is also increasingly engaged in regional "conflict management" initiatives, mediating between Kabul and Taliban, and organizing trilateral strategic engagements with Afghanistan and Pakistan. For example, in November 2014, representatives of the Taliban from its Doha-based office met in Beijing for talks. China, Pakistan and Afghanistan also initiated a new trilateral strategic dialogue in Kabul. Pakistan hosted a meeting in Murree, as part of the "Murree Peace Process", between the Afghanistan Government and representatives of Tehreek-e-Taliban Pakistan (TPP), the Pakistani branch of the Taliban, which was also attended by representatives of China and the United States.

India's responses to the above events and developments have been suboptimal and poorly thought-out. India is used to adopting a strategy of limited engagement when it comes to dealing with China—whether it is resolving border tensions or finalizing an agreement on the disputed border. While on the one hand India seeks to engage China on the trade front, on the other hand it fights shy of engaging China on larger regional security issues. With Pakistan, India also shows a tendency to indefinitely postpone the resolution of the troublesome issue of Kashmir. Thus, the limited engagement seems to be India's preferred policy option when it comes to dealing with complex issues. India also avoids addressing various emerging threats, failing to recognize them politically. For example, Islamic State (IS) hardly figures on India's list of strategic priorities, and nor does the geopolitical transformation of Afghanistan. This head-in-the-sand, inward-looking strategic posture is clearly not the exception but the rule in India's strategic thinking. Indian diplomacy has failed to think beyond bilaterally engaging with its neighbours for that matter. While India has engaged with China on a variety of bilateral issues, it has not been able to join forces with China and other neighbours in fighting terror, stabilizing Afghanistan, addressing the Islamic State (IS) threat, or even bringing Iran into the mainstream.

India is uncomfortably placed at the heart of a geopolitical landscape—India, China and Pakistan strategic triangle—that is beset with multiple strategic challenges. Even if one were to interpret China's attempts to engage in the reconciliation process in Afghanistan as commercially driven but benign, the perceived India-Pakistan rivalry in Afghanistan and the China-Pakistan partnership would effectively keep India out of the Afghanistan reconciliation process, hampering India's regional aspirations. China should consider the region as a security complex, *i.e.*, acknowledging that the security of each state cannot be considered separately from that of the others, and manage its relations with India in a cooperative manner. China cannot ignore the need to pacify the region and stabilize ties with India while it pursues its global ambitions.

On the other hand, India must view the region from a wider, long-term strategic perspective and avoid getting tied down in petty fights with Pakistan—for its own sake and for the sake of promoting a stable regional order. Such an order could lead to peaceful coexistence between India and China and conciliatory management of the region's problems. Similarly, Pakistan needs to adjust its strategic priorities, in the light of its growing inability to act as a modern, functioning state. Its deep-seated obsession with India, and the use of non-state actors as a tool of statecraft, need to end if it wants to get back on its feet as a viable nation state and contribute to a stable regional order.

Thus, it is important for India, China and Pakistan to move a step further in consolidating their similar goals and objectives with that of other countries of the region and help each of these nations in achieving economic liberty, strengthening their economy and energy security, in addition to pursuing their own goals of stabilizing the regional economies like Afghanistan, which would not be possible by excluding its neighbours. Each country should bring in more transparency in dealing with security issues in the region. If India, China and Pakistan can integrate their economic agendas and work in tandem to promote both economic integration and political stability in the region, the India-China-Pakistan axis could well be a reality.

CHAPTER 9

Cyber Warfare Doctrine

China's cyber spies are reported to have hacked into computers and stolen data from hundreds of government and private offices around the world, including those of the Indian embassies around the world. It is believed that Chinese army uses more than 10,000 cyber warriors to maintain an e-vigil on China's borders and monitor the border with great efficiency with electronic sentinels functioning 24 hours a day. While information about China's cyber warriors has begun to appear in the public domain only recently, People's Liberation Army's watchers across the world have known for long about China's well-conceived doctrine on information operations and cyber war. China's cyber war doctrine is designed to level the playing field in a future war with better-equipped Western armed forces that rely on Revolution in Military Affairs (RMA) technologies and enjoy immense superiority in terms of weapons platforms and intelligence, surveillance and reconnaissance (ISR) and command and control networks.

China is preparing its army to fight a war in the form of a 'local war under high-tech conditions' with increasing attention to the application of information technology. It is spending a lot of time and effort in assessing the implications of information technology and knowledge-based warfare on the modern battlefield and to applying the lessons to its own war concepts. It is also engaged in raising a private army of hackers who will wage cyber war against its enemies. Going with the tide of the world's military development and moving along the direction of informationalisation in the process of modernization, Chinese army is gradually achieving the transition from mechanization and semi-mechanization to informationalisation. Based on

China's national conditions and its army's own conditions, the Chinese army persists in taking mechanization as the foundation to promote informationalisation, and informationalisation as the driving force to bring forward mechanization. The Chinese army will promote coordinated development of firepower, mobility and information capability, enhance the development of its operational strength with priority given to the Navy, Air Force and Second Artillery Force, and strengthen its comprehensive deterrence and war-fighting capabilities.

The Chinese army works to improve its combat capabilities by taking advantage of scientific and technological advances and aims at building qualitative efficiency instead of a mere quantitative scale, and transforming the military from a manpower-intensive one to a technology-intensive one. Based on the transformation of modern warfare and the requirements of the socialist market economy, the Chinese army seeks to achieve development and breakthroughs in the process of reform and innovation. It develops its military theories in an innovative spirit and explores the laws of building the army and conducting operations under the condition of informationalisation.

Acupuncture Warfare

The denial of information, strategic deception and the achievement of psychological surprise have for long been an integral part of Chinese military doctrine. The Chinese army finds Information Warfare (IW) extremely attractive as they view it as an asymmetric tool that will enable them to overcome their relative backwardness in military hardware. China is devoting considerable time and energy to perfecting the techniques of Information Warfare to target the rapidly modernizing Western armed forces that are becoming increasingly more dependent on the software that runs modern communications. The Information Warfare presents a level playing field for projecting power and prevailing upon the adversary in future wars. China views information operations as

(a) Intelligence operations, which include intelligence reconnaissance and protection.

(b) Command and control operations to disrupt enemy information flow and weaken its capability while protecting one's own.

(c) Electronic warfare by seizing the electromagnetic initiative through electronic attack, electronic protection and electronic warfare support.

(d) Targeting enemy computer systems and networks to damage and destroy critical machines, networks and the data stored on them.

(e) Physical destruction of enemy sources like information infrastructure through the application of firepower.

China calls its pursuit of information warfare and other hi-tech means to counter Washington's overwhelmingly superior conventional military capabilities 'acupuncture warfare', a term that first surfaced in 1997. Acupuncture warfare, also known as paralysis warfare, is described as paralyzing the enemy country by attacking the weak link of its command, control, communications and information as if hitting a person's acupuncture point in kung fu combat. The Chinese army has also been simulating computer virus attacks in its military exercises. It is believed that China is developing a strategic information warfare unit called "Net Force" to neutralize the military capabilities of technologically superior adversaries. This unit will wage combat through computer networks to manipulate enemy information systems spanning spare parts deliveries to fire control and guidance systems.

China is assumed to re-direct its emphasis away from nuclear deterrence to information warfare and its overarching purpose is to deter the United States from intervening around China's peripheries and to seize Taiwan with minimum bloodshed and destruction. It has developed depth and sophistication in its understanding and handling of information warfare techniques and information operations. With Indian society becoming increasingly dependent on automated data processing and vast computer networks, India has become extremely vulnerable to such information warfare techniques, which can be practiced from virtually any place on the earth even during peacetime making acupuncture warfare even more diabolical. India is not prepared to face this new challenge to its security.

China's Cyber Warfare

China's recent cyber attacks directed against Taiwan and the United States are indicative of the efforts to develop new techniques, viruses and logic bombs. In future, cyber warfare will be crucial in the opening phases of a war aimed at the re-unification of Taiwan or a border conflict with India as it will be important to knock out the adversary's communications infrastructure by cyber as well as physical means. For this purpose, China is developing a private army of young civilian hackers on whom it can bank during crises. Compared with China's historically reactive stance of luring the enemy in deep and destroying it through strategic defence, the cyber warfare is essentially proactive and seeks to take the battle into enemy's territory. China also strives to achieve surprise in a proactive manner that is demonstrated by new 'quick-strike' tactics. Its aim is to catch the enemy unprepared in order to inflict substantial damage on strategic targets and disrupt logistics to gain psychological ascendancy. While the land frontier is expected to continue to generate some local tensions, the space and the oceans are identified as the new areas where future conflict might take place.

China has rejected the doctrine of deterrence as, in its view, it is associated with imperialism, amounting to military blackmail, glorifing the use of force and would be an empty threat if not substantiated by tangible power. The cyber warfare also calls for integrated deep strikes—a concentration of superior firepower that is to be utilized to destroy the opponent's retaliatory capabilities by employing long range artillery, short-range ballistic missiles and precision guided munitions. It emphasizes the effective use of advanced equipment wielded by elite units, with a focus on joint operations. The overall aim in this "limited war under hi-tech conditions" technique is to cause heavy attrition and disrupt the enemy's combat forces and logistics so as to bring about a negotiated end to the conflict or dictate terms if possible.

Unlike traditional warfare that moves at speeds measured in days or hours, cyber warfare happens in milliseconds. At such speeds, it is imperative that any strategy is comprehensive. But, in India, software developers are limited to developing defensive measures based on the current or known threat. However, new threats exploit flaws that have no current defense. This gap confers a significant advantage to the attacker. Therefore, a purely defensive strategy in cyber warfare does not ensure adequate protection and yields the initiative. A strategy designed around an offensive approach with defensive capability is the most logical. In such situations India should adopt an inter-ministerial, inter-departmental, inter-services, multi-agency approach to deal with emerging cyber warfare threats and must develop appropriate responses. No single agency in India is charged with ensuring cyber and IT security. A nodal agency must be created to spearhead India's cyber war efforts under a national cyber security advisor who should report directly to the national security advisor. The armed forces must be part of the overall national effort from the very beginning so that emerging tactics, techniques and procedures can be incorporated into doctrine and training. India also needs a Cyber Command to lead efforts within the military to safeguard computer networks from hackers and cyber-attacks. The strategy must be defensive to guard India's vulnerable assets, such as military command and control networks and civilian infrastructure dependent on the use of cyber space, as well as offensive to disrupt the adversary's communication systems and develop leverages that can be exploited at the appropriate time.

CHAPTER 10

Defence Cooperation and Military Engagement

As rising global economic and military powers, India and China have both committed themselves to promoting peace, stability and development in the present international context. Their improving bilateral relationship which has now become a focus of worldwide attention, is seen as a result of their shifting strategies and the ever-changing global politico-economic situation. On the political front, high-level interaction plays an important role in improving India-China ties. The political willingness to improve relations helps kick-start the significant process of building confidence and trust in different areas and at various levels. As two fast-growing economies and developing giants, both India and China have pledged to contribute to bilateral and multilateral cooperation. Enhanced political engagement and pragmatic strategic calculus have pressed both the countries to explore defence, security and non-traditional security cooperation. The burgeoning military interaction is of pragmatic significance to nurturing mutual trust on the strategic level and achieving reciprocal accommodation.

Military engagement between two countries is an important aspect of the bilateral relations between them. It is not only symbolic of maturing of their relationship but also builds trust and confidence between the defence forces which may be useful during any joint military operation such as fighting terrorism or natural disasters like flood and earthquake. Military engagement between two countries is possible only when there is higher degree of friendship and cooperation at the political level between the two governments, which is highly desirable because it reduces transaction costs and makes interstate relations more predictable.

Before we discuss the military cooperation and competition between India and China, let us have a look at the strengths of their defence forces.

Military Strengths of India and China

The Indian Armed Forces consist of three professional uniformed services, namely Indian Army, Indian Navy and Indian Air Force. Additionally, they are supported by the Indian Coast Guard and paramilitary organisations (Assam Rifles and Special Frontier Force) and various inter-service commands and institutions such as the Strategic Forces Command, the Andaman and Nicobar Command and the Integrated Defence Staff. The President of India is the Supreme Commander of the Indian Armed Forces, which are under the management of the Ministry of Defence of the Government of India. Here it should be noted that the Central Armed Police Forces which include Border Security Force (BSF), Central Industrial Security Force (CISF), Central Reserve Police Force (CRPF), Indo Tibetan Border Police (ITBP), National Security Guard (NSG), and Sashastra Seema Bal (SSB), are headed by officers from the Indian Police Service and are under the control of the Ministry of Home Affairs, not the Ministry of Defence.

The People's Liberation Army (PLA) of China consists of five professional service branches—the Ground Force, Navy (including the Republic of China Marine Corps), Air Force, Rocket Force, and the Strategic Support Force. It also has a militia service branch, the PLA Militia. Since 2002, the military comes under the full civilian control of the Ministry of National Defence and oversight by the Legislative Yuan. The Chinese army is under the command of the Central Military Commission (CMC) of the Communist Party of China (CPC). It is legally obliged to follow the principle of civilian control of the military, although in practical terms this principle has been implemented in such a way as to ensure the Chinese army is under the absolute control of the Communist Party of China. Its commander in chief is the Chairman of the Central Military Commission, who is also the General Secretary of the Communist Party of China.

The Ministry of National Defence, which operates under the State Council, does not exercise any authority over the army and is far less powerful than the Communist Party of China. A system of political officers embedded within the military ensures party authority over the armed forces so that the primary role of the Ministry of Defence is that of a liaison office with foreign militaries rather than a commanding authority. The political and military leadership have made a concerted effort to create a professional military force, the duties of which are restricted to national defence and to the provision of assistance in domestic economic construction and emergency relief. This conception of the role of the army requires the promotion of specialized officers who can understand modern weaponry and handle combined arms operations. Units around the country are assigned to one of five Theater Commands by geographical location. Military service is compulsory by law in China. However, compulsory military service in China has never been enforced due to large numbers of military and paramilitary personnel. In times of national emergency, the People's Armed Police and the People's Liberation Army Militia act as a reserve and support element for the PLA Ground Force.

A Brief Comparison of Military Strengths

Manpower: It is the actual manpower that drives a given military force. Wars of attrition traditionally favour those with more manpower to a given effort. Military equipment and perceived fighting strength come next.

	India	China
Total Population	1,281,935,911	1,379,302,771
Manpower Available	616,000,000	750,000,000
Fit of Service	489,600,000	619,000,000
Reaching Military Age	22,900,000	19,550,000
Total Military Personnel	4,207,250	2,693,000
Active Personnel	1,362,500	2,183,000
Reserve Personnel	2,844,750	510,000

Army Strength: Tank value includes Main Battle Tanks (MBTs) and light tanks as well as those vehicles considered "tank destroyers". Armored Fighting Vehicles (AFVs) value includes Armored Personnel Carriers (APCs) as well as Infantry Fighting Vehicles (IFVs).

	India	China
Combat Tanks	4,426	7,716
Armored Fighting Vehicles	3,147	9,000
Self-Propelled Artillery	190	2,000
Towed Artillery	4,158	6,246
Rocket Projectors	266	2,050

Air Power: It includes both fixed-wing and rotary-wing (helicopter) aircraft from all branches of service (Air Force, Navy, Army). Air power is the most important component of the modern military force. Attack aircraft represents fixed-wing and dedicated forms as well as light strike types. Some fighters can double as attack types and vice versa this is how multi-role aircraft can be of considerable value. Transport and trainer aircraft include both fixed-wing and rotary-wing.

	India	China
Total Aircraft Strength	2,185	3,035
Fighter Aircraft	590	1,125
Attack Aircraft	804	1,527
Transport Aircraft	708	722
Trainer Aircraft	251	353
Total Helicopter Strength	720	985
Attack Helicopters	15	281

Navy Strength: Aircraft carriers value includes both traditional aircraft carriers as well as helicopter carrier warships. Submarines value includes both diesel-electric and nuclear-powered types. Total naval assets is not simply a sum of the presented navy ship categories, instead it includes all showcased types along with any known/recognized auxiliary vessels.

	India	China
Total Naval Assets	295	714
Aircraft Carriers	1	1
Frigates	14	50
Destroyers	11	29
Corvettes	22	39
Submarines	16	73
Patrol Craft	139	220
Mine Warfare Vessels	4	29

Natural Resources (Petroleum): As much as any weapon system is vital to an ongoing military camping, wars still rely on the availability of natural resources, *i.e.*, petroleum. (bbl/dy --- Barrels per Day)

	India	China
Production (bbl/dy)	734,500	3,981,000
Consumption (bbl/dy)	3,510,000	10,120,000
Proven Reserves (bbl)	4,621,000,000	25,620,000,000

Logistics: War is as much a battle of logistics, moving man, and machine from-to points allover, as it is direct combat. A quantitative/robust labour force also adds to available wartime industry.

	India	China
Total Labour Force	521,900,000	806,700,000
Merchant Marine Strength	1,674	4,287
Major Ports/Terminals	7	15
Railway Coverage (Km)	63,974	86,000
Roadway Coverage (Km)	3,320,410	3,860,800
Serviceable Airports	346	507

Finance: War goes beyond simple physical "strength-in-numbers", relying heavily on financing and effort as much as any one piece of hardware fielded.

	India	China
Defence Budget	$ 47,000,000,000	$ 151,000,000,000
External Debt	$ 483,400,000,000	$ 1,649,000,000,000
Foreign Exchange/ Gold	$ 407,200,000,000	$ 3,194,000,000,000
Purchasing Power Parity	$ 9,447,000,000,000	$ 23,120,000,000,000

Geography: Geographical values primarily figure into a defensive-minded war, *i.e.*, invasion, but can also aid a nation when responding to such an act.

	India	China
Square Land Area (Km)	3,287,263	9,596,961
Coastline (Km)	7,000	14,500
Shared Borders (Km)	13,888	22,457
Waterways (Km)	14,500	110,000

Missiles and Nuclear Weapons: India has three air bases with four squadrons of Mirage 2000H and Jaguar IS/IB aircrafts, which are capable of nuclear strike. The estimated 68 nuclear warheads of land-based nuclear weapons of India are under the control of and deployed by the Indian Army, using a variety of both vehicles and launching silos. The Indian Navy has developed two sea-based delivery systems for nuclear weapons. The first is a submarine-launched system consisting of at least four 6,000 tonne (nuclear-powered) ballistic missile submarines of the Arihant class. The second is a ship-launnched system based around the short-range ship-launched Dhanush ballistic missile (a variant of the Prithvi missile).

On the other hand, China has up to 90 inter-continental range ballistic missiles (66 land-based ICBMs and 24 submarine-based JL-2 SLBMs), not counting MIRV warheads.

	India	China
Nuclear Weapons	110–120 Warheads	260–450 Warheads
Land-Based Ballistic Missiles	Prithvi Series (150–600 Km) Agni-I to Agni-IV (700–5000 Km)	DF Series (300–5000 Km)
Sea-Based Ballistic Missiles	Dhanush (350 Km) Sagarika (K-15) (700 Km) K-4 (3500 Km, Tested)	JL-1 (1770+ Km) JL-2 (8000+ Km)
Air-Based Ballistic Missiles	Astra (80–110 Km) Novator KS-172 (300–400 Km)	Hong-6 (3100 Km) Attack (3000–8000 Km)
Inter-Continental Ballistic Missiles	Agni-V (5000–8000 Km) Agni-VI (8000–12000 Km) Surya (12000–16000 Km, proposed)	DF-4 (5500+ Km) DF-31 (7200+ Km) DF-31A (11200+ Km) DF-5A (13000+ Km)
Ballistic Missile Defence System	Prithvi Air Defence (2000 Km) Ashwin Advanced Air Defense (5000 Km)	SC-19 (1100 Km) HQ-9 (500 Km) HQ-19 (3000 Km) HQ-29 (6000+ Km)

Military Engagements

The rationale and raison d'etre for defence cooperation and military engagement between India and China can hardly be overemphasized because of the fact that the two countries fought a boarder war in 1962 and they have a common border of around 4000 kilometers which remains undefined and disputed even after having thirteen rounds of fresh parleys. There always exists a persistent security dilemma between India and China. Although, there has been no major conflict between them after 1962, there have been border incursions from time to time leading to rise in tension across the border. In the post-1962 period and after the restoration of the diplomatic relations between the two countries in 1976, the relationship between the two reached its nadir when the Sumdorong Chu incident took place in 1986. This incident brought the two countries almost to the brink of war, which in turn impelled the two countries to explore ways and means for defence cooperation and military engagement. It is in this backdrop that it is significant to revisit the achievements between India and China in the field of defence cooperation and military engagement particularly at a time when these achievements built over the years as consequences of greater political engagement at various levels between the two countries and their leaders.

Agreement on Maintenance of Peace and Tranquillity, 1993: The path breaking visit of the then Prime Minister Rajiv Gandhi to China in December 1988, established the Joint Working Group (JWG), the groundwork for defence cooperation and military engagement. A milestone in the military relationship between the two countries was the visit of the then Defence Minister Sharad Pawar to China in July 1992. It was the first ever visit by a Defence Minister of India to China. During this visit, it was agreed to develop academic, military, scientific and technological exchanges between the two countries; and also, the Chinese military leadership emphasized the importance of force reduction in the border region due to prohibitive cost. The visit fructified in the signing of the Agreement on the Maintenance of Peace and Tranquility along the Line of Actual Control (LAC) in the India-China border area on 7th September 1993 during the visit of the then Prime Minister P.V. Narashima Rao. The salient features of this agreement are:

(a) The India-China boundary question shall be resolved through peaceful and friendly consultations and that neither side shall use or threaten to use force against the other by any means.

(b) The two sides shall strictly observe the LAC between the two sides and that no activities of either side shall overstep the line of actual control.

(c) When necessary, the two sides shall jointly check and determine the segments of the LAC when they have different views as to its alignment.

(d) Each side will keep its military forces in the area along the LAC to a minimum level compatible with the friendly and good neighbourly relations between the two countries.

(e) The reduction of military forces shall be carried out by stages in mutually agreed geographical locations sector-wise within the areas along the LAC.

(f) Each side shall give the other prior notification of the military exercises of specified levels near the LAC permitted under the agreement.

(g) In case of contingency or other problems arising in the areas of LAC, the two sides shall deal with them through meetings and friendly consultations between border personnel of the two countries.

(h) The two sides also agreed in the accord to take adequate measures to ensure that air intrusions across the line of actual control do not take place and that the two sides shall undertake mutual consultation in case intrusion occur.

As a follow up of this agreement, a senior level Chinese military delegation aimed at fostering Confidence Building Measures (CBMs) between the defence forces of the two countries made a six-day goodwill visit to India in December 1993.

Confidence Building Measures on LAC, 1996: An agreement between India and China on the Confidence Building Measures in the military field along the LAC in the India-China Border areas was signed on 29th November 1996 during the visit of Chinese President Jiang Zemin to India. This agreement while reiterating and reaffirming the intent and spirit of the 1993, state agreement, inter-alias, as Confidence Building Measures, envisaged the following:

(a) The major categories of armament to be reduced or limited include combat tanks, infantry combat vehicles, guns with 75 mm or bigger caliber, mortars with 120 mm or bigger caliber, surface-to-surface missiles, surface-to-air missiles and any other weapon system.

(b) The two sides shall exchange data on the military forces and armaments to be reduced or limited and decide on ceilings on military forces and armaments to be kept by each side within agreed geographically zones along the LAC in the India-China border.

In order to maintain peace and tranquility along the LAC in the India-China border areas and to prevent any tension in the border areas due to misreading by either side of the other side's intentions, Article IV of the Agreement states that:

(a) Both sides shall avoid holding large-scale military exercises involving more than one Division (15000 troops) in close proximity of the line of actual control in the India-China border areas. However, if such exercises are to be conducted, the strategic direction of the main force involved shall not be towards the other side.

(b) If either side conducts a major military exercise involving more than one Brigade Group (5000 troops) in close proximity of the line of actual control in the India-China border areas, one side will give the other side prior notification with regard to type, level, planned duration and area of exercise as well as the number and type of units or formations participating in the exercise.

(c) The date of completion of the exercise and de-induction of troops from the area of exercise shall be intimated to the other side within five days of completion or de-induction.

(d) Each side shall be entitled to obtain timely clarification from the side undertaking the exercise in respect of date specified.

With a view to preventing air intrusions across the LAC in the India-China border areas and facilitating over flights and landings by military aircraft, Article V states that:

(a) Both sides shall take adequate measures to ensure that air intrusions across the line of actual control do not take place. However, if an intrusion does take place, it should cease as soon as detected and the incident will be promptly investigated by the side operating the aircraft. The results of the investigation shall be immediately communicated, through diplomatic channels or at border personnel meetings to the other side.

(b) Combat aircrafts (includes fighter, bomber, reconnaissance, military trainer, armed helicopter and other armed aircraft) shall not fly within ten kilometers of the line of actual control.

(c) If either side is required to undertake flights of combat aircraft within ten kilometers from the LAC, it shall give the following information in advance to the other side, through diplomatic channels:

  (i) Type and number of combat aircraft;

  (ii) Height of the proposed flight (in metres);

  (iii) Proposed duration of flights (normally not to exceed ten days);

  (iv) Proposed timing of flights; and

  (v) Area of operations defined in latitude and longitude.

(d) Unarmed transport aircraft, survey aircraft and helicopters shall be permitted to fly up to the LAC.

(e) No military aircraft of either side shall fly across the LAC, except by prior permission. Military aircraft of either side may fly across the LAC or overfly the other side's airspace or land on the other side only after obtaining the latter's prior permission after providing the latter with detailed information on the flight in accordance with the international practice in this regard.

Notwithstanding the above stipulation, each side has the sovereign right to specify additional conditions, including at short notice, for flights or landings of military aircraft of the other side on its side of the line of actual control or through its airspace.

(f) In order to ensure flight safety in emergency situations, the authorities designated by the two sides may contact each other by the quickest means of communications available.

Similarly, with a view to preventing dangerous military activities along the LAC in the India-China border areas, Article VI states that:

(a) Neither side shall open fire, cause bio-degradation, use hazardous chemicals, conduct blast operations or hunt with guns or explosive within two kilometers from the LAC. This prohibition will not apply to routine firing activities in small arms firing ranges.

(b) If there is a need to conduct blast operations within two kilometers of the LAC as part of developmental activities, the other side shall be informed through diplomatic channels or by convening a border personnel meeting, preferably five days in advance.

(c) While conducting exercises with live ammunition in areas close to the LAC, precaution will be taken to ensure that a bullet or a missile does not accidentally fall on the other side across the LAC and cause harm to the personnel or property of the other side.

(d) If the border personnel of the two sides come in a face-to-face situation due to differences on the alignment of the LAC of any other reasons, they shall exercise self-restraint and take all necessary steps to avoid an escalation of the situation. Both sides shall also enter into immediate consultations through diplomatic and/ or other available channels to review the situation and prevent any escalation of tension.

Article VII of the agreement includes:

(a) Maintaining and expanding the regime of scheduled and flag meetings between their border representatives at designated places along the LAC.

(b) Maintaining and expanding telecommunication links between the border meeting points at designated places along the LAC.

(c) Establishing step-by-step medium and high-level contacts between the border authorities of the two countries.

Article VIII of the agreement includes:

(a) If the personnel of one side cross the LAC and enter the other side because of unavoidable circumstances like natural disasters, the other side will extend all possible assistance to them and inform their side, as soon as possible regarding the forced or inadvertent entry across the LAC. The modalities of return of the concerned personnel to their own side will be settled through mutual consultations.

(b) The two sides shall provide each other, at the earliest possible, with information pertaining to natural disasters and epidemic diseases in contiguous border areas which might affect the other side. The exchange of information will take place either through diplomatic channels or at border personnel meetings.

Article X mentions the following provisions:

(a) Recognizing that the full implementation of some of the provisions of the present agreement will depend on the two sides arriving at a common understanding of the alignment of the LAC in the India-China border areas, the two sides agree to speed up the process clarification and confirmation of the line of actual control. As an initial step in this process, they are clarifying the alignment of the line of actual control in those segments where they have different perceptions. They also agree to exchange maps indicating their respective perceptions of the entire alignment of the line of actual control as soon as possible.

(b) Pending the completion of the process of clarification and confirmation of the LAC, India and China shall work out modalities for implementing confidence-building measures envisaged under the agreement on an interim basis, without prejudice to their respective positions on the alignment of the LAC as well as on the boundary question.

Thus, from various provisions of different agreements and accords signed between India and China, it is found that every conceivable aspect of military contingency has been thoughtfully anticipated and ways and means to deftly handle them without precipitating the matter have been envisaged. It was against this backdrop of signing of various agreements providing for Confidence Building Measures (CBMs) that a slew of visits at various levels between the two countries were given further impetus. The most significant of the visit was that of the then Defence Minister, George Fernandes to China in April 2003 after a gap of more than one decade. This visit also helped to ease the post-Pokhran tension between India and China.

Defence cooperation and military engagement between India and China further received a boost during the visit of the then Prime Minister Atal Bihari Vajpayee to China in June 2003. The joint declaration between the two countries signed on 23rd June 2003 mentioned that "They agreed on the need to broaden and deepen defence exchanges between the two countries, which will help enhance and deepen mutual understanding and trust between the two armed forces. They confirmed that the exchange of visits by their Defence Ministers and of military officials at various levels should be strengthened."

Protocols on Confidence Building Measures along the LAC, 2005: The visit of then Chinese Premier Wen Jiabao to India in April 2005 gave an upward swing to the defence cooperation and military engagement between the two countries. The protocol between India and China on modalities for the implementations of confidence building measures in the military field along the LAC in the India-China border areas was signed on 11th April 2005. This protocol sought to further elucidate certain provisions of the 1996 confidence building accord while reiterating verbatim of some of the bilateral commitments in the accord. Some of the amplified provisions of the protocol are as follows.

Article III of the protocol describes the following provisions.

(a) In the case of an alleged air intrusion of its controlled air space by the military aircraft of the other side, either side may seek a Flag Meeting within 48 hours of the alleged air intrusion in order to seek a clarification. The investigation shall be completed by the other side and its results communicated through a Flag Meeting within a period of four weeks.

(b) If a military aircraft of either side is required to fly across the LAC or to overfly the airspace of the other side, prior permission shall be sought from the other side according to procedures and formats to be mutually agreed upon.

(c) If a military or civilian aircraft of either side is required to fly across the LAC or to land on the other side of the LAC in an emergency situation, the two sides will ensure flight safety in such a situation by adhering to procedures to be mutually agreed upon.

Article V of the protocol describes the following provisions.

(a) Both countries shall hold two additional border meetings each year at Spanggur Gap in the Western Sector; Nathu La Pass in the Sikkim Sector and Bum La Pass in the Eastern Sector respectively in celebration of the National Day or Army Day of either side. Specific arrangements shall be decided through consultation between the border forces of the two sides.

(b) Both countries are in principle to expand the mechanism of border meeting points to include Kibithu-Damai in the Eastern Sector and Lipulekh Pass/Qiang La in the Middle Sector. The precise locations of these border meetings points will be decided through mutual consultations.

(c) Both countries shall conduct exchanges between the relevant Military Regions of China and Army Commands of India. Specific arrangements shall be decided upon through mutual consultations between the relevant agencies under the Ministeries of Defence of the two countries.

(d) Both countries shall strengthen exchanges between institutions of training of the two armed forces, and conduct exchanges between institutions of sports and culture of the two armed forces. Specific arrangements shall be decided upon through mutual consultations between the relevant agencies under the Ministeries of Defence of the two countries.

Memorandum of Understanding (MoU), 2006: The then Defence Minister Pranab Mukherjee visited China on a five-day visit in May/June 2006 and held wide ranging talks with Chinese leaders including Chinese Premier Wen Jiabao and

Defence Minister General Cao Gangchaum. The most important point of this visit was the signing of the MoU, which was first ever of its kind between the two countries. The MoU envisages for the establishment of a mechanism to ensure frequent and regular exchanges between leaders and officials of the Defence Ministries and the armed forces of the two countries in addition to developing an annual calendar for holding regular joint military exercises and training programmes. As a result, in the past few years, the two countries have conducted joint naval manoeuvres, but the interaction between the ground forces has been limited to border meetings and mountaineering expeditions and there has been no interaction between the air forces of the two countries. Pranab Mukherjee also visited the sensitive Lanzhou Military Area Command which controls the largest physical area of China's seven military regions. The region holding the nuclear research and missile testing facilities in the Chinese West comes under the command of this area. This visit to the headquarters of the Lanzhou Military Command was a significant step in the process of building bilateral trust and confidence on part of China.

These achievements were further consolidated during the visit of Chinese President Hu Jintao to India in November 2006. In the Joint Declaration signed between the two countries on 21st November, it was mentioned that the exchange of visits in the field of defence has resulted in the building of mutual trust and enhancement of mutual understanding between the defence establishments of the two countries. Both the countries shall fully implement the provisions of the MoU for exchanges and cooperation in the field of defence signed on 29th May 2006, which provides a sound foundation and institutional framework for further development of defence cooperation. Certain concrete steps were taken as a follow-up of the confidence building measures. For example, Armed Forces of India and China hold a warm meeting at a new border point in Arunachal Pradesh, on 18th November 2006, on the eve of President Hu Jintao's visit to India. The two sides met at Kibithu in Anjaw district of Arunachal Pradesh and discussed modalities for the conduct of troops along the border. An official press release claimed that the meeting and exchanges were characterized by great warmth and bonhomie. It marks another milestone in the growing relationship and military exchanges between the armed forces of the two countries. Border meetings between personnel of the armed forces of the two countries have traditionally been held at Chushul in Ladakh, Nathu La in Sikkim, and Bum La in Kameng district of Arunachal Pradesh.

India-China Joint Military Exercise, 2008: Encouraged by the success of the first ever joint military exercise between India and China in Kunming in Yunnan in 2007, a week-long India-China joint anti-terrorists training kicked off on 6th December 2008 at Belgaum in Karnataka with performance of the Chinese Tai Chai and Indian martial arts. This joint training was aimed at promoting the two army's mutual understanding and trust. It was a way for the armies to develop their friendship and expand the fields for exchanges and cooperation.

Highlighting the need for the joint training, the Chinese Defence Ministry spokesman Huang Xueping said that such training was intended to enhance mutual understanding and trust and advance development of relations between Chinese and Indian armies. Emphasising the importance of such exercises, Lt. General Ma Xiaotian, Head of the Chinese Military Observer Delegation and also the Deputy Chief of the People's Liberation Army (PLA) said that the joint training showcased the resolution of the two sides to safeguard regional peace and stability and create a harmonious environment for development together. In an editorial of a China Daily it was mentioned that "China and India are looking after their fences, turning the Himalayas, the highest mountains on the earth, into a friendly border".

During 2009, defence cooperation between India and China maintained a healthy momentum. The Chief of Indian Naval Staff attended the International Fleet Review 2009 at Qingdao from 21st to 24th April 2009. Indian participation included guided missile destroyers INS Mumbai and INS Ranveer, the guided missile corvette INS Khanjar and the tanker INS Jyoti. On the other hand, Chinese "Shenzhen" Missile Destroyer made port call at the Kochi port from 8th to 11th August 2009. In

2009, Liberation Army of China also visited India. The Defence Secretary led a high level Indian delegation for third Annual Defence Dialogue held in Beijing on 6th January 2010. Although these military engagement and confidence building measures have somewhat helped in diffusing tension across the border, incidents regarding border incursions are reported from time to time. Every month the Indo-Tibetan Border Police (ITBP) reports around a dozen unannounced Chinese military patrols in the disputed border area, and this number have not decreased over the years. Most of these incidents are inoffensive. Often border-guards do not even make direct contacts, but leave behind subtle traces of their presence, like piles of stones, cigarette packets, or cans. From time to time, Chinese military officials reportedly enter the Indian side of LAC in civilian clothes and vehicles. In Ladakh, almost on a weakly basis, small Chinese boats tour around the Lake Pangong Tso.

In spite of all the confidence building measures, India is worried about a significant increase in the number of stand-offs between Indian and Chinese border patrols and more aggressive posturing by Chinese soldiers along the border. In the early September 2010, Chinese soldiers brought a bulldozer into a disputed area in the Ladakh region to construct a road. Even after the Indian side objected to it and asked the Chinese to take it back, the Chinese army unduly delayed the withdrawal of the machine and took it away only about four days later. The summer of 2010 had recorded an almost 100 percent increase in the number of stand-offs between the patrols of the two sides. These peaceful standoffs were reported from Depsang, Demchok and Pangong Tso areas of Ladakh region. The latest stand-off between the two sides was over Chinese construction of a road at Doklam on the India-Bhutan-China trijunction in the Sikkim sector. On 16th June 2017, Chinese troops with construction vehicles and road-building equipment began extending an existing road Southward in Doklam, a territory which is claimed by both China as well as India's ally Bhutan. On 18th June 2017, Indian troops, with weapons and two bulldozers, entered Doklam to stop the Chinese troops from constructing the road.

On 28th August, both India and China announced that they had withdrawn all their troops from the face-off site in Doklam.

Thus, defence cooperation and military engagement between India and China is an aspect of the complex mix of conflict and cooperation approach to bilateral relations between the two Asian giants. It is based on the presumption that there is a security dilemma between the two countries. It recognizes the framework and postulates of what is called cooperative security. China's acquiescence for military engagement and defence cooperation with India is another aspect of China's overall strategy of so-called peaceful and harmonious rise, which it initiated and pursues, arguably to project China as a soft-power, but really to consolidate its economic muscles and to use it as a leverage to enhance its influence, particularly at a time when there is greater degree of mutual economic inter-dependence between China and India.

Chapter 11

Comprehensive Trade and Economic Cooperation

Commercial links between India and China can be traced from ancient time. A large number of seashells from the coast of the Bay of Bengal was unearthed in Sichuan and Yunnan, which are assumed to be 3000 years old. These seashells were ancient currencies, indicating that there had been trade contacts between Sichuan, Yunnan and countries such as India and Myanmar at that time. India was the origin of Asiatic cotton, with a long history of producing cotton textiles. A piece of cotton cloth, which is about 3000 years old, was unearthed in Fujian, China, which is the earliest evidence of cotton cloth ever discovered. Since there was no cotton in China at that time, it is considered that this piece of cotton cloth probably came from India. During 4th century BCE, there were records about silk and Chinese silk in Kautilya's *Arthashastra*. Silk was also mentioned in other ancient works such as the two great Indian epics, the *Ramayana* and the *Mahabharata*. This indicates that Chinese silk had been introduced to India before the Common Era.

According to the *Shiji* (Records of the Grand Historian), in the Biography of Dayuan, cloth and bamboo cane produced in Sichuan had been seen in Bactria during Zhang Qian's mission to the Western Regions. This indicates that Sichuan products had long been introduced into India via Yunnan and then further transported to Bactria. It is recorded in the Chinese work, *Han Shu* (the Record on Geography) that there had already been sea trade between Southern India and China in the 2nd century BCE. The main goods from India at that time included "bright pearls, jewels (glass), rare stones and exotic things", and the goods from China were mainly gold and "za zeng" (all kinds of silk fabrics). Ancient coins of the Han Dynasty also have been unearthed in Southern India, which prove the existence of trade at that time. With the end of the age of the great ocean-going Chinese ships and Chinese merchants directly carrying their goods to Indian ports, the trade between India and China did not end but altered its form and orientation. This was the period of a flourishing junk trade between China and Southeast Asia. Indian and Chinese goods were often exchanged in Southeast Asian ports such as Malacca. However, there is evidence of the resumption of direct trade between Surat, the leading port on the West coast of India, and China from the last quarter of the 17th century AD. Chinese porcelain, tea, Chinese gold, lacquer work, copper and vermilion were exported to India in return for silver, spices, sandalwood and other items. However, some of the merchandise imported by Surat merchants was re-exported to the Persian Gulf and Red Sea area. There is also some evidence that by the early 18th century, this trade with China had entered a period of stagnation.

The entry of the European monopoly trading companies in the Asian waters was a new and significant feature of the 18th century AD. Initially, these companies participated in the trade without altering its structure significantly. However, Dutch Batavia (Central Jakarta) soon became an intermediate station in the trade between India and China. Western ships in the East Indies loaded up with spices and other goods which they carried to Guangzhou and from there, they carried porcelain and silk to Surat to exchange for cotton, sugar, gum and textiles, returning to Guangzhou with the monsoon winds. The rapid growth of the tea trade between China and Europe, and the establishment of the colonial power of the Western countries in India and other Asian countries, changed the nature of the trade between India and China substantially. From the last quarter of the 18th century AD, raw cotton from western India and opium from both Bengal and western India began to be exported to China in huge quantities to pay for the rapidly escalating import of tea into Britain from China. In the 19th century, raw cotton was one of the mainstays of Indian exports to China. Gujarat produced a short staple cotton that was suited to the handloom weaving industry of China at that time. British as well as Indian traders made considerable profits from the cotton trade, which also gave a boost to the shipbuilding industry in the western India. In the second half of the 19th century, manufactured cotton yarn, the product of India's earliest modern industry, the textile industry, started to become the main product exported to China by India. During 1872 to 1873, the total volume of export of Indian cotton yarn was 1.8 million pounds, of which 1.2 million pounds were exported to China only. After that, the volume of exports of Indian cotton yarn increased year by year. While from 1874 to 1879, the average annual exports were about 9 million pounds, by 1894 to 1899, it was 180.9 million pounds. Initially, Indian cotton yarn was mainly sold in Shantou and Guangzhou, and then it gradually extended to East China, Central China, North China, Northeast China and Southwest China. It was not until 1914-15 that the volume of export of Indian cotton yarn to China decreased to 134 million pounds due to entry of Japanese cotton yarn.

In the middle of 19th century, the volume of goods imported from China was much less than that of goods exported to China from India. China faced a huge trade deficit, which required silver to pay for the balance. The primary goods of exports to China from India were opium, cotton, wheat and jute; while the main goods of imports were raw silk, porcelain, tea and medicinal materials, mainly exported to Britain, USA, France, Netherland and Spain. During the period 1834 to 1845, the annual average value of the goods imported from China was only (1/80)th of the value of the goods exported from India to China. So, the net value of silver transported to India from China reached about 1.5 to 2.5 million pounds. The goods imported from China in this period included, besides raw silk, tea and porcelain, rock candy, white sugar, alum, silk and satin, camphor, paper, homespun, *etc*. From 1864 to 1891, the annual total volume of direct trade between India and China was 27.77 million haikwan tales (Chinese system of weights and currency) on an average. This figure rose in the 20th century. In 1926, the total volume of trade between the two countries reached 95,113,114 haikwan tales of which the total value of goods exported to China from India was 79,191,013 haikwan tales. During this period, products exported to China from India were mainly cotton, rice and cotton yarn. China also used to import from India flour, sugar, coal, kerosene, cement, tea, jute and various kinds of cloth. During this period, products imported from China were mainly silk, tea and beans. Besides these, other imports from China included eggs, peanuts, cowhide, sesame, China wood oil, coal, cotton yarn, pig iron, *etc*. Here, it is worth noting that while cotton yarn had earlier been exported from India to China, during this period China began to export cotton yarn to India.

In 1954, India and China signed the first trade agreement after the establishment of the People's Republic of China. During this period, India imported from China mainly rice, broomcorn, beans, raw silk, machines, transformers, wool, caustic soda, paper, *etc*. and exported to China mainly hemp articles, rice, beans, tobacco, chemicals, drugs, mica, electric fans, woolens, machines, *etc*. After a disruption of the trade in the 1960s and early 1970s, trade between India and China began to revive in the 1980s. In 1977, direct trade was resumed; in 1984, the two countries signed an official trade agreement; in 1985, the two countries signed a trade protocol; in 1988, there was established a minister-level economic, trade and scientific and technological cooperation group. During the 1980s, India imported from China mainly raw silk, silk products, edible vegetable oil, coal, mercury, antimony, petroleum, petrochemicals, drug, *etc*. and, at the same time, exported to China mainly iron ore, chrome ore, manganese ore, steel products, tobacco, leather, power generating equipment, *etc*. In 1982, the value of trade between India and China stood at USD 145 million. From 1984 to 1990, it grew year by year on the whole and by the year 2000 it had reached a total of USD 2.92 billion. Since then, trade between India and China has grown at a phenomenal rate and is the most dynamic element in the relationship at the present time. Currently, China has become India's largest trading partner. However, there is a distinct imbalance in the trade, with the balance of trade in China's favour, and the figure is only a small proportion in the total volume of foreign trade of the two countries.

India and China officially resumed trade in 1978 and in 1984, the two countries signed the Most Favoured Nation Agreement. India-China bilateral trade which was as low as USD 2.92 billion in 2000 reached USD 61.7 billion in 2010, making China India's largest goods trading partner, replacing the United States. By the end of 2009, as a result of the world economic downturn, bilateral trade dropped to USD 43.27 billion, a decline of 16.54 percent. However, in 2010 bilateral trade reached to USD 61.74 billion, a growth of 43 percent compared to the same period last year. India exported goods worth USD 20.86 billion to China and imported goods worth USD 40.88 billion from China, resulting in an adverse balance of trade of USD 20 billion. In the first 8 months of 2011, India-China bilateral trade reached USD 48.17 billion over the same period last year. India's total exports to China for this period were USD 15.68 billion and China's exports to India reached USD 32.49 billion, *i.e.*, the trade deficit for the first 8 months was USD 16.8 billion.

India-China bilateral trade in 2017 rose by 18.63 percent year-on-year to reach USD 84.44 billion. It was regarded as a landmark as the volume of bilateral trade for the first time touched USD 80 billion, well above the USD 71.18 billion registered in 2016. The trade touched historic high despite bilateral tensions over a number of issues including the China-Pakistan Economic Corridor, China blocking India's efforts to bring about a UN ban on Jaish-e-Mohammad leader Masood Azhar, China blocking India's entry into the Nuclear Supplier Group (NSG) as well as the military standoff at Doklam lasting 73 days. While the bilateral trade reached a new landmark, the trade deficit too continues to remain high at USD 51.75 billion—registering a growth of 8.55 percent year-on-year in 2017. One of the main reasons for this unfavourable trade balance is that India exports only raw materials like iron ore and copper to China. The deficit can be reduced only when India starts exporting value-added products. Unfortunately, the Indian manufacturing industries have to go a long way before they are geared up to export value-added products to China. According to India's trade figures, the deficit had crossed USD 52 billion in 2016. India has been pressing China to open the IT and Pharmaceutical sectors for Indian firms to reduce the massive trade deficit.

According to Chinese trade data, India's exports to China increased by 39.11 percent year-on-year to USD 16.34 billion in 2017. India's imports from China increased by 14.59 percent to USD 68.10 billion. India has emerged as the seventh largest export destination for Chinese products, and the 24th largest exporter to China. Significantly, diamonds along with copper, iron ore, organic chemicals and cotton yarn contributed to the increase in Indian exports to China. India's exports of diamonds grew 4.93 percent totaling to USD 2.59 billion. India was the second largest exporter of diamonds to China with a market share of 33.06 percent after South Africa. Also, Indian exports of copper registered a significant increase of 115.78 percent to reach USD 2.15 billion. India's cotton including yarn and woven fabric exports to China showed an increase of 1.86 percent to reach USD 1.30 billion. India was the second largest exporter of cotton to China with 15.04 percent market share in 2017. India's exports of Zinc to China showed a sharp increase of 802 percent to reach USD 240 million. On the other hand, China's exports were dominated by electrical machinery and equipment registering an increase of 28.23 percent to USD 21.77 billion. India was the largest destination for China's fertilizers exports registering 16.98 percent of its total fertilizers worth USD 1.03 billion to India. India was also the largest export destination for Chinese Antibiotics, with exports worth USD 783 million taking place in 2017. Chinese exports were also led by organic chemicals, worth USD 6.56 billion in 2017.

Institutional Framework of Bilateral Cooperation

There are several institutional mechanisms for India's economic and commercial engagement with China. India-China Joint Economic Group (JEG) on Economic Relations and Trade, Science and Technology is a ministerial-level dialogue mechanism established in 1988 during the visit of former Prime Minister Rajiv Gandhi to China. A Joint Study Group (JSG) was set up after former Prime Minister Atal Bihari Vajpayee's visit to

China in June 2003 to examine the potential complementarities between the two countries in expanded trade and economic cooperation. As per its recommendation, a Joint Task Force (JTF) was set up to study the feasibility of an India-China Regional Trading Arrangement. JTF Report was completed in October 2007. There are also Joint Working Groups on Trade, Agriculture and Energy. In 2010, both countries agreed to set up the India-China Strategic and Economic Dialogue (SED). The first SED took place in Beijing on 26th September 2011.

In the recent years the momentum generated by the visit of Chinese President Xi Jinping to India in September 2014 and the return visit of Prime Minister Modi to China in May 2015, has been kept high. President of India Pranab Mukherjee paid a successful state visit to China in May 2016. In the year 2016, Prime Minister Modi and President Jinping met thrice including for the G20 Summit in Hangzhou, the BRICS Summit in Goa, and the Shanghai Cooperation Organisation (SCO) Summit in Tashkent. In 2017, they met during the SCO Summit in Astana, G20 Summit in Hamburg and during the BRICS Summit in Xiamen. The other high-level visits include the Finance Minister Arun Jaitley's visit to China in June 2016, Defence Minister Manohar Parrikar's visit in April 2016, Secretary of Department of Economic Affairs (DEA) Shaktikanta Das's visit to Beijing in August 2016, Chairman of China's National Development and Reform Commission Minister Xu Shaoshi's visit to India in October 2016. The Chief Ministers of Madhya Pradesh and Andhra Pradesh also visited China in June 2016. The Chinese Finance Minister Xiao Jie visited India in March 2017 to attend the New Development Bank (NDB) board of Governance meeting and also held a bilateral talk with Indian Finance Minister. Indian side participated in all the BRICS related events. The Commerce Minister, Health Minister, Culture Minister, HRD Minister, Labour Minister, Minister of States (AYUSH) and Minister of States (Telecom) participated in respective BRICS Ministerial meetings.

India-China Strategic Economic Dialogue (SED): During Chinese Prime Minister Wen Jiabao's visit to India in December 2010, India and China agreed to set up the Strategic Economic

Dialogue (SED) mechanism. The SED mechanism looks beyond the immediate bilateral issues faced by the two countries and is a forum for both sides to discuss strategic macro-economic issues impacting both nations as a result of the changing international economic and financial landscape, to share their individual best practices and in handling challenging domestic economic issues and to identify specific fields for enhancing cooperation, learning and experience sharing. The first India-China SED took place in Beijing from 26th September 2011. The Indian side was led by Montek Singh Ahluwalia, Deputy Chairman, Planning Commission, while the Chinese side was led by Zhang Ping, Chairman, National Development and Reforms Commission. Some of the issues that was discussed during the SED included introduction to the 12th plan priorities of the two countries, a discussion on each country's monetary and fiscal policies, investment policies of the two countries, policies on energy conservation and environment protection, *etc.* Apart from the official meetings, the SED also included to a site visit to Tianjin, where the Indian delegation was introduced to water desalination facility. At the end of the official meetings both sides signed the Agreed Minutes of the 1st SED. The Indian delegation also called on the Chinese Premier Wen Jiabao. The fourth meeting of the India-China SED took place in New Delhi on 7th October 2016.

Joint Economic Group (JEG) Meeting: India-China Joint Economic Group (JEG) on Economic Relations and Trade, Science and Technology is a ministerial-level dialogue mechanism established in 1988 during the visit of former Prime Minister Rajiv Gandhi to China. JEG has so far met eleven times. The scheduling of the previous JEG's is as under:

Session	Place	Date
1st	New Delhi	18th September 1989
2nd	Beijing	6th February 1991
3rd	New Delhi	9th December 1991
4th	Beijing	4th January 1993
5th	New Delhi	13th June 1994

Session	Place	Date
6th	Beijing	19th February 2000
7th	New Delhi	16th March 2006
8th	Beijing	19th January 2010
9th	New Delhi	27th August 2012
10th	Beijing	2nd September 2014
11th	New Delhi	26th March 2018

During the 8th JEG Meeting, the Commerce Ministers of India and China agreed to work towards a more balanced trade. China had assured that it would import more from India.

During the 9th JEG Meeting, the two sides also set up three working groups on Economic and Trade Planning Cooperation, Trade Statistical Analysis, and Service Trade Promotion. The work programme of the three working groups was signed by China International Travel Mart (CITM) and Chinese Commerce Minister during the visit of Premier Li Keqiang to India from 19th May 2013.

During the 10th JEG Meeting, India and China acknowledged that the overall objective of trade cooperation was to achieve a balanced and sustainable level of bilateral trade. China had a favourable balance of trade in goods, while India had an unfavourable balance of trade in goods. According to Indian statistics, with an increase in the bilateral trade over the last decade, the trade imbalance against India also increased exponentially from USD 18.65 billion in 2009 to USD 36.86 billion in 2013. It was recognized that trade deficit with China was a matter of high concern for India. Against this background and in the spirit of mutual benefit, India and China should endeavor to strengthen cooperation and gradually achieve bilateral trade balance over the next 5 years. India and China should further endeavor to increase bilateral trade in services particularly IT and ITes services in the next 5 years. In order to bridge the bilateral trade deficit over the next 5 years, there was felt an urgent need for India and China to adopt measures for improving India's export capacity and competitiveness and expedite action on resolution of market access issues such as—

market access for Indian bovine meat, rapeseed meal and oil meals in China; market access for Indian basmati and non-basmati rice in China; market access for Indian fruits and vegetables in China; deepening bilateral trade cooperation; strengthen cooperation to promote export of Indian pharmaceuticals to China; strengthen cooperation to promote export of Indian IT services to China; strengthen bilateral cooperation in the tourism sector; and strengthen bilateral cooperation for resolution of trade disputes.

The 11th JEG Meeting was largely anticipated to address the widening trade deficit with China. The data for April-October 2017 shows a deficit of USD 36.73 billion, mainly due to Chinese exports of manufactured products for the telecom and power industries. At the 11th session of JEG Meeting, the two sides had reached a series of important consensus.

(a) The two sides would jointly promote the synergy between China's Belt and Road initiative and India's development strategies, including the "15-year Development Agenda", "Make in India", and "Digital India" to deepen mutually-beneficial cooperation and share development experience.

(b) The two sides would promote India's exports to China to address the trade imbalance between the two countries. China welcomed the participation of Indian businesses in the agricultural, pharmaceutical and IT sectors, and the participation of producers of manufactured goods. China would provide Indian participants with preferential arrangements.

(c) The two sides agreed to set up a special working group to draw a road map for developing two-way trade. The two sides supported the multilateral trading system and safeguard the interests of developing members. Both sides would demonstrate flexibility to reach at an early date a modern, comprehensive and mutually beneficial Regional Comprehensive Economic Partnership (RCEP) agreement of high standards. The two sides are also considering positively launching in due course negotiations on a regional trade arrangement or free trade agreement between India and China.

India-China Financial Dialogue: India-China Financial Dialogues are held in accordance with the Memorandum of Understanding (MoU) signed during Chinese Premier Wen Jiabao's visit to India in April 2005. Since then the two sides have successfully held 8 Financial Dialogues in April 2006, December 2007, January 2009, September 2010, November 2011, September 2013, December 2014, and August 2016.

Session	Place	Date
1st	New Delhi	7th April 2006
2nd	Beijing	4th December 2007
3rd	New Delhi	16th January 2009
4th	Beijing	2nd September 2010
5th	New Delhi	8th November 2011
6th	Beijing	27th September 2013
7th	New Delhi	19th December 2014
8th	Beijing	19th August 2016

The 5th India-China Financial Dialogue was held on 8th November 2011 in New Delhi. During the one-day dialogue, the two sides carried out in-depth discussions on international and domestic macro-economic situations and policies, the coordination among the G20 and inside other international financial organizations, as well as closer cooperation between the financial institutions and regulators of the two countries. During the Dialogue, both sides exchanged views on the global macro-economic situation and policy responses, with specific reference to current risks to the global economy and the role of India and China in the post crisis recovery phase. Both sides reached consensus on certain major issues, which would greatly boost bilateral financial cooperation and strengthen India-China strategic partnership.

The 6th India-China Financial Dialogue was held on 27th September 2013 in Beijing. During the Dialogue, the two sides held in-depth discussions on new challenges facing the global economy, macro-economic situations and policies in China and India, progress on structural reforms in both countries, cooperation under multilateral frameworks as well as bilateral financial cooperation. Both sides agreed to strengthen regular communication and coordination at various levels on macro-economic policies and major international economic and financial issues. Both sides recognized that global economic recovery was still fragile with downside risks remaining high. Volatility in financial markets has also intensified. With growth picking up in advanced economies, there is a need for them to collaborate with Emerging Market Economies (EMEs) on the pace and timing of recalibration of their unconventional monetary policies and strengthen communication with the market to avoid negative spillovers. As a group, the EMEs have continued to grow but the pace of growth has slowed in several countries. Under these circumstances, India and China called for greater international coordination on economic policies, particularly in the implementation of policy measures adopted by the G20 to boost growth and employment for promoting strong, sustainable and balanced growth of the world economy.

India and China recognized the importance of sound macro-economic policies and sustained structural reforms for improving long-term growth prospects. Both sides also acknowledged the effectiveness of bilateral coordination under multilateral frameworks such as the G20, BRICS and international financial institutions. They agreed to work together to promote the implementation of the important consensus reached in the G20 St. Petersburg summit, strengthen the momentum of global recovery, push for faster economic growth, generate better jobs, and build on the foundation for long-term growth. They urged the international financial institutions to increase their lending capacity to developing countries to expand the global aggregate demand. They also recognized the importance of strengthened fiscal and financial cooperation in the expansion of bilateral trade and investment. They agreed to maintain close communication, and work for more opportunities and better environment to enhance bilateral financial cooperation. Financial regulators from both countries exchanged views on market access regulation policies for foreign banks, agreed to support banks to establish branches and subsidiaries in each other's market, and advocated deeper cooperation between financial institutions from the two countries, especially in areas of infrastructure investment and financing.

The 7th India-China Financial Dialogue was held on 19th December 2014 in New Delhi. According to a joint statement issued at the end of the Dialogue, the two countries reviewed the prevailing global macro-economic situation and agreed to coordinate policy action in facing common external challenges. They underscored the need to strengthen cooperation under multilateral frameworks and fora. They also exchanged views on fiscal and taxation reforms and agreed to strengthen cooperation amongst financial sector regulatory agencies and encourage long-term Chinese investments in the Indian infrastructure sector.

The 8th India-China Financial Dialogue was held on 19th August 2016 in Beijing to strengthen trade and economic cooperation, with the two fast-developing nations underlining the need of building more solidarity to adopt more responsible macro-economic policies. Both the sides highlighted the steps for further cooperation between them with regard to trade, investment flows and participation of both Indian and Chinese companies in each other's economic development besides structural reforms and cooperation between the countries in multilateral forums like G20 and BRICS. They emphasized the need to build more solidarity, air common voice, urge developed countries to adopt more responsible macro-economic policies and lay foundation and enabling environment for global economic recovery. With unprecedented economic opportunities, relevant departments should seize the opportunity to deliver common consensus of two countries by adopting bold and innovative approach to overcome the fiscal, financial as well as investment impediments to achieve higher, better economic trade and investment collaboration.

NITI Aayog-DRC Dialogue: NITI Aayog-DRC Dialogues are held in accordance with the Memorandum of Understanding (MoU) signed between NITI Aayog and the Development Research Centre (DRC), State Council of the China, during the visit of Prime Minister Narendra Modi to China in May 2015. The NITI Aayog-DRC Dialogue provides an important platform for both sides to discuss key macro-economic issues impacting both countries and areas of mutual interest. The First NITI Aayog-DRC Dialogue was held in Beijing on 24th November 2015, co-chaired by Arvind Panagariya, Vice-Chairman, NITI Aayog and Li Wei, President, DRC. The second NITI Aayog-DRC Dialogue was held in New Delhi on 16th November 2017 and was once again co-chaired by Arvind Panagariya and Li Wei.

The 3rd edition of the NITI Aayog-DRC Dialogue was held in Beijing on 5th December 2017, co-chaired by Dr. Rajiv Kumar, Vice-Chairman, NITI Aayog and Li Wei, President, DRC. It enabled an in-depth interaction between the two delegations on the world economic prospects, India-China economic cooperation and practices for sustainable growth. In the context of global uncertainty and weak global growth, it was noted that as two large and rapidly growing developing countries, both India and China have a major stake in the path that the global economy is likely to take in coming years. Both sides exchanged views on policies and measures to address the challenges for attaining sustainable growth. In-depth discussions were held on sharing of experiences and best practices in the areas of Electric Mobility, Clean Energy, Higher Education and Special Economic Zones. They agreed upon the need to strengthen bilateral cooperation in trade and investment. The importance of pursuing balanced and sustainable bilateral trade was noted and opportunities for promoting Chinese investments in India were highlighted. They also agreed that the 4th NITI Aayog-DRC Dialogue will be convened in India in 2018.

Civil Aviation: The Memorandum of Understanding (MoU) signed during Premier Wen Jiabao's visit to India on 9th April 2005 provides for major liberalization of air links between India and China with multiple designation of carriers and an open skies policy for cargo, an increase in capacity entitlements, more points of call and an increase in the number of intermediary and beyond points. According to the Memorandum, the designated airlines of both parties are entitled to have unlimited third, fourth and fifth freedom traffic rights with unlimited capacity entitlement for dedicated cargo services. In terms of frequencies, the liberalized civil aviation agreement allows for 42 flights a week. It is now up to the airlines to utilize this capacity. Enhanced number of flights would be a function of commercial viability and availability of aircrafts. At present, five air service operators—Air China (5 per week), China Eastern (8 per week), China Southern (3 per week), Air India (4 per week), and Ethiopian Airways (4 per week) are currently operating a total of 24 flights between India and China every week.

Non-stop capacity between India and China in 2015 was up approximately 35 percent since 2008, with about 970 seats a day compared to 700 seven years ago. The market peaked in 2013 with 1400 daily seats. Three Chinese carriers (Air China, China Eastern and China Southern, all state-owned) and one Indian carrier (Air India) served the market. There are six routes, only one of which, Shanghai to Delhi, has overlapping service from Air India and China Eastern. All other routes have one operator. Only two routes have daily or more service—China Eastern's Kunming-Kolkata route has daily service while China Southern's Guangzhou-Delhi route has double daily service. Four Chinese cities have flights to India (Beijing, Guangzhou, Kunming and Shanghai) while three Indian cities have flights to China (Delhi, Kolkata and Mumbai).

Non-stop Flights between China to India

Carrier	Route	Weekly Frequency
Air China	Beijing-Delhi	4
Air China	Beijing-Mumbai	4
Air India	Shanghai-Delhi	4
China Eastern	Shanghai-Delhi	5
China Eastern	Kunming-Kolkata	7
China Southern	Guangzhou-Delhi	14

In 2015, the introduction of Air China's Beijing-Mumbai service has replaced the Air China's flight from Mumbai to Chengdu. Air China has also linked Beijing with Delhi, connecting the two capitals. Air India and China Eastern serve the Delhi-Shanghai route which carries more business traffic.

Although a small market, the India-China segment has been ripe for savvy intermediate carriers. Indian and Chinese carriers have lacked strong international networks, although Chinese carriers in recent times have been asserting themselves. Air India is growing but still faces challenges. Non-stop options between the two countries have been limited, as have city pair combinations. Chinese airlines are largely relying on their eastern hubs (Beijing, Guangzhou and Shanghai), reflecting demand and political ties. Despite the geographical strength of western hubs (funneling traffic through them using narrow body aircraft), Chinese carriers have a limited presence. China Eastern flies from Kunming while Air China moved its Chengdu-Mumbai flight to depart from Beijing.

Banking Links: Many Indian banks have established their presence in mainland China in the last few years. Four Indian banks, namely, State Bank of India (Shanghai), Canara Bank (Shanghai), Bank of Baroda (Guangzhou) and Bank of India (Shenzhen) have branch offices in China. However, State Bank of India is the only Indian bank to have authorization to conduct local currency business (RMB) at its branch in Shanghai. The following representative offices of Indian nationalized as well as private banks are also operating in mainland China—Axis Bank (Shanghai), Punjab National Bank (Shanghai), Union Bank of India (Shanghai), ICICI Bank (Shanghai), Bank of India (Beijing), Union Bank of India (Beijing), Allahabad Bank (Shenzhen), UCO Bank (Guangzhou), Indian Overseas Bank (Guangzhou), and State Bank of India (Tianjin).

More Indian banks are planning to upgrade their representative offices in China to branch offices and existing branch offices are applying for RMB license. Industrial and Commercial Bank of China (ICBC) secured a license to start banking operations in India in the early 2011. ICBC inaugurated its Mumbai branch on 15th September 2011. This marked the opening of the first branch of a mainland Chinese bank in India.

Various government institutions and agencies from India and China have also been interacting with each other for furthering cooperation in the areas such as taxation, human resource development and employment, health, urban development and tourism. There is a close exchange and interaction between the economic think tanks and scholars as well.

The Economic-Security and India-China Relations

The last two decades have witnessed significant growth in India-China trade, albeit from a very low starting point. Investment flows, though, have remained small compared to both countries' inward and outward FDI volumes. India-China economic ties have developed even as their political relationship from time to time has experienced setbacks and occasional tensions. Economic security considerations have increasingly factored into India-China trade and investment, especially in recent years, as China has aggressively pursued a policy of opening up new markets, cornering resources, and expanding economic influence, while India seeks to protect its domestic industry, gain market access for its niche sectors, and guard against external intrusion into its sphere of influence. While both India and China have benefitted from globalization since the late 1970s and early 1990s, respectively, by gradually opening up to the outside world, expanding trade, and drawing in investment, as Asia's two rising powers with growing ambitions and unresolved disputes they are also conscious of relative gains, dependence and vulnerability, and the economic foundation of military power and security, albeit with asymmetrical threat perceptions and different priorities.

Economic-security in an era of globalization refers to a state's ability to enhance its overall economic performance and competitiveness, reduce vulnerability in the areas of resources and energy supplies, and prevent dominance of critical sectors by foreign entities. This requires a combination of industrial policy and government intervention that enables the state to benefit from growing economic interaction and integration through trade and investment facilitation and active participation in the global marketplace. Advocates of economic security while recognizing the liberal international economic system of comparative advantage and accepting certain risks as a condition, nonetheless hold strong mercantilist views and are more concerned with relative gains. Such perspectives, in turn, could impose limitations on the scope and scale of international cooperation.

The notion of economic-security also relates to the concept of geo-economics, which describes how economic phenomena can both be the consequence of and further enhance national power, in the process changing the overall geopolitical order at the regional and international level. Geo-economics is increasingly trumping geopolitics in the absence of war. The critical issue here is how states can apply economic power to advance national interests, which in turn informs and supports economic diplomacy. There is a strong linkage between economic performance and security that can reinforce each other. Economic-security involves safeguarding the structural integrity and prosperity-generating capabilities and interests of a politico-economic entity in the context of various externalized risks and threats that confront it in the international economic system. In such a context, market access, techno-nationalism, protection of critical and sensitive domestic industries, reliable and affordable energy supplies, and so on, in contrast to the principles of free trade and laissez-faire, become the critical ingredients of economic-security.

In the context of India-China relations, the economic-security is a particularly useful prism through which some of the bilateral trade and investment issues can be understood. While expanding economic ties have benefitted both countries over the past two and a half decades and, in fact, India and China have sought to further promote their development, security and relative power have often been factored into economic decisions. For instance, perennial and worsening trade deficits deeply concern India as these are perceived to both reflect unequal terms of trade between the two countries as China primarily exports manufactured goods to India while India's exports to China are largely composed of raw materials. What is often characterized as securitization of economic issues also affects India's decisions on Chinese investments and sub-regional cooperation if these are perceived to result in strategic sectors being exposed to Chinese access, influence, and control.

India-China Economic Ties

Liberalization of foreign trade is a watershed in development policy of both India and China. To start with, both the countries adopted inward-looking import substitution policies with an emphasis on self-sufficiency. Later in 1978, China adopted the policy of opening up to the outside world and in 1991, India initiated an import liberalization policy. Comparative advantage replaced self-sufficiency as the basis tenant of trade and both the countries are now pursuing market-oriented and outward-looking policies. India has been a member of the WTO since its inception and China joined the WTO in the year 2001.

The former Prime Minister Rajiv Gandhi made a historic visit to China in December 1988, the first such visit by an Indian prime minister in 34 years. During this visit, one of the key decisions that the leaders of the two countries reached was that, given that territorial disputes could not be resolved in the near term, India and China should nonetheless set aside their differences in order to explore expanding ties in other areas, of which trade became one of the top priorities. Also, in that year, the two countries set up the India-China Joint Economic Group (JEG) on Economic Relations and Trade, Science and Technology.

China was able to preserve positive trade balance for a long period with the exception of early 1950s and in mid-1980s. Remittances from overseas Chinese have made an important contribution to the balance of payments. Besides, they also brought skill and knowledge of foreign markets to enhance production and exports. Investments from Hong Kong and Taiwan made a major contribution to China's rapid growth of foreign trade after the open-door policy. However, this was not the case with India. The NRI contribution was insignificant and FDI was not export-oriented. More importantly, the volume of FDI was also small as compared to China.

In spite of some similarities and dissimilarities, there is a scope for economic cooperation between India and China. Both the countries are growing fast and are home to the world's largest pools of skilled work force making them the engines of global economic growth in the 21st century. Both the countries are also developing closer economic relations with each other and with the rest of the Asian countries through bilateral and regional agreements. In recent years, bilateral trade and investment between India and China are growing, indicating the existence of a vast potential for economic cooperation. The complementarities exist between the countries, particularly in imports from China in electrical and electronics, chemicals and silk products. There are limited complementarities of Indian exports to China, which are confined more or less to primary, resource-based products, and low technology manufactured products.

India-China bilateral trade has increased rapidly after China's joining of WTO. It grew by 25.5 percent on an annual basis. Indian exports to China increased by 26.3 percent and imports from China increased by 24 percent on an average per annum. However, India's share in China's global imports remained just one percent, whereas China's share in India's global imports reached 5 percent. In recent years, China is gaining importance as destination for India's exports. India's export basket to China is dominated by primary and resource-based products. However, the product diversification is occurring gradually in most recent years. Imports from China are diversified and include resourced manufactured products and low and medium technology-based products. The product composition of India's exports to China has changed, but the level of product concentration has not changed much over the years. The number of products that India exports to China is much lower than the number of products that are imported from China. The Chinese exports to India are more diversified and Indian exports to China are less diversified. The degree of product concentration is high for India than for Chinese exports to India. There is a change in composition of China's exports to India. The shift is from resource based manufactured products to advance technology-based manufacturing products. The major change in product composition occurred in case of Chinese exports to India in 2003 when the manufacturing products with more advanced technology products, namely electrical and electronic products, dominated the Chinese export products to India. This change also has raised the Chinese potential for sustaining its export performance as compared to India.

Three reasons for increase in India's exports to China are:

(a) increase in Chinese demand for Indian products,

(b) increase in competitiveness of Indian products, and

(c) increase in product diversification by India.

However, the influence of competitiveness has declined in recent years. In case of Chinese exports to India, the reasons are:

(a) product diversification,

(b) increase in India's demand for the Chinese products, and

(c) increase in competitiveness of Chinese products.

When all the products exported from India are considered and compared with 0.25 percent export product list, a different picture emerges. The competitive factor becomes important and it accounts for over 50 percent changes in Indian exports. The demand factor responsible for increase in Indian exports will account for slightly more than one-third and increase due to product diversification shows about one-sixth of increase in exports. The increase in Chinese exports to India on all product basis shows the increase in competitiveness as the major factor, second is increase in India's demand for Chinese products, and third is the product diversification. The increase in Chinese demand is responsible for more than one-third of increase of India's export to China whereas competitiveness constitutes half of the increase in India's exports. The product diversification does not play an important role. As far as Chinese exports to India are concerned, competitiveness is the most important factor followed by demand factors.

The trade complementarities can develop in two ways—intra-industry trade and inter-industry trade between the two economies. Three types of indices, namely complementarity index, trade overlap index, and Grubel-Lloyd index, could measure the scope for trade cooperation. All the three indices show that in India-China bilateral trade, intra-industry trade seems to play a minor role. There is a huge gap between Chinese import need at individual product level and India's export to that country. The Revealed Comparative Advantage (RCA) index value shows that India has an advantage over its competitors in primary products, natural resource based or low technology manufacturing products. Further, it is found that India has an advantage over its competitors in product groups such as textiles, leather products, engineering, and granite. India could gain higher market share due to complementarities in product groups of leather, chemicals, textiles, engineering, granite, and food products. Advanced and medium technology products dominate the Chinese import basket and it accounts for 61 percent of the imports. To enhance trade complementarities with China, the country needs to diversify export products towards these technology-oriented products. Given the current state of Indian industrial structure, it appears that in the immediate future, the scope for building complementarities appears slim, as the potential for intra-industry trade is limited; the option is to enhance inter-industry trade.

China is the second largest recipient of Foreign Direct Investment (FDI). Further, it is successful in attracting huge export-oriented FDI in recent years. The foreign invested enterprises played a significant role in export expansion of China. The share of Multi National Companies (MNCs) in exports is over 50 percent in case of China as compared to mere 3 percent for India. More importantly, China is able to attract FDI to provide capital and expertise to achieve export competitiveness in a wide range of sectors. The FDI brought in the product design, specialized machine tools, intermediate inputs and knowledge of world marketing channels. The Chinese Government assured certain key conditions for profitability such as low taxes, reliable infrastructure, adequate power, decent logistics for imports and exports. As a result, the manufactured exports reached over 90 percent of the total exports in 2003. A substantial proportion of these exports constitute mechanical, electronics and electrical products. On the other hand, FDI inflow into India is relatively low and its focus is mainly on sectors such as infrastructure, power, capital goods and food processing. Among these sectors, many of them do not fall under export activities. A substantial proportion of FDI in case of India has gone to services, infrastructure and low technology intensive consumer goods manufacturing industries. As much as 40 percent of FDI in the late 1990s has taken the route of acquisitions rather than green field ventures. In contrast, the FDI is concentrated in export-oriented and high technology manufacturing industry in China. The FDI accounts for 45 percent of China's manufactured products and 80 percent of high technology exports. To some extent, the export-oriented production model is replicated in India in the service sector, particularly in software development and business processes. The FDI in India have not entered the export-oriented industries and have little impact on India's exports. Further, FDI in Indian manufacturing sector has been domestic market-oriented and not efficiency seeking in nature. The contribution of Special Economic Zones in India's export is around 10 percent whereas in China the same is over 70 percent.

India-China Bilateral Trade: Bilateral trade between India and China developed slowly and steadily in the formative years of 1950s. The trade volume increased from USD 8.68 million in 1950 to USD 26.62 million at the end of the decade; on an average, it grew about 20 percent. However, thereafter trade volume declined year after year, it was USD 2.37 million in 1962. Two countries resumed their diplomatic ties in 1976 and trade began to grow rapidly. It was USD 25.5 million in 1978 and touched a figure of USD 110.1 million in 1981. During this period, two countries signed trade protocols that largely facilitated the two-way trade to grow. However, the growth has been more or less steady. In 1981, India's export was USD 83.3 million that touched a figure of USD 97.3 million in 1990, at the annual growth rate of 1.7 percent and imports from China grew approximately 10 percent to reach the volume of USD 166.8 million in the same period. In most of the years, the trade balance remained in favour of China.

India and China signed a Trade Agreement (Most Favoured Nation Agreement) in 1984. During 1990s, India-China bilateral trade began to expand rapidly, particularly after mid-1990s. During the decade, total two-way trade increased by 30.6 percent per annum on an average to touch a figure of USD

2920 million by year 2000. By 2003, it has increased further to USD 7595.09 million. Exports from India touched a figure of USD 1350 million with the average annual growth rate of 34.3 percent. In 2003, it had become USD 3343.59 million. Compared to the year 2000 in 2003 Indian exports to China had increased by 2.47 times, experiencing an annual average growth rate of more than 36.89 percent. On the other hand, imports from China witnessed a figure of USD 1569 million by year 2000 with annual growth rate of 31.1 percent. In 2003, it had reached USD 4251.50 million. Compared to the year 2000, in 2003 India's imports from China had gone up by 2.70 times with an average growth rate of 31.04 percent.

India-China bilateral trade growth has been much faster in the recent years. In 1996, the total India-China trade was little more than USD 1.4 billion. By 2003, it had crossed USD 8.2 billion. In 2004, India became the 11th largest trade partner of China and bilateral trade between the two countries reached a total of USD 13.6 billion, representing an increase of 64.74 percent over the corresponding period of last year. Despite rapid growth, the share of India in China's import was just one percent and that of China in India's imports was around 5 percent in 2003. As an export partner, India was of very little importance to China. India's share in China's world exports was around one percent in 2004. In 1996, share of India's exports to China to total Indian exports was 2.60 percent. In 2003, it had become 7.03 percent. But now, China has become a very important destination for India's exports. In terms of important export partners for India, today, China stands second after the United States.

India-China bilateral trade reached USD 84.44 billion in 2017, an historic high notwithstanding bilateral tensions over a host of issues including the Doklam standoff. A rare novelty of the bilateral trade otherwise dominated by the Chinese exports was about 40 percent increase of Indian exports to China in 2017 totaling to USD 16.34 billion. The bilateral trade in 2017 rose by 18.63 percent year-on-year to reach USD 84.44 billion. It is regarded as a landmark as the volume of bilateral trade for the first time touched USD 80 billion, well above the USD

71.18 billion registered in 2016. The trade touched high despite bilateral tensions over a number of issues including the China-Pakistan Economic Corridor, China blocking India's efforts to bring about a United Nations' ban on Jaish-e-Mohammad leader Masood Azhar, China blocking India's entry into the Nuclear Suppliers Group (NSG) as well as the military standoff at Doklam lasting 73 days. The bilateral trade stagnated around USD 70 billion for several years despite the leaders of both countries setting USD 100 billion as target for 2015. Though it is still about USD 20 billion short, officials on both sides expect trade and Chinese investments in India to pick up further in 2018 as both the governments are trying to scale down tensions and step-up the normalization process. While the bilateral trade reached a new landmark, the trade deficit too continues to remain high at USD 51.75 billion, registering a growth of 8.55 percent year-on-year in 2017. According to India's trade figures, the deficit had crossed USD 52 billion in 2017. India has been pressing China to open the IT and Pharmaceutical sectors for Indian firms to reduce the massive trade deficit. As per the Chinese trade data, India's exports to China increased by 39.11 percent year-on-year to USD 16.34 billion in 2017. India's imports from China increased by 14.59 percent to USD 68.10 billion.

India has emerged as the seventh largest export destination for Chinese products, and 24th largest exporter to China. Significantly, diamonds along with copper, iron ore, organic chemicals and cotton yarn contributed to the increase Indian exports to China. India's exports of diamond grew 4.93 percent totaling to USD 2.59 billion. India is the second largest exporter of diamonds to China with a market share of 33.06 percent after South Africa. Also, Indian exports of copper registered a significant increase of 115.78 percent to reach USD 2.15 billion. India's cotton including yarn and woven fabric exports to China showed an increase of 1.86 percent to reach USD 1.30 billion. India was the second largest exporter of cotton to China with 15.04 percent market share in 2017. India's exports of Zinc to China showed a sharp increase of 802 percent to reach USD 240 million. India was the largest destination for China's fertilizers exports registering 16.98 percent of its total fertilizers worth USD 1.03 billion to India. India was also the largest export destination for Chinese Antibiotics with exports worth USD 783 million taking place in 2017. Chinese exports were also led by organic chemicals, worth USD 6.56 billion in 2017.

India-China Trade Pattern

Trade between India and China has been small relative to world totals. In 1990, total trade of India with China was less than 1 percent of its total trade with other countries of the world. Indian exports to China was just USD 17.94 million, while India's exports to the world was USD 17940.18 million and Indian imports from China was of the value USD 32.88 million while Indian imports from the world was equal to the value USD 23799.15 million. In the same way China's trade with India was very low as compare to its total trade with the world. China's trade with India was just 0.04 percent of total China's trade in 1990. Whereas Chinese imports from the world was equal to the value USD 53345.12 million.

But trade between India and China has been increasing, so is the percentage share of India-China trade in the total trade of both the countries with the world. The percentage share of India's trade with China went up to 16.96 percent of India's total trade in 2016. In the same way China's trade with India increased to 2.08 percent in 2010 and 1.90 percent in 2016, which was only 0.04 percent in 1990.

During the period 1990 to 2017, the trade between the two countries is mostly in favour of China except for the years 1991 and 1992. The balance of trade between India and China has been increasing continuously in favour of China. It was USD 14.94 million in 1990 and went up to USD 51567.03 million in 2016.

Trade between India and China is increasing year by year, and it is poised for a major leap forward and has tripled from USD 23468.23 million in 2006 to USD 69399.17 million in 2016, in a period of 11 years. The trade between India and China had doubled from USD 40983.42 million in 2009 to USD 72200.81 in 2011, in a period of just two years. The demand for each other's products is increasing in both the countries and producers and consumers in both the countries are getting more access to the products of the other country. The trade is opening up day by day and India is planning to give China the Market Economy Status (MES) very soon. Once they make a free trade agreement the trade volume between them will touch the sky. Since both the countries are developing their infrastructure very fast it can be recommended to India to capitalize on the growing demand of construction industry in China for products like iron ore, slag, ash, plastic and linoleum. While the demand for steel is strong in China, both due to the booming housing and industry construction, China is also emerging as a big importer of aluminium, especially for its communication and transport infrastructure. India can get a huge chance here to export a lot of raw materials and final goods related to construction. Also, the restructuring of China's textile sector could result in new opportunities for India to increase the exports of cotton yarn and fabrics to China. As of now the nature of trade between India and China does not go in favour of China because the exports of India to China mainly comprises of a few goods like ores, slag and ash, which is not an ideal situation for a country. The exported commodities from India to China are needed to be of various nature and Indian exporters are supposed to look for the opportunity of export to China in the fields other than the conventional exports. The exported commodities from India to China are needed to be of various nature and Indian exporters are supposed to look for the opportunity of export to China in the fields other than the conventional exports. In any discussion of the growing economic integration between India and China, it is important to remember also that trade is only one of the two major economic ties that bind nations. The other is investment. At present, investment links between the two countries are relatively modest. Haier and Huawei have significant presence in India. Similarly, Bharat Forge, TCS, and Infosys are building a noteworthy presence in China.

Given the sizes of their economies, strong growth potentials, and the low percentage of bilateral trade in their respective global trade, there is significant potential for growth. To

India's Trade with China, 2006–2016 (in million USD)

	2006	2007	2008	2009	2010	2011	2012	2013	2014	2015	2016
India's Exports to China	7829.17	9491.98	10093.93	10370.05	17439.99	16717.79	14729.32	16416.83	13434.25	9576.58	8916.07
India's Exports to the World	121200.61	145898.05	181860.91	176765.04	220408.49	301483.25	289564.77	376611.39	317544.64	264381.00	260326.91
Percentage Share	6.4596	6.5059	5.5503	5.8665	7.9126	5.5452	5.0867	4.8771	4.2307	3.6222	3.4249
India's Imports from China	15639.06	24575.77	31586.02	30613.37	41249.11	55483.02	54140.46	51635.44	58230.55	61604.43	60483.10
India's Imports from the World	178212.44	218645.29	315712.10	266401.55	350029.39	462402.79	488976.38	466045.57	459369.46	390744.73	356704.79
Percentage Share	8.7755	11.2400	10.0047	11.4914	11.7844	11.9989	11.0722	11.0795	12.6762	15.7659	16.9561
Balance of Trade	–7809.89	–15083.79	–21492.09	–20243.32	–23809.12	–38765.24	–39411.14	–35218.62	–44796.29	–52027.85	–51567.03
India's Total Trade with China	23468.23	34067.75	41679.95	40983.42	58689.10	72200.81	68869.78	68052.27	71664.80	71181.01	69399.17
India's Total Trade with the World	299413.05	364543.34	497573.01	443166.59	570437.88	763886.04	778541.15	802656.96	776914.10	655125.73	617031.70
Percentage Share	7.8381	9.3453	8.3766	9.2478	10.2884	9.4518	8.8460	8.4784	9.2243	10.8652	11.2473

Source: World Integrated Trade Solution.

China's Trade with India, 2006–2016 (in million USD)

	2006	2007	2008	2009	2010	2011	2012	2013	2014	2015	2016
China's Exports to India	14581.30	24051.38	31585.38	29666.56	40913.96	50536.42	47677.45	48432.41	54217.42	58228.03	58397.76
China's Exports to the World:	968935.60	1220059.67	1430693.07	1201646.76	1577763.75	1898388.43	2048782.23	2209007.28	2342292.70	2273468.22	2097637.17
Percentage Share	1.5049	1.9713	2.2077	2.4688	2.5932	2.6621	2.3271	2.1925	2.3147	2.5612	2.7840
China's Imports from India	10277.45	14617.16	20258.89	13714.29	20846.31	23372.28	18797.19	16970.27	16358.69	13368.55	11764.13
China's Imports from the World	791460.87	956115.45	1132562.16	1005555.22	1396001.57	1743394.87	1818199.23	1949992.31	1959234.63	1679564.32	1587920.69
Percentage Share	1.2985	1.5288	1.7888	1.3639	1.4933	1.3406	1.0338	0.8703	0.8349	0.7959	0.7409
Balance of Trade	4303.85	9434.22	11326.49	15952.27	20067.64	27164.14	28880.26	31462.14	37858.73	44859.47	46633.64
China's Total Trade with India:	24858.75	38668.54	51844.27	43380.85	61760.27	73908.7	66474.64	65402.68	70576.11	71596.58	70161.89
China's Total Trade with the World	1760396.47	2176175.12	2563255.23	2207201.98	2973765.32	3641783.3	3866981.46	4158999.59	4301527.33	3953032.54	3685557.86
Percentage Share	1.4121	1.7769	2.0226	1.9654	2.0768	2.0295	1.7190	1.5726	1.6407	1.8112	1.9037

Source: World Integrated Trade Solution.

explore opportunities for further economic cooperation, India and China have undertaken a number of initiatives. The two countries have set up an SED and five working groups on infrastructure, energy, environmental protection, policy coordination, and high technology. The two governments have also set up a joint study group to examine all trade-related issues, including trade imbalance. Meanwhile, Indian states and Chinese provinces are also beginning to explore economic opportunities at the substate level. An initial meeting of Indian chief ministers and Chinese provincial governors was held in Shanghai in mid-May 2015. When Prime Minister Narendra Modi visited China in May 2015, the two sides signed deals worth USD 22 billion in an effort to boost bilateral trade and overall economic ties. Topping the deals was Bharti Airtel, the Indian telecoms group, which received USD 2.5 billion in credit lines from Chinese bank. Given the difficulty of competing with China in the manufacturing sector, to address the deficit issue India is turning to those sectors where it enjoys relative comparative advantage. Five sectors are targeted—information technology, pharmaceuticals, textiles, agricultural products, and tourism, with special emphasis among those on pharmaceuticals and tourism, where India sees a potential Chinese market. Some of India's top exported products in its overall trade have not been able to gain access to the Chinese market, for example, pharmaceutical products have been one of India's top exports globally, but Indian drug companies face considerable lengthy procedures to get approval—three years as compared to one year in the United States for similar clearance.

Bilateral Investments and Service Sector

Despite growth in bilateral trade over the years, the investment level remains very low between India and China. Accumulated Chinese FDI to India is approximately USD 800 million, representing about 0.4 percent of all inflows of FDI into India, between 2000 and 2013 totaling USD 200 billion. In 2013, China invested USD 100 billion in other countries, making it the third-largest source of outbound FDI. However, its accumulated investment in India between 2000 and 2014 amounts to only USD 410 million, well behind the USD 22 billion from the United

Kingdom, USD 17 billion from Japan, USD 13 billion from the Netherlands, and USD 1.9 billion from Spain. By comparison, between 2005 and 2012, China invested more than USD 25 billion in ten members of the Association of Southeast Asian Nations (ASEAN). However, China is fast catching up in terms of investment in India. It was the 17th largest investor in India in 2016, up from 28th in 2014 and 35th in 2011, according to India's official ranking of FDI inflows. In 2017, Chinese business outfits invested an estimated USD 2000 million, compared with USD 700 million in 2016, thus tripling the investment in a single year.

In the past three calendar years, Chinese and Chinese-origin investors have poured in about USD 3.7 billion into Indian start-ups. Major beneficiaries are around 25 start-ups, including Truebil, ixigo, Paytm, Flipkart and MakeMyTrip. Chinese investors find Indian start-ups presenting a range of opportunities. Familiar and already tested business models and finance-based association work well for the companies. It is said that a potentially slowing Chinese economy and paucity of investment opportunities in their own country are bringing experienced Chinese investors to their neighbours's burgeoning start-up culture. Big spenders on start-ups such as Alibaba and Tencent have invested USD 1.2 billion and USD 650 million, respectively, in venture capital and private equity deals over the past two years. China wants more industrial parks allocated for Chinese firms, as well as expeditious discussion on an investment treaty. The bilateral engagement was under the aegis of the India-China Joint Group on Economic Relations, Trade, Science, and Technology. From 2016 onwards, the Government of India had terminated the Bilateral Investment Treaty (BIT) it had earlier entered into with various countries, including China. The government now maintains that all future investment pacts will be negotiated under the framework of the model BIT issued by the government in 2015. The one with China had come into force in 1996.

As on March 2012, 166 Indian companies were operating in China, with most located on China's rich East Coast and in the technology industries, such as IT/Software and pharmaceuticals.

These companies had been drawn to China both because of its relatively open economy and attractive tax incentives and because of India's more restrictive policies on investment at home. For example, Infosys and Wipro have followed a low-cost expansion strategy, taking advantage of their competitive edge in programming talent to carve themselves a niche in the growing Chinese market. India's major software companies, such as Tata Consultancy Services, Infosys Technologies, Satyam Computer Services, and Wipro Technologies have invested in China, and some of them have also developed collaborative projects with their Chinese counterparts. Tata Communications has entered into a partnership with China Telecom Global to offer live coverage of sports events in China, a market potential of USD 2.57 billion. Presence of some of the important Indian companies in major cities of China are given in the following table.

Beijing: Adani Global, Ashapura Minechem Ltd., Bank of India, Dr. Reddy's Laboratories Ltd., Electrosteel Integrated Ltd., Essar, Ispat Industries Ltd., Jindal Steel & Power Ltd., JSW Steel Ltd., Krsna Sourcetech Solutions, Mishra Ispat, Rashmi Metaliks Ltd., Reliance Anil Dhirubhai Ambani Group, Sasken Communication Technologies, Steel Authority of India, Suzlon Energy, Tata Information Technology Co. Ltd. (TCS), Tata Sons Ltd., Union Bank of India, VA Tech Wabag Water Treatment Technology Co. Ltd.

Fujian: Matrix Pharma Group

Guangdong: Allahabad Bank, Bank of Baroda, Bank of India, BEML, ESSEL Packaging, Godrej & Boyce Mfg. Co. Ltd., Guangzhou Sylvania Enterprises, Indian Overseas Bank, UCO Bank, Zee TV.

Hebei: NCPC Orchid Pharma Co. Ltd., Cumi Abrasives and Ceramics Co. Ltd.

Hongkong: JET Airways (India) Ltd.

Liaoning: Genpact, Liaoning Birla Carbon Co. Ltd.

Jilin: FAW Bharat Forge Co. Ltd.

Shandong: Apollo International Ltd., Gateway Exim Pvt. Ltd., Paprika Oleos (India) Ltd.

Shanghai: AIR India, Amol Biotech Ltd., Ashok Leyland, Asiatic Colorchem (India) Ltd., Aurobindo Pharma, Axis Bank Ltd., Bharat Heavy Electricals Ltd., Bharat Earth Movers Ltd., Bralco Steel Processing, Canara Bank, Cognizant Technology Solutions, Confederation of Indian Industry (CII), Covansys Software Technology Company Ltd., Daga Global Chemicals Ltd., Darbar Auto Spare Parts, Direct Logistics China Co. Ltd., EMCO, Engineers India Ltd., Evalueserve Export Knowledge Services, Gati-India-Centric Distribution Solutions, HCL Technologies (Shanghai) Ltd., ICICI Bank, India Grasim Industries, Infosys, Larsen & Toubro, Lucas TVS, Lupin, BRY-AIR, MI-ACE CNC Machinery Trading Co. Ltd., Navayuga Engineering Company Ltd., NIIT China Ltd., Pidilite Industries, Piramal Healthcare, Punjab National Bank, Raymond Ltd., Reliance Industries Ltd., Satyam Computer Services Ltd., Shipping Corporation of India, State Bank of India, Sun Pharmaceutical Industries, TCS, Tata Projects Ltd., Tata South-East Asia Ltd., Tata Steel Asia (Hong Kong) Ltd., Thermax Cooling and Heating Engineering, TKM Global China, Tractor & Farm Equipment Ltd., TVS Motors Co. Ltd., Union Bank of India, United Phosphorus Co. Ltd., Uni-world Logistics Pvt. Ltd., Virgo Engineers Ltd., Wipro, Zensar Technologies.

Zhejiang: Elgi Equipment Ltd., Sundram Fasteners Ltd., Tata Tea Extraction Co. Ltd.

Jiangsu: Igate Global Solutions Ltd., LMW Textile Machinery Co. Ltd., Mahindra Yeuda Tractor Co. Ltd., Tubular Precision Products Co. Ltd.

Nanjing: Tata Autocomp Systems

Sichuan: Zigong Safam Cast Iron Co. Ltd.

Tianjin: Ardee Business Services Pvt. Ltd., Beyond Frontiers Trading Ltd., Business Links Consulting Ltd., Monocon Refractories Co. Ltd., Monocon Aluminous Refractories Co. Ltd., State Bank of India, Therapeutics Chemical Research Corporation.

Major Chinese Companies in India are:

Sinosteel, Shougang International, Baoshan Iron & Steel Ltd, Sany Heavy Industry Ltd, Chongqing Lifan Industry Ltd, China Dongfang International, Sino Hydro Corporation, Huawei Technologies, ZTE, TCL, Haier, Shanghai Electric, Harbin Electric, Dongfang Electric, Shenyang Electric, Beijing Automotive Industry Corporation (BAIC), ZTE Kangun Telecom Company (I) P. Ltd., ESSEL Ahmedabad Godhra Toll Roads Ltd., Shanghai Electric India Pvt. Ltd., TBEA Energy (India) Ltd., TBEA Energy (India) Ltd., CHENGUANG Bio-Tech (India) Pvt. Ltd., Ecolutions Green Energy (India) Pvt. Ltd., YAPP India Automotive Systems Pvt. Ltd., XINDIA Steels Ltd., Nippon Paint (India) Pvt. Ltd., Cheetah Multitrade P. Ltd., Jushi India FRP Accessories Pvt. Ltd., WISCO (I) P. Ltd.

Infosys Technologies began its China operation in 2003 with an investment of USD 5 million. It had employed 6000 and built two development centers in Shanghai and Hangzhou. It has also invested USD 125-150 million to set up its own campus in Shanghai, the largest such investment outside India. Wipro intends to open a third China delivery center in the Northeast city of Dalian. India's ICICI bank is going to open several branches in different cities of China. Bharti Airtel, a top Indian telecommunications carrier, has teamed up with China Mobile for developing fourth-generation (4G) mobile data services. On the other hand, Huawei, a Chinese telecom giant, which has had business in India for 15 years, announced that it would open up a research and development center with a USD 170 million investment in India, the company's largest research and development center outside China.

Now, joint ventures and partnerships have become an effective approach to overcoming investment barriers, in addition to the wholly owned foreign enterprise model. Long-term strategy, local knowledge, local sourcing and employment, and a willingness to be open and transparent in business practices have proven to be the winning tactics of gaining trust, consolidating a foothold, and expanding business. For example, Huawei has made every effort to hire locals and source as many local components as possible. Of its more than 6000 employees in India, 95 percent are local hires. Huawei has built large Research and Development and service centers in India, including a 5000-seat one in Bangalore. Likewise, India's Tata Consultancy Services (TCS), the IT arm of the Tata Group, found its way into China through collaboration with the government to provide IT service training. Of its 3000 employees in China, 97 percent are local hires.

Increasing Chinese investment to India has been recognized as one way to address the trade imbalance issue. A memorandum of understanding on cooperation on industrial parks in India was signed by the two countries in June 2014 to compensate for India's growing trade deficits. Subsequently, during President Xi Jinping's first official visit to India in September 2014, China pledged USD 20 billion to develop the infrastructure of two industrial parks in Maharashtra and Gujarat over the next five years. The Commerce Ministers of both the countries signed a five-year trade and economic development plan that aims to promote sustainability and address trade imbalance, including access to Chinese markets for Indian pharmaceutical and agricultural goods. Also, under discussion were a possible USD 50 billion future Chinese investment in modernizing India's railway systems and a possible USD 50 billion for India's infrastructure development. China and India are likely to cooperate on railways, where India's out-of-date system could benefit from China's experience in developing the country's national high-speed rail networks. Indian Government has approved 100 percent FDI in India's high-speed rail system. An action plan was signed during Prime Minister Modi's visit to China, which includes cooperation in the following areas: the speed-raising of existing routes (Chennai-Bengaluru-Mysore), a high-speed rail (Delhi-Nagpur or Delhi-Chennai sectors), railway station re-development, heavy-haul training, and the establishment of a railway university. The Chinese side is pushing to start a pilot project covering part of the route from New Delhi to Chennai, in what one Chinese feasibility study has suggested could eventually become a mega USD 36 billion bullet train project.

It is believed that Chinese investment into India will total USD 30 billion between now and 2025, given the growing trade between the two countries, and with it, the necessity of manufacturing goods and developing infrastructure in India. Xiaomi, a Chinese cell phone company, has recently started production in India. Top executives have pledged to invest and undertake research and development in a fast-growing market currently dominated by Samsung Electronics and Micromax. Xiaomi also plans to invest in Indian tech start-ups, as the world's third-largest smartphone company expands its markets outside China, with the goal of becoming the number one handset brand in India by 2020. China's Alibaba has bought a stake worth approximately USD 550 million in India's One97 Communications Ltd., a major investment for Alibaba in India's fast-growing online business.

In 2015, India has given green light to the Bank of China to open its branch in Mumbai. This is part of the reform that India has undertaken to encourage foreign banks to expand their business in India. Currently, a single branch of just one Chinese bank, the Industrial and Commercial Bank of China, operates in India. In July 2015, India's Ministry of Home Affairs approved a 19-month old proposal from Huawei, China's telecommunications giant, to set up a unit in Tamil Nadu. However, separate security clearance is required for foreign nationals to be appointed top executives and the company is expected to reserve top technical positions for Indian nationals. India has also sought to attract investment from Chinese provinces, including those in its Western interior. China's accumulated outward foreign investment was an impressive USD 660 billion by 2014, and it has set its target to increase it to USD 1.25 trillion over the next decade; India sees an opportunity in this, particularly in attracting Chinese investment into its industrial parks.

The level and scope of investment in other countries reflect the investing country's confidence in the host country's overall investment environment, potential for economic growth, and long-term stable political relationship. Growing economic interdependence, of which investment is a good indicator, also can have a stabilizing impact on interstate relations, including in terms of conflicts and war. The fact that the level of India-China investment has remained low can be attributed to several factors, including legal, infrastructural, commercial, and security considerations. Infrastructure remains a major factor that can deter prospective investors, including Chinese ones. Security concerns are another impediment to investment. For example, the Indian Air Force has recently imposed a ban on the use of handsets manufactured by a Chinese mobile phone maker, Xiaomi, by its employees in the Air Force premises. It is also believed that security concerns have led the Modi Government to grant Japan the contract to build the Mumbai-Ahmedabad high-speed rail corridor. At the same time, Chinese companies neither are familiar with nor receive the services that Western and Japanese companies enjoy, given those companies' longer history of doing business in India. But, Chinese investment typically goes to resources and raw materials sectors, which are critical commodities that China seeks to exploit and import. At the same time, Indian investment encounters issues of intellectual property protection as well as regulatory clarity.

Challenges and Prospects for India-China Trade and Investment: The challenges that India and China face in their economic relations can be understood through the economic-security prism or the economics-security nexus. This is an area that should allow the two sides, given the complementary structures of their economies and their growing trade and investment ties, to benefit from comparative advantage, to further their economic interdependence and therefore raise the cost of conflict, and to bring about mutual gains corresponding exactly to the two governments' top priorities. However, this apparent win-win scenario has yet to materialize. Bilateral trade turnovers, while growing steadily over the years, remain disproportionately low relative to those of China's top ten trading partners. For example, China's total foreign trade in 2014 stood at USD 4.3 trillion and in 2016, it was 3.6 trillion, of which India-China trade accounted for only USD 70.58 billion and USD 70.16 billion, respectively, a dismal 1.6 percent.

There are various reasons, both political and economic, that explain the limitations and slow pace of what could have been much larger volumes of trade and investment. Strategic mistrust or even rivalry, along with unresolved issues ranging from territorial disputes to China's special relationship with Pakistan to the Tibet issue, will continue to impede the pace and scope of bilateral economic ties. Even where purely economic matters are concerned, the much-touted India-China complementarity, where China's manufacturing prowess (hardware) and India's information edge (software) combined to present a rosy picture of India-China relations, is now under serious reconsideration in both geopolitical and economic terms. A closer examination of the bilateral economic structure reveals the fact that the relations between these two emerging economic giants are as much competitive as they are complementary. In some areas, competition can become even more intensified as the two countries continue their development trajectories. For example, competition for energy has already become an area of concern in terms of security for both, India and China.

The two countries are likely also locked in competition for capital and resources while their respective comparative advantages do not automatically translate into expanded trade opportunities, largely because of bureaucratic impediments, security concerns, and cultural barriers. For example, major Chinese telecommunication firms, such as Huawei and ZTE, have been banned from bidding for contracts to supply GSM lines in India's Northern and Eastern Zones, because Indian national security officials are concerned that Chinese telecom equipment can be used for spying or infected with malware. On the other hand, China's own ambition to become a software power means it is reluctant to cede market access to the Indian software industry even though the latter has gained significant prestige globally. Indeed, more than 70 percent of India's software service exports go to Western markets but only 10 percent is sold to China.

One of the major obstacles in India-China economic ties is the perennial trade imbalance where India sustains significant and growing deficits. It is evident that the more the two countries trade, the more deficits it seems India will suffer. A constant complaint from India is the flooding of the Indian market with cheap Chinese goods. From low-value products such as toys to higher-value consumer goods like electronics, Chinese imports have been a major problem for small Indian businesses. For example, Chinese solar panels sell at half the price of Indian-made ones and take up approximately 60 to 70 percent of the Indian solar market share. However, Indian Government is seeking to gain more market access to China and attract Chinese investment to India to address the trade imbalance issue.

The ever-increasing trade imbalance has led India to take drastic measures. India is already imposing a 21 percent duty on power equipment imported from China. It has also raised the import duty on steel, the goal of which is to stem cheap supplies from China and Russia. Between 1995 and 2011, India initiated 147 anti-dumping cases against China, 120 of which ended in Chinese products being hit by penalties. In effect, every fourth anti-dumping case from India is directed towards China. India is asking the Chinese side to invest in India to manufacture these products as a way to provide job opportunities in India but earn profits for Chinese companies. The Federation of Indian Export Organization (FIEO) has also come out proposing to sign a free trade agreement with China to boost Indian exports. However, Indian manufacturing industry lobbying groups, such as the Federation of Indian Chambers of Commerce and Industry (FICCI), are opposed to such an arrangement, believing the further reduction of tariffs would harm Indian industry. China remains much more competitive than India in manufacturing and therefore any further reduction in tariffs would only result in greater Chinese exports to India. Cheap Chinese imports are considered in India as a "slow killer", a threat to India's manufacturing industry, and it is assumed that 75 percent of Indian manufacturing depends on imports from China. At the same time, Indian companies, even those in the more competitive sectors such as pharmaceuticals and IT technology, find it difficult to penetrate China's market. Even in the case of pharmaceutical sector, where India has a comparative advantage, an anomaly exists whereby India, which produces one-third of the world's medicines in the form of generic drugs, has to rely on China, as more than 80 percent of the raw materials for these drugs come from there.

It is pointed out that India's paranoia about its trade deficit with China misses an important point—India typically runs deficits with most of its trading partners (16 out of 25) simply because it does not produce enough goods to meet domestic market demands. India's deficit as a percentage of bilateral trade with some countries is much higher than it is with China, which was approximately 55 percent in the 2013-14 fiscal year. By comparison, it is 90, 83, and 62 percent, respectively, vis-à-vis Iraq, Switzerland and Australia. It is argued that Indian imports of Chinese consumer goods help to raise people's living standards while Chinese capital goods at lower prices allow Indian businesses that depend on imported machinery and power equipment to use the savings elsewhere to create new jobs.

There are lot of obstacles in the way of developing a bilateral strategic relationship between India and China, which is a key factor in facilitating trade and investment expansion. There are political-strategic (including territorial disputes), the Tibet issue, and the India-China-Pakistan triangle (especially China's continuing support of Pakistan and the United States factor). On the economic front, India has yet to recognize China's market status even though India itself is much less open with its numerous non-tariff barriers. India remains reluctant to negotiate a Free Trade Agreement (FTA) with China, even though a joint feasibility study was concluded in 2007. Formal negotiation has yet to begin and there is a lack of consensus, largely due to uncertainty about the likely negative impacts on those sectors that are most vulnerable to competition because of significant reduction or even elimination of tariffs. As the two markets open up to each other, there are bound to be major disruptions, and the two countries need to set up dispute resolution and contingent protection measures. It is believed that an FTA would benefit China much more than it would

India, as the lowering of tariffs would allow for massive inflows of Chinese made goods into the Indian market, aggravating the trade imbalance problem.

Despite growing economic ties, India's understanding of China and vice versa remains shallow, misconstrued and at times misguided by ignorance and stereotypical perceptions. Neither country has made any serious attempt to address these perceptual problems. In recent years, especially since the Xi Jinping–Li Keqiang administration and the Modi Government came into power in 2014, significant efforts have been made to expand economic ties, through liberalization of some of the restrictions and incentives to attract capital. This is in response to the chronic trade imbalance in India-China trade and the existing market barriers in both countries. However, realizing the potential and making investment work still requires a whole set of policies that must be implemented in both countries to provide the regulatory and facilitating environments. It is believed that if managed well, and if certain perennial issues such as the trade imbalance can be properly handled and addressed, there is no reason why India-China economic ties cannot grow further, given the size of their economies and their rising middle classes. There are several factors which are favourable to India-China economic ties.

(a) There is significant commitment from both sides to further developing bilateral economic ties, as economic development remains a top priority for both India and China. In China, the goals set for the two "Hundred Years" (2021 to mark the 100th anniversary of the Communist Party of China, 2049 to mark the 100th anniversary of the founding of the People's Republic of China) require balanced and sustainable economic growth. The 2008 global financial crisis and economic recession have greatly affected Chinese exports to their traditional markets due to declining consumer demands. This has forced China to make adjustments, including seeking new markets as well as encouraging domestic consumption. On the other hand, India has all the incentives to attract investment and promote "Make in India".

(b) The sizes of the two economies and their growing middle classes provide potential future markets for goods, services and investment opportunities. India's economic reform began in 1991 and within years bilateral trade crossed USD 1 billion mark in 1995. Although it has experienced significant slowdown in the past few years, the growth rate of India's economy is poised to rival, perhaps even overtake China in the coming years, and that could lead to an expanding market and growing demands for consumer goods. Chinese power equipment already accounts for over 60 percent of Indian orders, and Chinese telecommunications and smartphone manufacturers are also expanding their market shares in India. Chinese consumer goods remain competitive in India. However, as China continues to pursue economic reforms and expand its service sector, India's IT sectors, pharmaceutical, and financial services could also tap into China's market. The complementary nature of the two economies is conductive to further expansion of bilateral economic ties.

(c) In recent years, economic ties between India and China have expanded to include subnational and subregional interactions. The BCIM-EC (Bangladesh, China, India and Myanmar-Economic Corridor), when fully operating, could inject much-needed energy into India's Northeastern Region and China's Southwestern provinces, both landlocked, while at the same time connecting Bangladesh and Myanmar, as well as China and India, in order that the subregion's rich resources be explored and flows of trade, investment, and people-to-people contacts be facilitated, turning the BCIM-EC into an important intersection in the "One Road, One Belt" initiative. The transportation connectivity will greatly reduce the time and cost of doing business between the two countries and assist development in each country's less developed regions. Also, Indian states and Chinese provinces are exploring areas of cooperation, in particular where the latter could provide financial resources to assist infrastructure development and form economic partnerships. For example, recent years have seen growing interactions between Indian state chief ministers and Chinese provincial leaders, and the establishment of sister-city arrangements.

(d) A free trade agreement between fast-growing BCIM economies could also unleash tremendous market growth in both India and China. It is argued that a free trade agreement between India and China could significantly enhance bilateral relations, strengthen the strategic partnership, and benefit the two emerging economies in many positive ways, including promoting growth in trade and investment, deepening economic reform and restructuring to be more open and competitive in the global economy and reducing poverty in the relatively poor and underdeveloped regions of both countries, enhancing mutual political trust, improving the management of bilateral disputes, and cooperating in nontraditional security areas such as energy, food, health, and terrorism, among others.

"Hindi-Chini Buy, Buy"—The Concept of Chindia: The term "Chindia", which refers to the combination of China and India, was coined by the then Indian Minister of State for Commerce Jairam Ramesh in 2004. The fact that India and China declared the year 2006 as the "Year of India-China Friendship" was hailed as a realization of the Chindia concept and the resurrection of "Hindi-Chini Bhai Bhai". The expectation behind this concept was that India and China would emerge as the fastest growing economies and the economic cooperation would act as the driving force and the focal point of bilateral ties.

Growing middle classes in India and China want to consume high quality goods for affordable prices in a secure environment. War and insecurity are not an option for them and if there are conflicts they should be solved peacefully because securing the prosperity of the nation and its citizens through peaceful means is the main objective of the state. Rising trade has itself contributed to an easing of the border issues. For example, China's recognition of Sikkim as part of India enabled an agreement to open the Nathu La and Jelep La Passes in Sikkim as trading links in 2004. Closed since 1962, the Nathu La Pass finally reopened in July 2006. However, trade through the pass, once the route for 80 percent of bilateral trade, has been limited, primarily benefiting areas in close proximity to the pass. While the opening of the pass has been broadly interpreted as a goodwill gesture, there is still mutual mistrust. Both sides have placed restrictions on items that can be traded across the pass.

China is one of the largest trading partners of India, but the trade comes with a frustrating deficit for India as it is difficult to sell Indian made products in China, while Chinese goods are flooding the Indian market. India wants to reduce the dominance of primary products and raw materials, like iron ore, in India's export basket by including manufactured goods therein. For India it is very important to solve these issues with China because the trade deficit is a factor in the depreciation of the Indian currency. It has also put enormous pressure on India to attract foreign investment. The trade imbalance shows that India's manufacturing infrastructure is still weak and that Indian manufacturers are not capable to produce high quality goods which consumers like to buy, like their Chinese counterparts. Indian firms are pressuring the Indian Government to protect them from Chinese dumping prices. But this policy might backfire and hurt the economy as well as the Indian consumer. The pros and cons of a stronger Chinese engagement in the Indian market is a matter that the Indian Government and the Indian public must evaluate themselves. Economic stability and profit are the main motives for India and China to work together. They have signed a draft bilateral investment promotion and protection agreement during President Hu Jintao's visit to India in November 2006. The agreement was one of thirteen trade pacts signed between India and China during the official visit and provides an institutional and legal framework for increased foreign investment flows between them. They have also agreed to encourage cooperation in oilfield bidding and exploration and the development of hydrocarbons in third countries. For example, in Sudan both countries work together—India drills the oil and China provides the infrastructure by building the pipe lines. This is an example where Chindia happens.

It is believed that if India and China join together they would be able to resolve global challenges, such as climate change or energy issues. They are also two of the biggest oil consumers. If they work together they could put great pressure on the oil producing countries along with G7 states. This is the basic concept of Chindia and this term is often used for the possible synergies in the IT sector or business in general, where China produces the hardware (manufacturing) and India provides the software (service).

However, Chindia is not limited to the economic aspect, but is also being applied to broader political issues. It reflects the optimistic expectations about the coming together of India and China, and is seen as a prelude to the emergence of a World Commonwealth. Thus, despite their bitter experiences and differences over disputes, it is believed that India and China will stand together in international affairs as a powerful combination. Indeed, there is a possibility that both countries can enhance cooperation in the establishment of a new international order. A certain convergence of views on the international order enables them to project a distinctive developing countries' perspective on global affairs. On the other hand, their viewpoints on international issues are not always identical or compatible, which also restrains India and China from expanding cooperation.

Strategy Objectives and Policy Suggestions to Promote Bilateral Trade

India and China are two important trade partners. In the year 2006, bilateral trade was valued at USD 23468.23 million and has grown rapidly since then at average annual rate of 25 percent. In 2016, bilateral trade amounted to USD 70161.89 million, out of which China's exports to India valued USD 58397.76 million and China's imports from India valued USD 11764.13 million. According to the statistics from the Indian authorities, in 2016, the trade volume between India and China stood at USD 69399.17 million, out of which India's exports to

China stood at USD 8916.07 million and India's imports from China were USD 60483.10 million.

In terms of product structure, China's major exports to India are manufactured goods including mechanical and electrical products, chemical products, and base metals and related products. According to an estimate, principal commodities of import from China during the year 2016-17 included electronic goods, machinery, organic chemicals, transport equipment and fertilizers. Chinese products find a market in India due to their competitive prices and growing domestic demand. On the other hand, China has a high import demand for raw materials and primary products as Chinese industries face a resource crunch due to rapid industrialization and urbanization in China. Therefore, at present, India's exports to China mainly comprise raw materials, primary products and intermediate products mainly iron ore, copper, mineral, cotton, *etc.* During the year 2016-17, export of nonferrous metals, cotton, iron ore and petroleum constituted nearly 50 percent of Indian exports to China.

Bilateral trade in services between India and China started relatively late and has been rapid growth in recent years with a growth in China's deficit against India in service trade. There is great potential for growth of trade in services between India and China. India has emerged as a major service exporting country and services contribute to 60 percent of the gross domestic product (GDP) of the country, whereas India's secondary and primary sectors accounted for 26.1 percent and 13.9 percent of GDP respectively. On the other hand, China has a dominant secondary sector which accounts for 45 percent of GDP and the tertiary and primary sectors represent 40 percent and 10 percent of GDP respectively. As per Chinese statistics, India's service exports to China focus mainly on commercial services, while China's service exports to India focus mainly on the three traditional service fields of tourism, transport services and construction services. Under the aegis of the 9th session of India-China Joint Group on Economic Relations, Trade, Science and Technology held on 27th August 2013, a Joint Working Group on Trade in Services was constituted and entrusted with the task of enforcing mutual cooperation between the two countries for the development of bilateral trade in services. The 1st meeting of the JWG was held on 13th December 2013, where four key sectors were identified for promoting bilateral trade in services—software and IT services, IT enabled services, audio visual and entertainment, and tourism and tourism related services.

India has a significant advantage in trade in services, particularly in IT and IT enabled services (ITeS). It has more than 20 years of experience in IT services outsourcing and established its position as the world's largest outsourcing destination. Indian IT industry has set up over 560 global distribution centers and serves 85 percent of the Fortune 500 enterprises and 20 of the top global financial institutions. According to China, India occupies 65 percent share of the global software outsourcing market and 46 percent share of the global outsourcing market of other services. China also has ambitious plans to become a global business and IT services hub and is taking aggressive steps to drive growth in the IT sector. India and China recognize the strong potential for cooperation and are keen on leveraging each other's strengths in this sector. To materialize this understanding, both countries signed a Memorandum of Understanding (MoU) in March 2014 for enhancing cooperation in the fields of software applications and services, e-commerce and e-governance and collaborating in the field of emerging technologies.

The overall objective of trade cooperation between India and China is to achieve a balanced and sustainable level of bilateral trade. China has a favourable balance of trade in goods, while India has a favourable balance of trade in services. With an increase in the bilateral trade over the last decade, the trade imbalance against India also increased exponentially from USD 7809.89 million in 2006 to USD 51567.03 million in 2016. In order to bridge the bilateral trade deficit, there is an urgent need for India and China to adopt measures for improving India's export capacity and competitiveness and expedite action on resolution of following market access issues.

Market Access for Indian Bovine Meat, Rapeseed Meal and Oil Meals in China: India has consistently sought market access from China for certain products where it has global competitiveness for exports and the issue of market access for Indian bovine meat, rapeseed meal and oil meals in China requires urgent attention as it would help India ease the trade deficit to an extent. In May 2013, a Memorandum of Understanding (MoU) for the export of buffalo meat was signed by Agriculture and Processed Food Products Export Development Authority (APEDA) of India and General Administration of Quality Supervision, Inspection and Quarantine (AQSIQ) of China. As regards Indian rapeseed meal and oil meals, an MoU on trade and safety of feed and feed ingredients was signed between the Export Inspection Council (EIC) of India and AQSIQ in May 2013 and in July 2014, the terms of a "Protocol of Health and Safety Regulations on Improving Indian Rapeseed Meal" were negotiated between EIC and AQSIQ.

Market Access for Indian Basmati and Non-basmati Rice in China: India is a leading producer and exporter of rice including basmati rice and other variants of rice. Whereas China has emerged as one of the world's largest importer of rice. In November 2006, India and China signed a protocol for exporting of rice from India to China. In 2009, to ensure that Indian basmati rice is free from quarantine pests, a standard operating procedure setting out the monitoring and control measures for quarantine pests was agreed upon by Indian and Chinese authorities. Consequently, in the year 2012, China provided market access for Indian basmati rice. However, despite the provision of market access, Indian exporters face practical bottlenecks and have complained that the Chinese authorities are not aware of the quarantine clearance given by the Chinese Government for import of Indian basmati rice. Further, enhanced cooperation in export of Indian non-basmati rice possesses strong potential for mutually beneficial trade between India and China. Given that Indian non-basmati rice producers follow the same monitoring and quality control standards as agreed under the standard operating procedure, China should endeavour to promote import of rice, both basmati and non-basmati varieties from India.

Market Access for Indian Fruits and Vegetables in China: According to the bilateral agreements executed with China in

2000 and the MoU on phytosanitary measures executed with China in 2002, India had requested market access in China for 17 varieties of Indian fruits and vegetables. Upon conducting a risk analysis, China provided market access for mangoes in 2004 and for grapes and bitter gourd in 2005. India has identified 5 fruits and vegetables (out of the remaining 14 fruits and vegetables for which market access is pending) and requested China to take a fast track decision to provide market access for these 5 products on priority.

Deepening Bilateral Trade Cooperation: India and China are looking forward to strengthening cooperation in bilateral trade and deepening integration in global value chains. Following the new trends in international trade, both sides stand to benefit from establishment of supply and production chain linkages between them. China can facilitate the creation of such linkages through policy initiatives which promote imports from India of intermediate goods such as Indian textiles, casein and caseinates, diamonds and oil seeds. These Indian intermediate products are highly regarded for their global export competitiveness and present a win-win potential for bilateral trade. Exports of these products would enable China to strengthen its position in the global and regional value chains in the food processing, jewelry, textile and garment industries. In addition, this would help reduce the bilateral trade deficit of India.

India has also requested China to consider lowering tariffs and facilitating imports of the above-mentioned products from India. It is believed that it is important for China to consider reducing tariffs on Indian textiles and handmade carpets, casein and caseinates, diamond and oil seeds in the spirit of mutual cooperation and reciprocity. In this regard, China has suggested that the discussion on tariff reduction for the above-mentioned products can be taken up under the framework of the Asia-Pacific Trade Agreement.

Export of Indian Pharmaceuticals to China: India has attained global recognition for the manufacture of high quality, affordable generic medicines and is fast becoming a hub for contract research, biotechnology, clinical trials, and clinical data management. Indian pharmaceutical industry is the fourth largest in the world in terms of production volume and has approximately 1400 WHO cGMP (World Health Organisation's current Good Manufacturing Practices) approved pharmaceutical plants. It is a major supplier of pharmaceutical products to international agencies as well as diverse markets including the United States of America, European Union and Africa. Therefore, enhanced cooperation in pharmaceuticals trade would be to the mutual benefit of both India and China. A strong partnership in export of formulations from India to China would go a long way in catering to the Chinese public healthcare programme. Indian pharmaceutical companies can leverage their expertise for providing innovative generic drug formulations, late stage intermediaries and high end active pharmaceutical ingredients for the Chinese public healthcare programme as well as to meet the requirements of the Chinese healthcare industry.

The strength of China's pharmaceutical industry lies in hardware and equipment. However, China seeks to fill gaps in aspects such as research and development, world-class national laboratories, and excellent clinical trial centers. Besides, Chinese enterprises lack experience in international operations. Therefore, the pharmaceutical is one of the best sectors where both sides can strengthen economic and trade cooperation. With the aim to promote bilateral trade in the field of pharmaceuticals, both sides are working towards finalization of a work plan on drug administration and cooperation between Ministry of Health and Family Welfare of Government of India, and Food and Drug Administration of China.

Export of Indian IT services to China: India and China are strongly complementary to each other in terms of electronic information software and hardware industries and service fields, enjoying a broad space for cooperation. The rapid development of the Indian IT and ITeS industries has transformed India's image on the global platform. With outsourcing experience spanning more than 20 years, the Indian IT/BPO industry has presence in more than 70 countries and delivers services in more than 35 languages. In view of India's experience and competence in software outsourcing, a strong partnership between Indian and Chinese IT industry would help in positioning China as an attractive offshoring destination. India's extensive experience and competence in software when combined with China's strength in hardware offers a strong proposition for embedded software industry on a global level.

Indian IT companies have significant experience in servicing clients across diverse geographies and verticals through their unique Global Network Delivery Model (GNDM). An enhanced partnership with India in the IT sector will help in improving the competitiveness of Chinese companies and transforming their operations through innovative outsourcing solutions. The Indian IT industry has been focusing on reconfiguring its resources to be socially and economically efficient and provide services tailored to specific jurisdictional requirements. The Indian IT/BPO industry employs approximately 20,000 Chinese citizens in China. Therefore, a strong IT partnership with India will help in improving the employment opportunities of Chinese students. With their well-established global presence, Indian IT companies are well positioned to service and partner with the Chinese IT companies. In March 2014, the Ministry of Communications and Information Technology of Government of India and Ministry of Industry and Information Technology of China signed an MoU to enhance trade and economic cooperation in the IT and ITeS sector.

Bilateral Cooperation in the Tourism: India and China are major emerging tourist markets. With the economies of both India and China developing rapidly and with the improvement in people's standards of living, the number of Indians and Chinese travelling abroad, including Indians to China and Chinese to India, has been surging. In 2017, more than 10 million tourists came to India, showing an impressive growth of 15.6 percent over 2016. More interestingly, China which stood at 13th overall for India's inbound tourists in 2014, has moved six rungs up the ladder in just three years taking 8th position. The number of Chinese visitors has clocked a fourfold increase in the last ten years—from a mere 62,300 in 2006 to 2,51,313 in 2016.

In the first meeting of the JWG on Trade in Services held on 13th December 2013, India and China identified tourism as a key service sector and recognized that there is immense potential for cooperation in the tourism sector. In the same meeting, both sides discussed the prospect of promoting bilateral investments in the tourism and hospitality sector in each other's countries. In 2013, with a view to expand cooperation in the tourism sector, China launched "Beautiful China" tourist promotion activities in India, and India began its "Incredible India" marketing campaign in China. Each year, China invites Indian exhibitors and purchasers to participate in the China International Travel Mart (CITM), sends delegations to attend the Outbound Travel Man (OTM) in India, and invites 100 Indian travel businessmen and media journalists to visit China. It is believed that such tourist and business promotion events would contribute towards enhancing the understanding of India and the Indian people in China and vice-versa.

For fostering cultural relations and promoting trade in tourism, India and China designated 2014 as the 'year of friendship and exchange for India and China'. Both sides had planned a series of activities and exchanges to be held during the year, including high-level visits, bilateral dialogues, defence cooperation, engagements in the fields of trade and economy, and cultural, educational and people-to-people contacts. 'Glimpses of India Festival' was observed in 12 cities of China. It was jointly organized by the Indian and Chinese authorities, and well received and featured an array of Indian performing arts, exhibitions of modern Indian art and calligraphy, visual and photographic exhibitions on Buddhist heritage of India and links with China, scientific achievements of India, as well as events involving eminent Indian and Chinese scholars and writers. India also participated in the China International Fair for Trade in Services (CIFTIS) held in June 2014.

With a view to expand tourism cooperation, the year 2015 was designated as the "Visit India Year in China" and the year 2016 as "Visit China Year in India". China also agreed to favourably consider a proposal from the Indian side for the joint development of a Xuanzang Circuit in India to promote tourism and people-to-people linkages inspired by Xuanzang's historical travels, keeping in view his significant contribution to promoting deep contacts between the two countries. Both sides may also strengthen cooperation for publishing tourism related literature in the Chinese language and facilitate availability of recorded audio guides in the Chinese language at all major Indian tourist sites. Training of Indian tour guides in the Chinese language is another policy initiative which merits consideration. Given the visual impact of films and audio products, shooting of films in Indian and Chinese cities would go a long way in promoting India and China as attractive tourist destinations. Further with a view to increase trade in tourism, it is suggested that greater involvement of the Indian and Chinese governments in providing travel advisories and familiarizing Indian and Chinese tourists about the tourist destinations in each other's countries would yield significant benefits.

To encourage Chinese tourists to travel to and within India, the Indian Government has started e-visa facilities for Chinese tourists in May 2015. In 2017, e-visa usage marked a sharp 57 percent increase over 2016, which shows China fairing even better, emerging as the 5th largest user of India's e-visa facility, leaving advanced nations like Canada, France and Germany far behind.

Strengthen Bilateral Cooperation for Resolution of Trade Disputes: India and China are working for strengthening cooperation for creation of a robust dispute resolution mechanism to address disputes arising between commercial entities in the two countries. A bilateral dispute resolution mechanism would facilitate speedy redressal of grievances of exporters and importers in the two countries on matters pertaining to fraud and intellectual property infringement. On a bilateral level, the mechanism of dispute resolution would foster a relationship of mutual trust and partnership between both the governments and their industries.

Potential of Bilateral Investment Cooperation

There has been an increase in Chinese foreign direct investment inflows into India since 2000. Up to the end of 2016, Chinese cumulative investment in India amounted to USD 4.07 billion, which represents a share of 0.18 percent of the total FDI in India, and India has invested USD 650 million in China. According the

Department of Industrial Promotion and Policy (DIPP), Ministry of Commerce and Industry, Government of India, China ranked 17th among countries infusing FDI in India.

Cumulative FDI Inflows from China

Period	Rank	FDI Inflow (in USD Million)	Percentage of Total FDI inflows
April 2000—December 2016	17	1611.66	0.50
April 2000—December 2015	17	1322.81	0.48
April 2000—December 2014	28	453.82	0.19
April 2000—December 2013	30	313.02	0.15
April 2000—December 2012	31	240.87	0.13
April 2000—December 2011	35	102.56	0.06
April 2000—December 2010	36	53.05	0.04

Source: Department of Industrial Policy and Promotion.

In 2011 total Chinese FDI in India was USD 102 million. However, in 2016, USD 1 billion of Chinese FDI reportedly came to India, but official Indian and Chinese statistics differ on cumulative figures. The DIPP estimated that total FDI from China between April 2000 and December 2016 was USD 1.6 billion. Nonetheless, Chinese investment flows into India remain relatively low, both in terms of total FDI flows into India and Chinese outward investment globally. China's share of total FDI in India is only 0.5 percent, despite its being the second largest economy in the world and India's largest trading partner. However, this is higher than other BRICS countries' investment in India—Brazil chalks up 0.01 percent and Russia 0.37 percent despite historically robust relations. Yet, China's 0.5 percent share pales in comparison with fellow Asian powerhouse Japan (7.7 percent). Meanwhile, the United States, which China recently replaced as the world's largest economy in purchasing power parity terms, has a 6.13 percent share in total FDI in India. While China's FDI flow into India in 2016 showed a relatively significant rise, the figure was negligible when viewed against China's outbound investment of over USD 170 billion across 164 countries, including USD 45.6 billion in the United States alone.

China's investment in India involves only a few industries, such as metallurgical, automobile, industrial machinery, services and power. According to DIPP, Indian metallurgical industry has received the highest percentage of FDI from China (*i.e.*, 33 percent) and Indian automobile sector has been the recipient of 25 percent of FDI from China. Indian industrial machinery, power and services sectors account for 7 percent, 4 percent and 7 percent FDI from China respectively. On the other hand, as per Chinese statistics, India's investment inflows in China stood at USD 88.05 million in 2008 and were valued at USD 27.05 million in 2013. Key Chinese industries which have received investment from India are software development, IT services, pharmaceuticals, steel, auto parts, beverages, and shipping agency.

Thus, there are broad prospects for bilateral investment cooperation between India and China given that both countries are fast-growing economies with enormous market potential and complementary industrial structures. China has introduced a series of preferential policies on sectors such as IT, medicine and pharmaceutical, and on the other hand, India has developed a range of measures aimed at promoting infrastructure investment and manufacturing development. India has also progressively liberalized its FDI regime and is keen on leveraging Chinese investment in development of industrial parks in India. It is believed that industrial parks would provide a platform for cluster type development of enterprises of both countries. Such industrial clusters are aimed at building a production network with a strong ability to provide auxiliary products and have the potential to transform and upgrade related industries. In this connection, an MoU on Cooperation on Industrial Parks in India was signed between India and China in June 2014 with the objective of strengthening cooperation and encouraging Chinese enterprises to enhance their engagement in development of industrial parks in India. These industrial parks will enjoy the support that the Chinese Government grants to overseas economic and trade cooperation zones as well as benefits under the prevailing policy frameworks in India, including the Special Economic Zones (SEZ) and National Investment and Manufacturing Zones (NIMZ) in India. The development of industrial parks is based on the principles of government facilitation, enterprises as major players, and market operation. India and China are also endeavouring to explore the feasibility of arriving at a memorandum or work framework on infrastructure investment by Chinese companies in India. Enhanced investment cooperation between the two countries would help in improving the international competitiveness of Chinese and Indian enterprises. To achieve this objective, India and China shall strive to maintain a transparent, stable and investor friendly business environment and policy framework on an ongoing basis and endeavour to enhance cooperation for attracting more FDI inflows from China in India in the following areas.

(a) *Selecting priority sectors for investment in India*: India and China need to strengthen cooperation to promote investment from Chinese firms in India's infrastructure sector and advance the development of industrial parks in India. For this, China may encourage Chinese enterprises to invest in India under the FDI route and through the capital markets, including the newly established infrastructural debt funds and trust funds. In the manufacturing sector, there are significant opportunities for Chinese investment in machinery, telecom equipment, hardware, electronics, communications, home appliances, autos and parts, pharmaceuticals, textiles, plastics and chemical engineering industries. Both countries share a strong potential for market cooperation in the field of electronics, radio and mobile communication as China has state-of-the-art technologies for digital TV and radio and mobile communications as well as remarkable advantages in costs for related system construction. They may also extend cooperation for investment in the power sector given that China has rich experience in power generation and power grids and has obtained global recognition for equipment manufacturing. Also, from the perspective of enhancing India's capacity in food processing and export of agricultural products, they may cooperate for increasing investment from China in the food processing machinery, logistics and warehousing equipment sectors in India.

(b) *Strengthening the role of various chambers of commerce involved in trade and investment cooperation between India and China*: The role of various chambers of commerce needs to be increased to promote trade and investment cooperation between the two countries and act as a bridge between governments and enterprises. An increase in the role of chambers of commerce in trade and investment cooperation between India and China would bring into full play their role as a bridge between governments and enterprises and as a mouthpiece for overseas investment enterprises, and help to effectively maintain the interests of enterprises and create a sound local business environment.

(c) *Encouraging enterprises from both countries to fulfil corporate social responsibility*: The enterprises from both countries are encouraged to incorporate corporate social responsibility (CSR) in their corporate development strategies in accordance with country specific laws and create a sound framework for their implementation.

(d) *Encouraging Indian and Chinese enterprises to establish Research and Development centers in each other's countries*: Both sides have recognized the benefits of encouraging Chinese and Indian enterprises to establish research and development centers in each other's countries.

(e) *Encouraging Chinese and Indian enterprises to organize investment and trade fairs*: Investment and trade fairs will facilitate cooperation by providing a platform for interaction of Chinese and Indian enterprises and promote exchange between enterprises and local governments. To increase awareness about the Indian investment framework and business environment amongst Chinese enterprises, India has started to stage Indian fairs and festivals in various cities in China on a regular basis.

(f) *Improving law enforcement for better intellectual property protection:* India and China should endeavour to provide appropriate protection to intellectual property rights consistent with their respective laws, rules and regulations and other international agreements to which they are committed.

India's and China's Roles in Global Trade and Finance

India and China constitute unprecedented stories of economic development. Owing to vibrant growth rates in the last decade, they have already reached heavyweight status in the global economy. Indeed, after adjusting for the price of non-tradable, India is already the fifth largest economy, just behind Japan, while China is the world's second largest economy, still behind the United States. The determinants of such rapid development, and whether it can be sustained in the longer run, are important research and policy issues. The findings of several studies in respect of India's and China's long-term growth prospects have indeed been startling. According to one such study, by 2050 India and China will regain their pre-industrial revolution status as the world's third and first largest economies at market prices.

From a global perspective, India and China are poised to play a key role in four of the most pressing policy debates of recent years.

(a) China's large current account surplus and accumulation of hefty foreign reserve assets are inherently associated with discussions on global imbalances.

(b) Strong growth in India and China, together with other emerging economies, is also considered to have contributed to recent increases in the prices of energy and other commodities, which may have been a source of upward pressure on inflation over the past few years.

(c) The rapid pace of India's and China's economic development is often related to mounting concerns about the risks of outsourcing manufacturing activities to China and services to India.

(d) The integration of India and China into the world economy has also deeply affected international capital flows, for instance, through China's large-scale purchases of the United States Treasury bonds or growing merger and acquisition activities by both Indian and Chinese companies abroad.

From Euro area perspective, India and China are becoming increasingly important in the Euro area's external environment, particularly with regard to trade and financial relations. In terms of trade in goods, China is already one of the two main sources of Euro area imports, with a share of over 10 percent. The Euro area's trade relations with India have not developed to such an extent thus far, with India accounting for about one percent of Euro area imports and exports of goods. Nevertheless, the Euro area has been an active investor in the two emerging economies, accounting for around 7 percent of direct investment flows into China since the turn of the millennium, and 14 percent of such flows into India. In turn, China and India have gained in importance as a source of capital for the Euro area. In this respect, direct investment received by the Euro area from China and India averaged EUR 400 million per year since the introduction of the Euro, or about 0.2 percent of all FDI inflows. Thus, direct exposure of the Euro area banking system to India and China has far remained contained, as it is to emerging economies in general—claims of Euro area reporting banks to the Bank for International Settlements to India and China accounted for less than 1 percent of their foreign claims.

The overwhelming size of India's and China's population is the most important similarity between the two economies, and the main reason why their economic development attracts so much attention from other countries of the world. Taken together, India with about 1.35 billion inhabitants and China with 1.42 billion accounted for close to 37 percent of the world's population in 2018. However, this apparently undisputed similarity hides noticeable differences in terms of demographic structure and prospects. In particular, India's population is currently significantly younger and is growing at a faster pace than China's. As a result, long-term projections suggest that India's population will increase in the next few decades, while China's will decline from 2030 onwards, implying also that India could then overtake China as the world's most populated country. These demographic differences have important economic repercussions. Therefore, the period of demographic dividends—characterized by faster labour force growth than population growth, a support to economic activity—is expected to end in China but not in India. In fact, India's growth potential is anticipated to increase relative to China's, supported by more favourable demographics, to the extent that structural reforms continue. Also, there is a strong prospect that, all things being equal, China's sizeable current account surpluses may turn into deficits due to capital account liberalization, population ageing and lower savings. On the other hand, India's saving rates will be supported by its favourable demographic trends. Altogether, this could profoundly affect global current account patterns, with implications for the roles of both economies in global trade and finance.

Although, India and China are currently growing vigorously, marked differences exist between the two economies on this account, with China's performance steadily exceeding that of India for more than two decades. Since the early 1980s, real GDP growth in China has averaged 9.9 percent, compared with 6 percent in India—a gap of close to four percentage points. If both economies are key engines of world growth, together accounting for about 40 percent, their contributions are far from balanced, with China alone responsible for about 30 percent. Still, there are signs that India is starting to close the gap. Since the turn of the millennium, the growth differential between India and China has narrowed to about three percentage points, with real GDP growth averaging 6.8 percent in India, compared with 9.6 percent in China. In 2006 the differential was even smaller, at below two percentage points, with real GDP growing by 9.7 percent in India and 11.1 percent in China. In line with this, the remaining productivity gap between India and China also bodes well for India's future growth performance. The average level of productivity in India is currently only 9 percent of that in the United States and 75 percent of that in China. Therefore, India is able to reap large productivity gains by enlarging and modernizing its fixed capital stock, including infrastructure, by improving the skill level of the workforce and by shifting resources towards higher productivity sectors, particularly from agriculture to services.

The contribution of capital accumulation and efficiency gains (factor productivity) to growth are roughly equal in both India and China. Therefore, aside from faster productivity gains, China's higher investment rate explains its stronger growth performance. Investment in China is further supported by a higher rate of personal and government saving. China saved more than one-half of its GDP in 2006, compared with one-third in India. In part, India's lower saving rate is due to high public deficits, which absorb a large share of private savings. The strong growth performance of India and China has been considered by some as almost unsurprising. Its reliance on strong capital accumulation, high rates of saving and dynamic exports (notably in China), emulates the development patterns of other Asian economies in the past, such as Japan in the 1960s and the "Asian Tigers—Hong Kong, Singapore, South Korea, and Taiwan" in the 1970s and 1980s.

The aforementioned trends hide marked sectoral differences in the contribution of productivity to growth. China's productivity performance has been especially strong in industry, as has India's in services. China's growth rate of output per capita in industry was almost 10 percent a year in the period 1993-2004. Of this, no less than two-thirds (6.2

percentage points) was generated by efficiency gains. Over the same period, India's growth rate of output per capita was just 3.1 percent a year in the same sector, to which capital accumulation contributed one-third and productivity two-thirds. In services, India's growth rate of real output per capita was close to China's (5.4 percent, compared with 5.1 percent in China). However, Indian productivity growth surpassed China's; efficiency gains contributed 3.9 percentage points to Indian growth (a contribution of around 70 percent), compared with just 0.9 percentage points in the case of China. Such growth patterns have had a profound, but distinct, impact on relative standards of living. GDP per capita was comparable in China and India in the mid-1980s (at around USD 300, at market prices), but it is now more than twice as high in China (at USD 2000, compared with USD 800 in India). However, both countries' future growth could be constrained by similar environmental and social challenges. Those raised by environment protection, including access to water and efficient use of energy sources, have been singled out as among the most pressing. A large share of the population in both India and China does not have access to sanitation facilities or improved water sources. Similarly, while CO_2 emissions, electric power consumption and energy use are still lower than in mature economies, including the United States, they are expected to grow markedly in the period ahead. Another possible constraint that may weigh on future growth is the prevalence of large inequalities, with the corresponding waste of talent and risks of political strains. Almost 30 percent of the population in India (over 300 million) lives below the poverty line, compared with 10 percent in China (about 150 million). Moreover, both India and China score poorly in terms of prevalence of malnutrition, infant mortality rate and life expectancy.

India's and China's Roles in Global Trade: The most salient difference between India and China lies in the patterns of their integration into global trade, which differ in almost all areas, although their starting points were comparable. About a quarter of a century ago, both India and China accounted for a relatively small share of global trade in goods and services. However, in subsequent years their respective experience has been drastically different. Since the early 1980s, China's share in global trade in goods and services has risen almost continuously, reaching 7 percent in 2006, while India's share has risen far more slowly, standing at close to 1 percent in 2006. These trends partly mirror differences in output growth. Yet, the discrepancy in terms of trade integration remains, even after accounting for these differences. China's relative share in world trade (about 7 percent) is now about 30 percent higher than its share in world output (about 5 percent), while the converse holds true for India (1.3 percent against 1.8 percent). China's share in global trade has surpassed its share in global output since the early 2000s. Although, India joined the World Trade Organisation (WTO) six years earlier than China, its share in global trade has remained steadily below that in global output. To some extent, these differences also mirror dissimilarities in terms of trade openness. China has gradually opened up to world trade since the mid-1980s, encouraging the export of manufactured goods as an engine for domestic development. By contrast, India has started to open up more than a decade later and Indian import tariffs have been progressively reduced—from about 35 percent in 1999 to around 10 percent in 2005—although they remain high and dispersed relative to other emerging economies. The breakdown of India's and China's current account balance also reveals very noticeable differences between the two countries, which seem to differ on all accounts. While China has a very large current account surplus (9.9 percent of GDP in 2007, 1.8 percent of GDP in 2016, and 1.4 percent of GDP in 2017), India has a small current account deficit (0.7 percent of GDP in 2016 and 2 percent of GDP in 2017). Separating goods from services, China has a large surplus in trade in goods, which roughly equals India's large deficit (both at 8 percent of GDP in absolute values). A similar difference can be found for services, but in other direction, with India registering a small surplus and China a deficit. To some extent, these features reflect the domestic economic structure of India and China, as industry dominates in the latter and services in the former. More specifically, industry contributes almost half of China's GDP, but less than one-third of India's, where services represent around half of GDP.

Trade in Goods: India and China differ markedly in terms of the overall degree of their trade intensity and the depth of their bilateral trade linkages. China is remarkably integrated, both multilaterally and regionally, whereas India is not. On a bilateral basis, China imports predominantly from other emerging Asian economies and exports to mature economies, such as the United States and the Euro area, while no such pattern can be observed for India. China is also an important trade partner for India, whereas India is a minor trade partner for China. India has emerged as the seventh largest export destination for Chinese products, and the 24th largest exporter to China.

From the perspective of the mature economies, China accounts for a substantial share of foreign trade in goods vis-à-vis the Euro area, Japan, the United Kingdom and the United States, particularly on the import side, whereas India accounts for a minor share of their trade flows. The overall degree of China's trade intensity is higher and its bilateral trade linkages stronger than economic size, location and other relevant fundamentals would suggest. Conversely, the overall degree of India's trade intensity is lower and its bilateral trade linkages weaker than fundamentals would suggest. Notwithstanding, a number of constraints may weigh on India's capacity to produce competitive goods for foreign markets in the same way as China, including:

(a) *Infrastructure*: China is better endowed with modern infrastructure and invests significantly more than India on developing it. However, an exception is the telecom infrastructure, which has improved significantly in India in recent years. China has greatly benefited from facilities offered by Hong Kong, as a distribution depot, a source of capital and a source of modern management and production techniques. India has no comparable resource.

(b) *Labour Laws*: India's labour market is relatively more regulated than China's, where labour laws (for instance in terms of working hours) are sometimes circumvented. China has taken advantage of this in conjunction with the end of trade barriers in, for example, the apparel and textile industries. At the same time, the Indian labour market is characterized by a high degree of informality. People with regular employment contracts account for only 15 percent of total employment and most of these are concentrated in urban areas.

(c) *Foreign Direct Investment*: It is sizeably lower in India than in China, with a corresponding loss in expertise, productivity spillovers and benefits from competition. Emulating China, Indian authorities have created "Special Economic Zones", which offer tax benefits to and simplified procedures for export-oriented investments, in order to attract foreign direct investment.

(d) *Indirect Taxes*: In India, indirect taxes are among the highest in Asia. Tax collection efficiency is low and high fiscal deficits limit the scope for tax rebates.

Considering the strength of bilateral trade linkages, it is found that those of China are stronger than fundamentals would suggest, while those of India are weaker. In particular, China is highly integrated with other emerging Asian economies relative to what economic size, location and other relevant fundamentals would warrant. This reflects China's insertion into a regional production network for export activity with both domestic and foreign investors exploiting China's comparative advantage in low cost labour. Consequently, China has a central role as a processing and assembly location for inputs imported from other emerging Asian economies, which are then re-exported to mature economy markets with a new value about 20 to 30 percent higher than their original value. China is also very well integrated with commodity exporters such as Canada, Peru and Australia. India, by contrast, is less integrated with other economies, particularly other Asian economies, than suggested by fundamentals.

A key difference between the roles of India and China in global trade in goods is their uneven ability to climb the technological ladder. Since the early 1990s, China has increasingly specialized in high-tech goods, while India has continued to concentrate on low-tech exports. From a global perspective, China is becoming a dominant player for both high-tech and low-tech goods. In 2004, China became one of the world's first exporters of high-tech goods, together with the Euro area and the United States. In addition, China has become the second largest exporter of low-tech goods in the world, after the Euro area, owing to the strong growth in its overall exports. Thus, it can be seen that China has become a direct competitor of mature economies, while India does not. China's revealed comparative advantage is in the high-tech sector, although it still withholds a relatively strong comparative advantage in the low-tech sector. This makes China's exports comparable with those of mature economies, which also have high indices in the high-tech sector. China's export basket has switched towards high-tech exports and that the share of high-tech goods China exports is now significantly higher than would be expected given its income level.

Within product markets, Chinese exports to the United States have lower prices than exports from the Organisation for Economic Cooperation and Development (OECD) countries (OECD is an intergovernmental economic organization with 37 member countries, founded in 1961 to stimulate economic progress and world trade), suggesting that OECD exporters attempt to react to competition from Chinese products by producing goods with a higher technological content. Chinese exports are also comparable with those of several other emerging Asian economies, probably echoing the complementarities between China and its neighbours within the "Asian production chain". By contrast, India has a revealed comparative advantage in the medium and especially low-tech sectors. This makes India's exports closer to those of non-Asian emerging economies, such as Brazil, Russia, Tunisia and Turkey. The different nature of India's and China's respective competitors in goods markets can be further illustrated by a synthetic measure of economic distance between countries in terms of export composition. China is close to markets of many emerging Asian economies, such as South Korea, Taiwan, Thailand, Indonesia and Singapore. On the other hand, India is found not to be particularly close to any economy, whether emerging or mature, its Euclidian distance always being higher than (or equal to) that of China. This is because India's export structure has thus far been highly concentrated on one category of goods (jewellery, works of art), which accounts for 20 percent of total Indian exports but only 1.4 percent of world trade.

The composition of Chinese and Indian imports also matters when it comes to evaluating the impact of their development on the rest of the world. Chinese imports are particularly rich in electronic components (partly because of processing trade activities). China also heavily imports manufactured goods that are essential to its economic development, such as specialized machines or electrical apparatus. This could have beneficial effects on Japanese exports, in particular, which are strong in these two categories. Also, China imports significant quantities of commodities such as iron, steel, non-ferrous metals and ores, and plastics. Accordingly, strong demand from China is often seen as a key driver of the rise in world commodity prices. By contrast, India does not import many electronic and investment goods. Neither does the Indian economy imports many primary products, except non-monetary gold, presumably owing to its production of jewellery and works of art. With regard to oil imports, India imports proportionally more crude oil than China—this category accounts for 27 percent of goods imports, compared with 6.3 percent in the case of China.

Trade in Services: China's role in trade in services also remains more important than that of India, although the latter is growing rapidly but only in deregulated sectors such as IT and IT-enabled services—India's flagship of integration into global trade. In 2006, China accounted for a larger share of global trade in services than India, 3.1 percent compared with 2.7 percent. However, India's share has been rising very markedly since the turn of the millennium. Over the last four years it has more than doubled in the wake of the liberalization of the telecom and IT sectors by India. In line with this, both India and China already rank among the top ten exporters of services in the world. Furthermore, India is the most specialized economy among the world's main exporters of services, which account for about 38 percent of India's total exports, compared with 32 percent in the case of the United Kingdom and 29 percent in that of the United States, the world's leading exporters of services. In China, by contrast, services represent only 9 percent of total exports, given the even larger magnitude of manufacturing exports. Fifteen years ago, India's and China's shares were roughly equal (at 16 percent and 20 percent, respectively), which suggests that India's specialization in services is rising sharply over time.

The take-off in India's services exports is mostly dependent on deregulated sectors, mainly IT and IT-enabled services. By contrast, China's exports of services are more broad-based and somewhat complementary to its manufacturing exports, thereby reflecting its importance in global trade in goods. IT-related exports have increased sharply in India since the late 1990s. The sector has been among the fastest-growing in the economy at close to 30 percent per year since the late 1990s, with its contribution to output doubling from close to 2 percent to 5 percent. At the same time, direct employment has grown by over one million from about 280,000 to 1,300,000, although this is barely 1 percent of the labour force. In 2006, the service sector had contributed over USD 36 billion in revenues, of which one-quarter from business process outsourcing activities. Exports accounted for two-thirds of all revenues, with the main destinations being the Americas (70 percent) and Europe (8 percent, including the United Kingdom). Notwithstanding, India's export performance in the other types of services has stalled. To a great extent, this reflects the fact that a large share of India's services is still in the informal sector, is often not open to competition (both in terms of market entry and labour regulation) and, thereby, scarcely productive. On the other hand, in China, a large variety of services exports has experienced strong growth in the last decade. China is notably strong in IT services exports and has emerged as a potential rival to India. It is strong in (maritime) transportation, which is seemingly linked to its increasingly large role as a manufacturing hub in Asia. Reflecting these complementarities, it is interesting to note that services exports in China have grown hand-in-hand with goods exports, as their ratio has remained broadly stable over time. On the other hand, in India the ratio of IT services exports to IT goods exports has sharply risen over time, underscoring its increasing specialization in, and dependence on, this particular service activity.

India's and China's Roles in Global Finance: India's and China's roles in the global financial system are far more limited compared to their prominent roles in global trade. In certain areas they mirror the differences in India's and China's integration into global trade. As an overall measure, India's and China's international investment position, which captures the two countries' total external assets and liabilities, suggests that both economies are still relatively small players in global finance. In 2005, China's creditor position vis-à-vis foreigners stood at below USD 300 billion, around 13 percent of its GDP and less than 19 percent of the net foreign assets of Japan, which is the world's largest creditor economy. Unlike China, India is a debtor vis-à-vis the rest of the world. In 2005, India's debtor position was about USD 50 billion, around 6 percent of its GDP, which was less than 2 percent of the net foreign liabilities of the United States, the world's largest debtor economy.

However, one area where India's and China's roles in the global financial system is evident, is their large and growing reserve holdings, which dominate on the asset side of both economies' international investment position. In 2005, China's reserve holdings accounted for about 37 percent of

GDP, compared with 20 percent of GDP in the case of India. In this respect, China's reserve holdings surpassed the USD 1 trillion mark in October 2006 to reach about USD 1.1 trillion in December 2006. India has recently been one of the fastest reserve accumulators. In 2017, India's reserve assets have quintupled to reach nearly USD 426.0824 billion. India's holdings are largest than those of Singapore or Hong Kong, making it the seventh largest holder of reserves in the world. However, a major difference between the two economies lies in the origin of the reserves accumulated. Since 2000 about two-thirds of China's reserves have originated from current account surpluses, while the remaining third has stemmed from private capital inflows, essentially foreign direct investment. Conversely, the bulk of India's reserve accumulation has originated from hefty private capital inflows, mostly portfolio flows and bank lending, while current account surpluses have turned into deficits since 2005. Their large reserve holdings aside, both India and China hold little other foreign assets. This stems partly from capital account restrictions, for example, Indian banks are not allowed to acquire foreign assets, rather they are encouraged to hold government bonds in order to lower the cost of financing public deficits. Accordingly, India and China hold relatively small amounts of foreign equities (both securities and foreign direct investment) and foreign debt securities (in the order of 8 percent of GDP in the case of China and 2 percent of GDP in that of India). Foreign bank loans outstanding (included in the category 'other investment assets') are of a similarly small magnitude.

While their foreign assets are rather similar, India's and China's foreign liabilities are markedly different, which translates into uneven risk exposures. Foreign direct investments are China's dominant source of foreign liabilities, accounting for 27 percent of its GDP. Given that foreign direct investment is of a rather long-term nature, China's exposure to volatility in international capital flows is relatively contained. Reflecting this, the activity of foreign portfolio investors in China is limited by capital controls, although since late 2002 restrictions have been gradually lifted, in particular in the equity market. Debt markets also remain highly regulated, since debt flows are considered by authorities as potentially volatile. Unlike China's, the composition of India's foreign liabilities is more diverse, ranging from foreign direct investment and equity securities (each accounting for around 7 percent of GDP) to bank lending (about 15 percent of GDP). In particular, registered foreign institutional investors are allowed portfolio investments through stock exchanges and debentures, albeit subject to ceilings. However, restrictions on purchases by foreigners in the government and corporate bond markets are much stricter. The higher share of portfolio equity in India's foreign liabilities suggests that it is, perhaps, more exposed than China to volatility in international capital flows.

In line with India's and China's relatively modest roles in the global financial system, Indian and Chinese securities account for a relatively minor share of global portfolios, although their importance is growing. Gross purchases of Chinese equities by foreigners have risen six-fold since the mid-1990s, reaching about USD 30 billion in 2006. At the same time, equity inflows into India have doubled to reach about USD 10 billion. Taken together, India and China account for about 20 percent of cross-border holdings of foreign mutual funds dedicated to emerging economy equities. Reflecting the prevalence of capital controls, equity markets in both countries are still largely dominated by domestic investors. Foreign mutual fund holdings of Chinese equities were USD 39 billion in late 2006. This represented only about 3 percent of the combined capitalization of the Shanghai and Shenzhen stock markets. Likewise, foreign mutual funds held USD 28 billion in Indian equities (about 7 percent of the capitalization of the Mumbai stock market) in 2006. However, taken together, these amounts were still very small by global standards. Owing to the capital controls, bond inflows remained small, averaging below USD 1 billion to China, while those to India were negligible.

Foreign Direct Investment and Complementarities with Role in Global Trade: One of the most distinctive features between India's and China's roles in the global financial system is foreign direct investment. China has attracted much more foreign direct investment than India to date, which has been central to the development of its export-oriented manufacturing sector and, thereby, growth performance. Promoting inward foreign direct investment was one of the early steps made by China towards financial liberalization in the 1980s and 1990s, on account of its contribution to technology transfer and export promotion, and its putative stability effect. There are now no major restrictions on inward foreign direct investments to China, which has helped the economy become the world's third largest recipient of such investments.

Foreign direct investment in India amounting to USD 12 billion, is only 18 percent of that of China. One reason for India being less attractive is that foreign direct investment remains subject to a range of restrictions. In certain strategic sectors, including atomic energy, FDI is prohibited, whereas in a wide range of other sectors it is subjected to ceilings.

A common trait of foreign direct investment in both India and China is its concentration in terms of investor countries. Since the turn of the millennium, about one-third of the investment flows received by India and China have originated in Mauritius and Hong Kong, respectively. This underscores the importance of these offshore centers as entry points for investment into India and China, as well as the existence of round-tripping activities. Another one-third of investment flows to China comes from the Chinese diaspora and, therefore, would unlikely be invested elsewhere. The rest is related to vertical integration and China's role as a processing and assembly location for inputs imported from other emerging Asian economies. The sectoral allocation of foreign direct investment follows rather different patterns and perhaps mirrors India's and China's roles in global trade. FDI in China is concentrated in the manufacturing sector, which received about two-thirds of investment flows between 1999 and 2006. Electronic equipment and the textile industries together received one-fifth of such investment, mirroring China's ability to exploit its comparative advantage in labour-intensive products. By contrast, investment flows to India are relatively more diverse. As many as four sectors received one-half of all foreign direct investment flows in the period 2000-06, namely electrical equipment, the transportation industries and, in particular, services and telecommunications. The importance of the latter two sectors echoes India's strong performance in services exports.

China is increasingly investing abroad, a further sign of its growing role in the global economy, while India lags somewhat behind. Investment patterns seem to echo India's and China's roles in global trade, at least in part. Since 2001, China has started to liberalise outward investment relating to projects of national strategic importance. China's direct investments abroad, typically in the order of USD 3 billion per year from the mid-1980s to 2004, rose to USD 120.08 billion in 2017. India's direct investments abroad were more modest, amounting to about USD 46.8 billion in 2017. A large share of these investments was destined to other emerging economies, while mature economies received a much smaller share. China's investments in the Euro area, Japan and the United States together accounted for about only 3 percent of the country's foreign direct investment. A large share (one-third) of China's investment abroad involved strategic resources (mining), probably with a view to catering for the growing energy needs generated by the economy's rapid development and its orientation towards exports of manufactured goods. However, some other sectors were involved, including leasing and commercial services, as well as manufacturing, each with a share of one-fifth. Data on recent mergers and acquisitions by Indian and Chinese companies confirm these broad trends. The bulk of mergers and acquisitions initiated by Indian and Chinese companies targeted other emerging economy companies (42 percent and 78 percent, respectively). Euro area companies were more frequently targeted by Indian companies than by Chinese companies and accounted for

28 percent of the targets of the former, compared with 18 percent in the case of the latter. However, the market value of the mergers and acquisitions targeting Euro area companies and initiated by Chinese companies was double that of those initiated by Indian companies. In terms of sector choice, a large share (two-thirds) of China's mergers and acquisitions abroad targeted strategic resources, including oil, gas, chemicals and basic resources. The sector targets of Indian companies were more diverse, with telecommunications, technology and consumer services accounting for the largest share (almost 40 percent), the smaller share of strategic resources in India likely reflecting the stronger orientation of the economy towards services.

CHAPTER 12

Regional Competition and Cooperation

India and China, two oldest civilization-states and once great powers of the world, are back as claimants to preeminence in Asia and the world. Now, both are contributing a greater part in the global economy and possess nuclear powers with expanding military capabilities to match their growing ambitions. However, they have a paradoxical and challenging relationship, where growing cooperation goes hand in hand with mounting rivalries. Only during the last few years, they have begun to shed their wariness toward each other by initiating measures to stabilize their relationship, including regular high-level visits. This rapprochement is based on a mutual need to focus on social and political stability, and strong economic growth and a sense of security, so each of them can avoid the perils of stagnation or decline.

During a visit to India in 2015, Chinese Premier Wen Jiabao said that there is enough space in the world for the development of both China and India. This statement clearly highlights that the two countries have developed a shared common conception of their role on the global stage. As two large developing countries, India and China are aware of each other's role in the process of promoting the establishment of a new international political and economic order. They are supportive of the democratization of international relations and multilateralism, establishment of a new international political and economic order that is fair, rational, equal and mutually beneficial, and promotion of North-South Dialogue and South-South Cooperation. They have also agreed at the time that the United Nations should undergo comprehensive reform, with emphasis on increasing the representation of developing countries.

The incipient India-China entente has the potential to radically alter these countries security environment and restructure Asian geopolitics. However, India-China ties remain fragile and as vulnerable as ever to sudden deterioration as a result of misperceptions, unrealistic expectations, and eruption of unresolved issues. Internal issues of stability and the external overlapping spheres of influence forestall the chances for a genuine India-China rapprochement. The issues that bind these two countries are also the issues that divide them and fuel their rivalry. With their ever-expanding economies and widening geopolitical horizons, the bilateral relationship between the two rising Asian giants could be characterized more by competition than cooperation. As India and China are moving ahead simultaneously on their relative power trajectories, geopolitical equations and power relations in Asia are bound to undergo significant realignment. Despite growing interaction at the political, cultural, and economic levels, the gulf between the two countries, in terms of their perceptions, attitudes, and expectations of each other, has widened over the years. China has a deep distrust over India and it does not want to see India play a role beyond South Asia or emerge as a peer competitor. It has made its displeasure known over Southeast Asian countries' recent attempts to draw India into the region. In the power competition game, China has clearly surged far ahead of India by acquiring potent economic and military capabilities and the existing asymmetry in power and status serves China's interests very well. Therefore, China has very limited expectations from India which can be described by its "five No's" principles.

(a) Don't peddle—China threat theory.

(b) Don't support Tibet or Taiwan's independence.

(c) Don't object to the China-Pakistan strategic partnership.

(d) Don't align with the United States and/or Japan to contain China.

(e) Don't see or project yourself as an equal of China or as a nuclear and economic counterweight to China in Asia.

Based on these principles, China is trying to make relationship with India as part of its friendly neighborhood strategy. China would be happy if India's relations with the United States and Israel cool off and lose the momentum that was developed in the transfer of advanced weaponry such as the Phalcon airborne early warning system to India.

On the other hand, for India, emotions range from the euphoria of misperceived India-China brotherhood in the 1950s, to the bitterness of India's 1962 military defeat by China, and back again to the euphoria of imagined togetherness in the twenty-first century. With its current focus on economic progress, China is seen as a restrained power interested in managing, if not resolving, conflict. Guided by this perception, India hopes that intensifying trade and commerce would facilitate a resolution to their protracted boundary dispute. India also believes that a sound India-China relationship will help induce Pakistan into a negotiated settlement of the Kashmir dispute.

Though, India and China are competitors for power and influence in Asia, they also share common goals of maintaining regional stability, maintaining access to capital and markets, and benefiting from globalization. Cooperation will allow them to balance the influence of United States and increase their negotiating positions with the sole superpower.

Continued hostility between India and Pakistan, China's involvement in the India-Pakistan conflicts, and competition between the superpowers had turned South Asia into a significant area for rivalry between India and China. In the wake of the 1962 India-China war and the China-Soviet split, China chose to go with Pakistan to counter India, as well as to retain its influence in South Asia. Thus, China became involved in India-Pakistan conflict. As the competition for regional leadership remains a significant element in post-Cold War India-China relations, the regional competition has contributed a culture of rivalry between India and China. Also, India-China interaction on regional issues reveals both the country's asymmetrical perceptions of threat. India tends to be mired in the traditional security concept that China is seeking to enclose India in a South Asian straitjacket by engaging other South Asian states. On the other hand, China appears comparatively confident about threats from India although it is mindful of India's relations with ASEAN states and Japan.

Over the years bilateral relations between India and China have improved, but they still have misgivings about each other's engagement with their neighbours. India keeps a wary eye on China's ties with its South Asian neighbours, especially Pakistan. Both India and Pakistan saw threats emanating from each other as being major threats to their security. China and Pakistan still see each other as reliable partners whenever India-Pakistan relations sour. As a result, China-Pakistan relationship, especially China-Pakistani arms nexus, has been a cause of grave concern for India. China also encouraged other smaller South Asian states such as Nepal and Bangladesh to stand up to India's aspiration to dominate South Asia. India's longstanding conflicts with other South Asian states would drain and weaken India and, thus, serve China's strategic interests. However, from the Indian point of view, China has consistently sought to constrain Indian power and confine it essentially to the region of South Asia.

On the other hand, China is concerned with India's increasing efforts to extend its influence eastward and is conscious of the ongoing deep engagement between India and other Asian countries. While China has issues with some of its marine neighbours over the South China Sea, India has embarked on a "Look East" policy to engage the ASEAN states of Japan, South Korea and Taiwan. In addition to the traditional antagonism in South Asia, Southeast Asia emerges as a new area of India-China competition. Thus, along with the competitive dimension, there is linkage between the perception of threat and cooperation in India-China relations. In fact, India and China have reasons to cooperate even over regional issues. In addition to geopolitical competition, sub-regional economic cooperation and anti-terrorism campaigns have been added to the agenda of India-China relations in recent years. These developments, along with China's cautious neutrality towards the India-Pakistan conflict, show that India and China are willing to scale down their enmity. Hence, from a regional perspective, India and China are not always bound to clash in their journey from regional to global power. They are acting as both competitors and partners in regional affairs. India-China relations are a mixture of competition and cooperation, although the latter might be somewhat less noticeable.

India's Look East Policy

Feeling pressure from China's engagement with South Asian states, India has been able to take some balancing initiatives to counter its perceived encirclement by China. For example, it has tried to strengthen its engagement with China's neighbouring states, such as the countries in East Asia, to put pressure on China's security environment and, thus, distracting China. In the early 1990s, when India began to undertake economic reforms, there was an appraisal of India's policy towards the countries in East Asia. The steady economic development of the region, especially before the financial crisis, attracted much of India's attention. Against this backdrop, P.V. Narasimha Rao's government unveiled the "Look East Policy" to revive India's relations with East Asia, particularly ASEAN states. During the initial phase, this policy had gained favourable results on the economic and trade fronts, and in 1992, India became a Sectoral Dialogue Partner of ASEAN. The two sides had identified four broad sectors for cooperation—trade, investment, science and technology, and tourism—that had the aim of contributing to a closer economic link between India and ASEAN countries. Japan, Korea and ASEAN countries also emerged as a lucrative export market and source of foreign investments for India.

As India embarked on the Look East Policy to reach out to countries in East Asia, it showed its ambition to extend its influence beyond the subcontinent and identified Southeast Asia as its "extended neighbourhood" with strategic implications for India and wished to maintain the momentum of the Look East Policy to forge a closer partnership with ASEAN countries. It can be seen that geography inevitably predetermines India as having close and cooperative relations with countries of ASEAN and the Asia-Pacific region. This policy could be seen as one of India's successful geo-strategies because India's relations with the countries in the region have since improved significantly. This policy also provides a possible approach for India to challenge China's status in the region. On the other hand, China is closely monitoring India-ASEAN ties to prevent the formation of an anti-China collaboration in the region.

Security Dimension of Look East Policy: The economic interactions between India and ASEAN countries might have slowed down with the Southeast Asian economic meltdown, but India changed its previous perceptions of ASEAN countries and so tended to attribute more significance to relations with ASEAN countries. As a result, in October 2003, India joined the Treaty of Amity and Cooperation in Southeast Asia. In November 2004, India and ASEAN further concluded the "India-ASEAN Partnership for Peace, Progress and Shared Prosperity". This signifies India's commitment to work with ASEAN countries in maintaining regional peace and stability. In 2005, India was also allowed to take part in the East Asia Summit. Meanwhile, the economic and trade fronts remain as important elements of the relations between India and ASEAN countries. In 2003, India and ASEAN signed the Framework Agreement on Comprehensive Economic Cooperation, which aimed to establish a free trade area by 2011. An India-ASEAN Free Trade Agreement (FTA) in goods was signed in August 2009, besides India has been actively conducting bilateral FTA negotiations with the countries in the region. For example, India signed a bilateral FTA agreement with Thailand in July 2003, and the Comprehensive Economic Cooperation Agreement with Singapore in June 2005. India has also concluded trade-related institutional arrangements with Vietnam, Philippines, Laos, Myanmar and Malaysia. With the conclusion of such arrangements, India is poised for greater economic integration with ASEAN countries and the region.

The Look East Policy of India was premised on trade and economic interaction with Southeast Asian nations, but subsequently it expanded to other areas of common interest. Despite the economic engagement, during India's search for an association with new friends in the region, security ties and military cooperation have been identified as being among the areas of India-ASEAN cooperation. However, the motivation for the Look East Policy was primarily economical, but the political relations and security ties between India and the ASEAN nations have also gradually progressed. On security and political front, India joined the ASEAN Regional Forum (ARF) in 1996, which is an organization aimed at fostering dialogue and consultation on political and security issues of common interest and concern, and at making significant contributions to efforts towards confidence-building and preventative diplomacy in the Asia-Pacific region. In 1996, India was accepted as a full dialogue partner of ASEAN and participated for the first time in the Post Ministerial Conference (PMC) of ASEAN in Jakarta. The first India-ASEAN summit was held in 2002 and India became the fourth country, after China, Japan and South Korea, to establish the summit mechanism with ASEAN.

India has also shown interest in strengthening military cooperation with ASEAN nations by offering training slots to ASEAN nations and holding joint military exercises with them, which have over the years increased in scope and content, and at the same time enhanced interoperability. Conducting the exercises has been institutionalized between India and Singapore, and joint patrols continue with Indonesia and Thailand. In addition, India has also made military relations with Vietnam and Myanmar. For example, during the Indian Defence Minister George Fernandes' visit to Vietnam in March 2000, the two countries signed a wide-ranging agreement paving the way for greater military cooperation, which included the sale of advanced military light helicopters, assisting in the repair and overhaul of Vietnam's mainstay MiG fighters and raising the level of military contacts.

Due to its common border with India and China, Myanmar has traditionally sought to maintain a balance between these two neighbours. But, both India and China want to have Myanmar as their ally against the other state. India sees China's aid to Myanmar as China's intention to infiltrate its military strength as far as the Indian Ocean. For example, with China's help, Myanmar is expanding its naval facilities in Great Coco Island, which is the site of a major signals intelligence facility situated near India's Andaman and Nicobar Islands. To counterbalance

China's strategic link, India has also increased its cooperation with the Myanmar Military Junta. Particularly, there has been a substantial increase in bilateral defence cooperation between the Indian Army and the Myanmar Army in training and other fields. There have been exchanges of high-level visits, such as that of the Indian Chief of the Army Staff to Myanmar and the Commander in Chief of the Myanmar Navy to India. India is also willing to expand the ambit of military cooperation between the two countries, including military transfers, and has promised to give a favourable response to the Myanmar Government's request for military equipment. In April 2007, the Indian and Myanmar security forces had conducted joint military operations along the 1643 km India-Myanmar border to neutralize insurgent groups. Thus, India's impulses to continue "Look East Policy" are not only dictated by the economic engagement, but also are grounded in the consideration of geopolitics.

The expansion of India's profile in the defence sector has created interests among the regional powers in partnering with India. China thinks that ASEAN nations welcome Indian military presence in this region because they consider that India could contribute to maintain the balance of power. This is why ASEAN nations did not follow the United States or Japan's example in criticizing India's nuclear tests of 1998. China interpreted the mild response by ASEAN nations as their acknowledgement of India as a rising political power that has near-parity with China and a balance against its influence. India has gradually revealed its potential as an economic power and now it is ASEAN nations that are turning to India. The region sees India as one of its growing partners in trade and as a major source for future investments.

There are two major drives behind India's Look East Policy.

(a) The essence of this policy is the recognition that India's aspirations for a larger global role cannot be realized while its foreign policy and national security preoccupations are limited to the subcontinent. It is a necessary step if India wishes to achieve the goal of being a world power. India has also to establish closer contacts with the relevant region to prevent marginalization in the context of the trend towards regionalism. In other words, this policy is part of India's grand strategy for securing global-power status.

(b) This policy became one of India's ploys to counter China's "omnidirectional pressure". The presence of India's navy in the South China Sea was a particular source of concern to China. India's navy stayed in the South China Sea even after concluding a joint military exercise with Singapore, Vietnam and so on. Given the territorial disputes between China and some ASEAN nations, it was argued that India's attempt to maintain a substantial military presence in the South China Sea would have a profound and long-term implications for China's policies towards the region.

India commands the geo-strategic location at the heart of the world's vital commercial shipping lanes in the Indian Ocean and can play a significant role in the safety of the "new silk route", which extends from the Persian Gulf and straddles the Indian Ocean till it enters the Strait of Malacca, the gateway to South-East Asia. Given the high stakes involved in the uninterrupted flow of commercial shipping, India's area of interest extends from north of the Arabian Sea to the South China Sea. The overlapping claims over the sovereignty of the oil-rich Spratly Islands in the South China Sea have placed additional pressure on China's security. China does not want to see countries in the region working together with outside powers against China over the South China Sea issue, therefore it has a deep concern about the propensity of India to extend its areas of operation and interests eastward to the South China Sea. China, looking at the South China Sea as its special domain, does not like India's presence in the area. The improvement in India-ASEAN relations and the establishment of a cooperative partnership have made China's security environment more complicated, putting pressure upon China's western and southern regions, challenging China's maritime security, and increasing its difficulty in solving the boundary problem and the territorial claims in the South China Sea.

Nuclear Proliferation and Military Competition

China's nuclear and missile proliferation is one of the most important sources of contention for India. It is the adversarial nature of the India-China relationship that has driven India's and Pakistan's nuclear weapons program. Majority of Western powers have grudgingly acknowledged India's *de facto* nuclear status, but China shows no sign of softening its demand that India should initiate a complete rollback of its nuclear weapons program and unconditionally participate in the Comprehensive Test Ban Treaty (CTBT) and the Nuclear Non-Proliferation Treaty (NPT) as a Non-Nuclear Weapons State. China always objected India's entry into the exclusive Nuclear Five Club and distanced itself from any move that would acknowledge, legalize, or legitimize India's status as a Nuclear Weapons State. It has also consistently rejected India's proposals for bilateral nuclear confidence-building measures (CBMs). It has also objected India's call for a "common nuclear doctrine for India, China and Pakistan based on no-first-use (NFU) pledge". The idea of a common nuclear doctrine, though impractical and unrealistic given their different security imperatives, talks of "credible, transparent, and verifiable CBMs in treaty form to minimize the risk of nuclear and missile conflict with China or Pakistan". China has withdrawn its NFU pledge to India in 1995 when it amended its nuclear doctrine to make the NFU pledge applicable only to NPT member-states. Since neither China nor Pakistan follows a policy of NFU of nuclear weapons vis-à-vis India, India wants to bind them to an NFU pledge.

It is ironical that China demands India's denuclearization, but itself is continuing to proliferate in violation of its legal commitments under the NPT. China has also offered nuclear reactors to Pakistan despite growing international concern over Pakistan's troubling nuclear proliferation record. On the positive side, a regular security dialogue has begun, and navies of India and China have conducted their first search and rescue exercise in November 2003. In March 2004, the two countries agreed to enhance bilateral defense relations and, for the first time, granted observer status to military officers at each other's exercises. India and China have supported Europe's challenge to

American space supremacy by investing Euro 300 million and 200 million respectively in the Galileo global satellite navigation system. Both see the Galileo project as a real alternative to the *de facto* monopoly of the American Global Positioning System (GPS) and the Russian GLONASS system.

However, Indian and Chinese militaries view each other as future rivals and each point to threatening trends and behaviour in the other. Both countries keep a close watch on changes in military doctrines, defense spending, capabilities and related activities and remain committed to neutralizing perceived security gains of the other side. They support nuclear disarmament but continue to expand their own nuclear arsenals and capabilities. Possession of nuclear arsenals may be vital to preserving strategic autonomy for India and China, but it also raises the stakes in their competitive relationship.

Energy Security to Maritime Rivalry

India and China are facing growing demand for energy and are locked in fierce competition for stakes in overseas oil and gas fields in Russia, Burma, Iran, Iraq, Sudan, Vietnam and Libya. For example, a USD 600 million acquisition in Angola by Indian oil company was won after a fight with a Chinese bidder. Competition between India and China has also intensified in Central and Southeast Asia as both view these regions as vital sources of natural resources and markets for their goods. But China has a lead over India both economically and diplomatically, and each has put forward its own proposals for multilateral cooperation that exclude the other. Nearly 70 percent of China's trade is through the Strait of Malacca, the Indian Ocean, and the Suez Canal. The predominance of the United States and Indian navies along these sea-lanes of communication is viewed as a major threat to Chinese security. To protect its long-term economic security interests, China is now laying the groundwork for a naval presence along maritime chokepoints in the South China Sea, the Malacca Straits, the Indian Ocean, and the Strait of Hormuz in the Persian Gulf through acquisition of naval bases in Cambodia, Burma, Bangladesh, and Pakistan. On the other hand, India has countered by promoting defense cooperation with Iran, Oman and Israel in the west while upgrading military ties with Burma, Singapore, the Maldives, Thailand, Vietnam, Taiwan, Philippines, Australia, Japan and United States in the east. Its new naval doctrine is to influence events around the Indian Ocean and beyond. Maritime competition is likely to intensify as Indian and Chinese navies show off their flag in the South China Sea and the Indian Ocean with greater frequency.

India and China in the Middle East: India and China have long lasting commercial ties with the Middle East. However, it is only in 1993, as China became a net oil importer country, that the Middle East countries took a strategic importance, and that China gave up its ideological foreign policy for a more pragmatic approach based on its internal development and stability. Today, both India's and China's relationships with the Middle East are mainly, but not exclusively, based on energy. To meet their increasing energy requirements, both countries have become increasingly dependent on the supply from the Middle East countries and their energy diplomacy has been playing a crucial role in their global foreign policy. First, on an economic point of view, the economic growth of India and China opened the Middle East countries to new export markets for their oil and investors, at a time where the West started losing its economic attractiveness. Secondly, it has counterbalanced the United States' hegemony over the region—on the one hand giving a new importance to countries such as Iran, which remained in the shadow of the American sanctions, and on the other hand putting Western companies in direct competition with Asian firms in countries such as Saudi Arabia which were considered as part of the Western sphere of influence.

Indian and Chinese policies in the Middle East are rather characterized by fragmented, bilateral relations, and their relations with the Middle East countries are based on the mutual respect for sovereignty and non-intervention in internal affairs, and consequently mainly about mutual economic interests. However, it does not mean that they are excluding all political or strategic considerations.

In spite of adopting similar approaches towards their relations with the Middle East countries, India and China remain competitors, in a region already faced by fierce international competition. First of all, they compete for oil. Both have encouraged their state-owned companies to acquire so-called "equity oil" contracts at premium prices in order to be able to control the production and the prices. This approach has exposed them to criticism from the West, which considers it to be a distortion of market mechanisms and which repeatedly encouraged them to respect the rules of the international market. In this competition, Chinese companies have so far proven to be more efficient than Indian ones, who lost several contracts against their Chinese competitors. Yadavaran oilfield in Iran seems to be a perfect illustration of the ongoing India-China competition, but also potential cooperation. In Yadavaran oilfield, Indian companies have 20% stake whereas their Chinese counterpart has 50% stake.

Thus, India has succeeded in developing a real strategic relationship with Iran while maintain a good working relationship with the United States. India has been developing a defence and military cooperation with Iran since 2001. This can be explained by the geographical position of Iran at the Western border of Pakistan, and by the strategic interest of India to have allies within the Muslim world which could support it in case of war over Kashmir. Concerning the China-Iran relationship, it has been suffering of the consequences of the American pressure on China during the Iranian crisis, which has led China to officially stop supporting Iranian nuclearization since 2006.

If India-Iran partnership is on a better track than China-Iran one, China on the contrary is in a better position in Saudi Arabia, which has replaced Iran as China's major supplier in 2009. On the other hand, politically the relations between India and Saudi Arabia have been not so good due to the Saudi support to Pakistan, and financing of Islamic schools in India at a time of increasing internal interreligious conflicts. Yet India considers Saudi Arabia as a possible counterweight to Pakistan in the Islamic world.

The most important and strategic issue of competition between India and China is the control of the Indian Ocean, of the main Sea Lanes of Transportation, and of the Straits of

Hormuz through which 80 percent of the oil passes, and of Malacca through which 70 percent of Chinese oil passes. India and China worry that a blockade of these chokepoints would lead to supply disruption. The Indian Ocean region, through which most of the oil passes, is considered by India as its natural zone of influence, and by China as a strategic zone that needs to be controlled. Therefore, a fierce competition exists between China which considers India's claim as illegitimate as illustrated by the quote of the Chinese General Chi Haotin according to which the Indians must understand that "it is Indian Ocean not India's Ocean", and India which sees itself encircled from all sides by the Chinese construction of ports. While India has engaged itself in modernization of its navy, in which it has been supported by the United States in the framework of the Indo-US defence cooperation agreement signed in 2005, China has been leading a policy called by the United States and India "The String of Pearls Strategy", consisting in participating in the construction of infrastructure in strategic ports in countries along the Sea Lanes of Communication, in order to secure their oil supply. China has been building ports in Myanmar, Cambodia, Bangladesh, and the most important is the Deep-Water Sea Port at Gwadar in Pakistan, 400 km from the strait of Hormuz, which can be used as a means to avoid the Malacca Strait and to diminish the cost of sea transportation, by transporting the oil and gas through land to China.

As a response to Gwadar Port, India has collaborated with Iran to build the Port of Chabahar, which is also very strategically located and would represent both a strategic point for alternative routes of transportation, and a strategic point in case of a war with Pakistan. The Iran-Pakistan-India pipeline projects, which is so far victim of poor India-Pakistan relations, Pakistan's internal security, and American pressure in favour of the alternative Turkmenistan-Afghanistan-Pakistan-India pipeline, is another sign of the well-functioning Indo-Iranian cooperation.

Thus, there is a tough competition for transportation routes, which gives to the Indian Ocean and Central Asian regions a strategic importance. In these sectors, the role of the United States and of Pakistan is central, and the evolution of their positions will have an essential influence on future developments. The Indo-American cooperation seems to place India in a comfortable position in the Indian Ocean, while the Sino-Pakistan cooperation could give China an advantage once the Gwadar port will really be operational.

Due to competition for energy markets between China and India within the Middle East, the prices of oil and gas had increased. To deal with such situation, in 2005, India and China had developed a dialogue on energy cooperation under Indian initiative. In the same year, they signed the Sino-Indian partnership for peace and prosperity and have since then conducted several joint military exercises in the Indian Ocean. These developments, if one can doubt whether they really reflect the reality of the India-China relationship, illustrate the reciprocal awareness of the needs for cooperation in areas where both have mutual interests. For example, Chinese and Indian oil companies jointly purchased shares of 36 Syrian oilfields. The Syrian joint venture was their first common acquirement of oil assets.

Regional Cooperation between India and China

Common interests between India and China far outweigh their differences, so both countries could focus on expanding cooperation rather than fighting over differences. As far as the geographic proximity is concerned, it not only generates competition between India and China, but also presents an opportunity for cooperation in some areas. According to Chinese President Jiang Zemin, geographic proximity could be an advantage for China-India cooperation, along with the vast land masses, rich natural resources, large populations and huge markets. Unfortunately, in the past, border disputes have prevented both sides from exploring the possibility of benefiting more from their geographic proximity. In order to move forward India-China relations away from the notion of competition and towards cooperation, both countries are seeking opportunities to make use of the geographical advantages, rather than focusing on the disputes. In a development likely to forge more benign interactions, India and China are working to place the issues regarding regional cooperation on their agenda, with the expectation of imparting additional momentum to improve their relations.

Anti-Terrorism Cooperation: India and China have a common concern over malignant cross-border activities. During Chinese President Jiang Zemin's visit to India in 1996, India and China signed an agreement on combating drug trafficking. The common willingness to combat Islamic militancy and fundamentalists emanating from Central Asia and Afghanistan is likely to provide a fillip to the India-China relationship. Although both the countries have worked hard to repress the terrorist activities in their respective regions, the internal-external linkage has created difficulties. External sympathetic groups in Central Asian states, Afghanistan, and Pakistan have provided sanctuary, support, and training for the terrorists. Therefore, seeking international cooperation to block extremist movements inside their own territories and cut the links across the border is a fundamental aspect of China's and India's policies to combat cross-border terrorism.

China has expressed its willingness to share intelligence with India on terrorism in Kashmir and unrest in Northeast in exchange for India's intelligence on the Uighur separatists. The first India-China counter-terrorism dialogue took place in April 2002 and the second was held in June 2003. However, the extent to which the dialogue mechanism can being India and China closer remains debatable. The key to further cooperation on counter-terrorism will depend on whether the two countries can reconcile their differences over the definition of terrorism. China tends to equate religious extremists and national separatists with international terrorists. Therefore, according to the Chinese definition, there is no difference between Uighur and Tibetan separatists and both should be crushed without mercy. But it is difficult for India to accept this sort of concept in view of fact that India still provides sanctuary to the Dalai Lama and his government-in-exile.

China has claimed that it opposes all forms of terrorism, no matter when, where or in what form terrorism strikes, and no matter against whom it is directed. But this definition finds China difficult to assent to India's definition regarding international terrorism, particularly its accusations about Pakistan. China has dismissed the charge that Pakistan has rendered training to the Uighur terrorists, and will not agree to expand the war on terrorism to include Pakistan. Chinese sensitivity to the issue is evident from the fact that the Chinese officials play down the significance of this dialogue mechanism on countering terrorism. Such differences could exacerbate divisions between India and China and limit the scope of cooperation. Since both India and China insist that there should be no double standards in addressing the issue of terrorism, they have to forge a consensus on the definition of terrorism. However, the common course of anti-terrorism has provided a platform for the two countries. The armies of two countries conducted the first-ever India-China Joint Anti-Terrorism Training Code named "Hand-in-Hand 2007" in December 2007 in Kunming, China's Yunnan province. It was followed by the "Hand-in-Hand 2008" joint military training and exercise at Belgaum in Karnataka, India.

The Kunming Initiative: The improved relations between India and China since the late 1980s and the introduction of India's economic reform have provided a new setting for stronger economic engagement. By focusing on economic development, China has been keen to promote sub-regional economic cooperation by adopting an opening-up policy towards its neighbouring countries. For example, back in 1991, Sichuan's officials had publicly demanded that the entire region of Southwest China should be open up for India, along with Myanmar, Bangladesh, Pakistan, Thailand and Malaysia. Similarly, Yunnan's officials said they wanted to make the province an "international hub" for transport through Southeast Asia and the South Asian subcontinent. Like Southwest China, India's Northeast region comprising the seven states of Assam, Arunachal Pradesh, Manipur, Meghalaya, Mizoram, Nagaland and Tripura, is interested in engaging with contiguous regions of Bangladesh, Myanmar, Bhutan and Tibet. Economic backwardness of Northeast India has contributed to the development of various insurgencies and other riot activities, making it one of the most volatile and sensitive regions of India. The fact that this region shares less than two percent of its borders with the rest of India reflects the importance of opening it up for its neighbouring countries. Therefore, exchanges between the two land-locked sub-regions, Southwest China and Northeast India, should be increased to boost the economy. In order to transform geographic proximity into an economic advantage, some initiatives have been taken. Since, there is no common border between the two sub-regions, it was decided the engagement had to be carried out in a multilateral framework, involving a third party, such as Myanmar. The proposal centered round the theme of transportation infrastructure links and the development of a sub-regional economic integration forum, because the lack of transportation links was chiefly responsible for the sluggish growth of foreign trade between Southwest China and India.

Sub-regional economic integration is a major initiative that involves China's Sichuan and Yunnan provinces, and India's Northeastern states, Myanmar and Bangladesh. This track-II Kunming initiative, named after the capital of China's Yunnan province, came out of an academic symposium called the "Conference on Regional Cooperation and Development among China, India, Myanmar and Bangladesh". The "Kunming Initiative" was discussed and signed by the leaders of the four delegations. The main thrust of the exercise was to exhort the governments concerned to establish a forum for sub-regional economic cooperation comprising China, India, Myanmar, and Bangladesh. It was believed that the economies in the sub-region can be strengthened significantly through increased cooperation by the quadrangle.

India's and China's Cross-Border Cooperation

In the start of 21st century, there has been a seismic shift in the global order from Western economies to Asian economies in terms of economic growth. According to the World Bank report, the South Asian region has become an important player and is recognized as an economic powerhouse with remarkable development along with its ability to attract foreign investments.

In order to boost cooperation in the region, India's Cabinet Committee on Economic Affairs (CCEA) has approved for enhancement of a 65 km road project between Manipur and Myanmar. This will expedite the road connectivity program of South Asian Sub-regional Economic Cooperation (SASEC). It will also be a progressive step in the development of the Great Asian Highway, a 141000 km network of roadways connecting 32 Asian countries. On the other hand, China has joined Central Asia Regional Economic Cooperation (CAREC) program to boost its regional integration.

Central Asia Regional Economic Cooperation (CAREC) Program: It is a partnership of 11 countries—Afghanistan, Azerbaijan, China, Georgia, Kazakhstan, Kyrgyz Republic, Mongolia, Pakistan, Tajikistan, Turkmenistan, and Uzbekistan—supported by 6 multilateral institutions, working together to promote development through cooperation, leading to accelerated growth and poverty reduction. Its long-term vision is Good Neighbours, Good Partners, and Good Prospects. With the rapid economic expansion of the China and Japan to the East, the Russia to the North, and India and Pakistan to the South, there is unprecedented opportunity for CAREC countries to emerge as a center of trade and commerce, achieve higher levels of economic growth, and reduce poverty. CAREC helps Central Asia and its neighbours realize their significant potential by promoting regional cooperation in four priority areas—transport, trade facilitation, energy, and trade policy.

Greater Mekong Subregion (GMS): It comprises Cambodia, China, Laos, Myanmar, Thailand and Vietnam. In 1992, with Asian Development Bank's assistance, the six countries entered into a program of subregional economic cooperation, designed to enhance economic relations among the countries. The GMS Program, with support from Asian Development Bank and other donors, helps the implementation of high priority sub-regional projects in transport, energy, telecommunications, environment, human resource development, tourism, trade, private sector investment, and agriculture. Substantial progress has been achieved in terms of implementing GMS projects since 1992. Priority infrastructure projects worth around USD 11 billion have either been completed or are being implemented. Among these are the upgrading of the Phnom Penh (Cambodia)–Ho Chi Minh City (Vietnam) highway and the East-West Economic Corridor that will eventually extend from the Andaman Sea to Da Nang.

South Asian Sub-regional Economic Cooperation (SASEC) Initiative: Launched in 2001, it brings together Bhutan, Bangladesh, Nepal, India, the Maldives, Sri Lanka and Myanmar. It intends to boost cross-border cooperation in six priority sectors—trade, transport, information and communication technology (ICT), investment and private sector cooperation, energy and power, and the environment. Being developed with assistance from Asian Development Bank (ADB), the project-based partnership focuses on promoting regional prosperity, improving economic opportunities and providing a better quality of life to the people in the region.

To establish sustainable growth of South Asia in a climate of global uncertainties and challenges, SASEC is integral to enhance regional cooperation. SASEC's Trade Facilitation Sector Strategy and SASEC Energy Sector Strategy focus on upgrading infrastructure and promote intra-regional exchanges and cooperation. Other notable projects include North Eastern State Roads Investment Program in India, SASEC Road Connectivity Project in Nepal, SAARC Road Connectivity Project to upgrade international road corridor in Bangladesh, BBIN (Bangladesh, Bhutan, India, and Nepal) Motor Vehicles Agreement (MVA) for seamless cross-border movement of vehicles and goods, Dhaka-Chittagong Expressway Public-Private Partnership Design Project, and Air Transport Capacity Enhancement Project.

***India—A Passage for Connectivity*:** India's geographic position in South Asia makes it the only country that shares physical boundaries with all states in the region. It further functions as a bridge between Southeast Asian economies and South Asian states, including landlocked countries of Nepal and Bhutan. An important aspect of India's connectivity projects is that it focuses on its policy towards integrating the East. This demonstrates India's commitment towards its "Act East Policy", launched in November 2014 to build close-knit relations with

ASEAN nations. Partnership in this region will promote the growth of regional trade via improved connectivity that will facilitate smooth cross-border movement of goods as well as passengers thereby reducing transport costs and time.

A Response to China: The development in SASEC project comes against the backdrop of China's ambitious geostrategic initiative labelled "One Belt One Road" (OBOR), now known as Belt and Road Initiative (BRI), which proposes to connect countries from Asia to Europe through a network of rail routes, highways, oil and gas pipelines, sea lanes and port infrastructural projects. For China, this is not just an economic drive but a long-term vision of securing its continental, maritime, and geo-strategic domain. BRI is an integral part of China's economic strategy to dispose of its problem of labour surplus in its domestic industries. Besides exporting skilled and partially skilled manpower, China will also provide for the vast amount of capital and construction materials required for BRI, solving its problem of an overcapacity of unused capital. In addition, even the funding of BRI is undertaken by the Chinese led Asian Infrastructure Investment Bank (AIIB).

The BRI-SASEC Face Off: India is critical of China-Pakistan Economic Corridor (CPEC), an indispensable element of the BRI, as it passes through Gilgit and Baltistan regions of Pakistan-occupied Kashmir (PoK). While BRI is disguised as a harbinger of reverse colonization, SASEC symbolizes collective power among developing countries. SASEC rekindles the role of regional collaboration as a catalyst for growth and development.

India is currently engaged in developing two road corridors under SASEC initiative. One of them shall connect India and Nepal, Bhutan and Bangladesh through the sensitive and heavily patrolled Siliguri corridor also known as "chicken neck" area. The other will connect India and Myanmar. In line with its "Act East Policy" and with ADB as its primary financial aid, India is also developing East Coast Economic Corridor (ECEC) along its Eastern coast to establish connectivity with East and Southeast Asia. Enhancing connectivity across all dimensions—physical, regional, institutional and cultural with the South Asian community as well as the rest of Southeast Asia is a strategic and progressive move towards growth and prosperity.

The BCIM Economic Corridor: One of the major policy initiatives among Asian countries in recent years is directed towards developing sub-regional, regional and trans-regional corridors with the aim to further connect and integrate their economies. One such corridor is the Bangladesh—China—India—Myanmar Economic Corridor (BCIM-EC) involving four nations. While the former focuses on its potentials, particularly in transforming landlocked and underdeveloped border regions of the countries involved, the latter pays more attention to the strategic implications it might have on the region.

In the late 1990s some ideas emerged from China's Yunnan Province about a possible sub-regional cooperation involving Southwestern China, eastern India and the whole of Myanmar and Bangladesh. One of the first tasks was in defining this "zone" as a sub-region. The proponents of the idea argued that this zone contains a few key essential characteristics based on which cooperation at the level of sub-region could be explored. Among other features, this zone is seen as "the meeting point of the three markets of China, Southeast Asia and South Asia" and thereby connecting "two major markets of China and India and even the whole of Asia". Second, even as the sub-region suffers from poor infrastructure, its rich natural resources promise huge potential for large-scale development. Third, the sub-region is isolated from global markets and is characterized by relative poverty. Lastly, all the four countries have actively participated in regional and sub-regional organisations with the aim to integrate into the global economy. Having argued that this zone shares certain characteristics that could form the basis for cooperation, a few likely benefits were visualized, such as:

(a) It was felt that if India and China could cooperate in regional affairs through such a mechanism, it would contribute to promoting peace and stability of Asia and the world.

(b) Such cooperation at the sub-regional level could also help in rooting out social evils such as drug production and trafficking.

(c) It would also assist in the alleviation of poverty and promote social development.

(d) It would connect the unlinked markets of Asia and thus integrate the whole continent.

Five key areas were outlined as the immediate plan:

(a) Building modern communication and transportation networks, thus connect the sub-region by rail, road and air routes;

(b) Expansion of intra-regional trade;

(c) Development of tourism;

(d) Institution of economic and technological cooperation by leveraging ancient ties; and

(e) Promotion of cultural exchanges.

Conceived as a sub-regional economic cooperation, the above ideas formed the basis of launching the BCIM initiative in 1999 in Kunming, the capital of Chinese Yunnan province. Two prominent objectives had driven the BCIM initiative since the beginning—one is economic integration of the sub-region that would also enable integration of Asia and the other is development of the border regions.

The BCIM priority agenda has evolved over time. From the 3-T's of Trade, Transport and Tourism, the BCIM priority agenda has moved to TTE (Trade, Transport, and Energy). Apart from these items, social, cultural and environmental issues were also brought on the table for discussion, but the focus increasingly has favoured trade, connectivity and energy cooperation. Some proponents continue to argue for the "soft" agenda to be brought back in the BCIM dialogue as this is seen "more feasible" in the sub-region and will have direct positive impact on "the livelihoods and aspirations of the peoples in the borderlands". The idea of multi-modal transportation was also added to the BCIM connectivity agenda with the focus on Inland Water Transportation and the promotion of port development and coastal shipping.

In a major development in realizing the BCIM-EC, the first meeting of the BCIM-EC joint study group held in December

2013 in Kunming, thus officially setting up the mechanism to promote cooperation. This development has given a clear indication that India and China are prepared to work together in their common peripheries. Now, the BCIM initiative has moved away from the state of stalemate and uncertainties that had defined the initiative for a long time. This is evident from the fact that Modi Government has continued with the same enthusiasm of the Manmohan Singh Government in acknowledging the progress made in promoting cooperation under the BCIM-EC framework and to implement the understandings reached between the two sides.

The BCIM initiative can be seen as an emerging opportunity that could be a game changer for the region. Such assessments are driven by the prospects of economic benefits at a time when bilateral trade in the BCIM countries are growing rapidly in recent years. However, there are other issues and challenges that are still at play when the initiative is seen from the political prism. Some issues have been inherent in the BCIM initiative since the beginning. Government involvement in the BCIM initiative has been not different in terms of both the attitude and level of participation. Since the beginning the BCIM was a Track I activity for China and Myanmar with the Myanmar Central Government on the one hand and the Yunnan Provincial government taking the lead role. For India and Bangladesh, the BCIM began as a Track II initiative and soon Dhaka decided to move towards Track I. The BCIM remained largely a Track II activity as far as India was concerned until the India-China Joint Statement of May 2013 when the BCIM was officially endorsed at the highest level, thus moving towards Track I venture. An extension of this issue has also been reflected in the level of involvement and role of government. For example, Yunnan province of China has played a leadership role in the BCIM discussions, but this has not been the case for the states from Eastern India.

Economics of Influence: India and China in South Asia

India has enjoyed substantial regional influence across South Asia due to its size, comparative economic might, and historical and cultural relevance to the region. On the other hand, China's history of involvement in South Asia is limited in comparison, though its long-standing ties to Pakistan are a notable exception. But over the past decade, China has become a significant economic partner to countries throughout the region, forging particularly strong ties with smaller states through trade, diplomacy, aid and investment. China's increased involvement in South Asia poses a challenge to India as the regional economic and diplomatic heavyweight.

Despite India's eclipse by China, several threads of economic interaction continue to link India with its neighbours quite deeply. China has not eclipsed India across South Asia, but it is catching up in its trade and investment, and in some cases, its economic diplomacy has been accompanied by expanded strategic cooperation with India's neighbours. As China steps up its engagement with the region and promotes Asian connectivity, largely through its "One Belt One Road" vision, it can marshal extensive resources on initiatives such as the Asian Infrastructure Investment Bank that will likely outpace other financial sources. With an eye on India's own regional position, Indian Government has doubled down on its outreach across South Asia, stressing infrastructure development, people-to-people connectivity, and a "lift all boats" approach to help India's neighbours gain from its own rise.

Trade with South Asia: The South Asian region is one of the least economically integrated regions in the world. Intra-regional trade remains well below its potential due to high transport costs, protectionist policies, and political tensions. The South Asian Association for Regional Cooperation (SAARC) agreements, the South Asian Preferential Trading Arrangement, and the South Asian Free Trade Arrangement, have failed to break down trade barriers. The deep-seated enmity between India and Pakistan, punctuated by four wars, has stood in the way of broader regional trade expansion, slowing the flow of goods to a mere trickle across the India-Pakistan border. Most SAARC countries rely heavily on developed countries as export destinations, and increasingly import from China.

Due to its size and location, India was a natural top trading partner for South Asian countries for decades. India and Nepal share an open border; India signed its first free trade agreement with Sri Lanka; India and Bhutan share mutually beneficial economic inter-linkages; and India has been a major economic partner to Bangladesh since its independence in 1971. With the exception of China's extensive economic relationship with Pakistan, China's growing influence in South Asia is a relatively recent phenomenon. The China-Pakistan axis stands as a special and separate case, one that reflects a unique strategic logic unparalleled with other South Asian countries. China's most recent economic commitment to Pakistan, a declared package of USD 46 billion in infrastructure development and assistance, thus represents an intensification of, but not a strategic change in, a longstanding relationship going back five decades. Their current two-way trade volume surpasses USD 16 billion.

In the past decade, China has emerged as a top exporter of goods to the region, including to India, breaking into South Asian markets with its export-led growth strategy. Bangladesh provides the starkest example of this trend. Around 2005, China overtook India as Bangladesh's top trading partner and displaced many Indian goods in Bangladesh, offering cheaper Chinese products without the visa, transport, and customs challenges that had limited trade between India and Bangladesh. However, the 2015 Land Boundary Agreement between India and Bangladesh positions both countries to address border issues affecting trade in the near future. China's trade with Nepal and Sri Lanka still lags behind India's, but the gaps are narrowing. Sri Lanka is among India's top trading partners in South Asia, and India is Sri Lanka's largest trade partner. However, since 2005, Chinese exports to Sri Lanka have quadrupled to close to USD 4 billion, coming closer to Indian levels. China and Sri Lanka are also negotiating an FTA (Free Trade Agreement) to further boost trade and provide better access for Sri Lankan goods in Chinese markets; the current trade balance overwhelmingly favours China. Given Nepal's strategic location, it attracts significant attention from both of its neighbours. A 1996 trade agreement between India and Nepal increased bilateral trade volume, which now accounts for more than half of Nepal's total trade. In 2005, at the peak of Nepal's Maoist insurgency, a low point in its relations with India, Sino-Nepali relations shifted both economically and politically. Chinese goods flooded Nepali markets as Nepal diversified its imports and lessened its dependence on India. In Afghanistan, both India's and China's trade volumes with the landlocked country are under USD 1 billion, but expected to grow. India's plans for sea-land access to Afghanistan via Iran's Chabahar port are expected to materialize very soon, which will allow India to bypass Pakistan, dramatically cutting transportation costs that hamper India's trade with Afghanistan. However, increased Chinese involvement in Afghanistan and the completion of its economic corridor connectivity plans through Pakistan could also alter trade dynamics by opening up routes to markets in Afghanistan through Pakistan.

Migration and Remittances: Labour migration reflects economic and cultural linkages among South Asian countries. Here, India is linked much more deeply than China across South Asia. The remittances resulting from such migration represent substantial economic ties. According to the World Bank, around five million South Asian migrant workers in India sent more than USD 7.5 billion in remittances back to their home countries in 2014, while just twenty thousand workers in China sent USD 107 million. In the case of Bangladesh, remittances from India inject the Bangladeshi economy with more than USD 4 billion, nearly eight times the value of the USD 557 million in Bangladeshi goods imported by India in 2014, making remittances a vital economic component of the relationship. Looking in the other direction, hundreds of thousands of Chinese workers and millions of Indian workers in South Asia also send significant remittances home. India received almost USD 9 billion from migrant workers in the region, while China received more than USD 1 billion in 2014. Here it should be noted that nearly USD 958 million of China's remittances from South Asia came from Bangladesh which has cultivated extensive trade ties with China.

Aid and Investment: China is now focusing on development assistance and government investment programs in South

Asia, particularly for large infrastructure projects. Overseas development assistance requires a grant element of at least 25 percent; meanwhile, the debt-servicing conditions on Chinese loans often fall outside of OECD (Organisation for Economic Cooperation and Development) standards. According to China's 2014 foreign aid white paper, concessional loans represent more than half of China's aid. Projects funded by Chinese concessional loans must also be awarded to Chinese companies and source Chinese goods, linking Chinese aid to its government investment activities. The allocation of India's foreign aid prioritizes Bhutan, demonstrating the special economic relationship that India and Bhutan share. It is likely also designed to ensure that Bhutan continues to opt out of diplomatic ties with China and continues to look to India as the regional power. India's help of an additional USD 1 billion to Nepal for post-earthquake reconstruction shows that India can move quickly and at scale when needed. Afghanistan is also a significant recipient of Indian aid, and to date, India's pledged assistance to Afghanistan nears USD 2 billion.

Sri Lanka has been the paradigmatic case for the sudden rise of Chinese influence in South Asia. The uptick in Chinese development assistance to Sri Lanka, mostly in the form of concessional loans, began in 2009 after the Sri Lankan civil war and then spiked dramatically in 2011. Chinese support for a port, airport, and cricket stadium in Hambantota revealed an increasingly close relationship between the two countries. The upgrade of the China-Sri Lanka relationship to a strategic cooperative partnership in 2013 demonstrated the geopolitical influence of China's generous support to Sri Lanka. Detailed loan disbursements available from the Sri Lankan Government show a dramatic gap between Indian and Chinese contributions. Between 2012 and 2015, China disbursed almost USD 2.5 billion, of which more than 75 percent came from the Export-Import Bank of China. During the same period, India extended USD 660 million in lines of credit. Sri Lanka also features prominently in China's Maritime Silk Road project. China's focus on deep seaport development played on India's fears of a Chinese "string of pearls" encircling India.

Both India and China share a common interest in a stable Afghanistan and have been stepping up their engagement. Indian companies won a USD 10 billion tender in 2012 to the Hajigak iron ore deposit, and China invested in the Aynak copper mine in 2007. However, India's and China's mining projects face security threats from the Taliban that could jeopardize or delay operation.

Future of Competition and Cooperation

With an unresolved border and a contentious history, India takes China's activities in the South Asia neighbourhood warily. However, India's and China's efforts in South Asia can overlap, such as in the development of the Bangladesh-China-India-Myanmar economic corridor, opening up new opportunities for constructive cooperation. India's "Act East" policy aims to facilitate commerce, culture, and connectivity throughout Southeast Asia, an area that also captures China's focus. The two countries' efforts will likely be complementary since the region's infrastructure needs are so pressing and require trillions of dollars in capital. Greater connectivity will enable both India and China to tap further into Asian markets through trade and investment, although India will be hard-pressed to provide products as inexpensive and plentiful as China can in the near term.

In the Western South Asia, the competitive edge will more likely go to China. With the international troop drawdown in Afghanistan, South Asia faces security challenges that require coordination between India, China, and other regional countries. China's connectivity plans have the potential to help stabilize and strengthen not only Afghanistan but also all of Asia by opening up trade routes and creating new economic opportunities and linkages. When the China-Pakistan Economic Corridor, a vision to link Western China by road and rail down to the Gwadar deep water port, will come to fruition in the near term, India may find itself on the outside of a new transformational supply chain in the middle of the region. In addition, China's infusion of resources to create its Silk Road Economic Belt will position China as a benefactor without parallel. It is the major donor to the Asian Infrastructure Investment Bank (capital pool of USD 100 billion), and to the reserve fund of the New Development Bank (the "BRICS bank"), and on top of those multinational institutions, has created its own Silk Road Fund of USD 40 billion in capital. India can gain from greater connectivity and the redevelopment of trade ties across Asia, but India will also need to step up its economic diplomacy if it plans to keep pace.

सत्यमेव जयते

Chapter 13

India and China in the Global Arena

The future of India-China relations is believed to be a crucial factor in shaping the international order. India and China with their huge population are rising players in the international arena and, therefore, their interactions not only affect the two countries, but also international society. The India-China relation has gone beyond the bilateral context and acquired a global dimension. Therefore, a stable, normal and friendly relationship between India and China not only conforms with the fundamental interests of the two countries, but also helps promote peace, stability and development not only throughout Asia, but also in the world as a whole. On the other hand, if India and China work to counterbalance each other, it will serve the interests of the so-called "hegemonist". There are several possibilities regarding how India-China interactions could shape the international order. Of these, the most noticeable are Indo-American alliance against China, an India-China-Russia strategic triangle against the United States, and "Chindia" as a dominant player in international society. These in fact are related to two different strategies of reducing threat perception—balancing and bandwagoning.

Multilateral Engagement with Mistrust

India and China often come together when it comes to oppose demands from western, developed countries. For example, in climate policy, India and China signed a five-year agreement in October 2009 to jointly fight climate change and to negotiate international climate deals using common positions. This agreement was made prior to the United Nations' climate change summit in Copenhagen in December 2009. India and China, both members of G20, consistently argue that developing countries should not be required to set and meet the same targets for reducing greenhouse gases as developed countries who carry a greater historical responsibility for the increase in atmospheric greenhouse gases. They rejected calls by developed nations to set legally binding targets, and both countries signed a modified Copenhagen Accord in March 2010.

On the economic arena, India and China together did not consent to a bilateral Free Trade Agreement (FTA) because of fears of the Indian industry that it would not be able to compete with cheap Chinese imports. Nonetheless, an indirect arrangement came into effect in 2010, when an India-ASEAN FTA and a China-ASEAN FTA was signed, respectively. India and China have also joined hands in the World Trade Organisation (WTO). In 2008, at the Doha Development Agenda (DDA) trade talks in Geneva, the main cleavage was between the developed countries led by the United States and the European Union, and BASIC (Brazil, South Africa, India and China). After years of negotiation, and after almost reaching an agreement, talks broke down after the United States refused to discuss "special safeguard agreements" in agriculture as India has requested. China backed India's stand. Although this mutual support drew widespread criticism from not only developed countries but also from Brazil, the joint position of the two neighbouring countries has continued ever since.

In multilateral forums, both Asian giants share a geo-strategic interest, but the seemingly strong solidarity between India and China vanishes when it comes to what both assume to be their own respective backyards. The Shanghai Cooperation Organisation (SCO) is a group of Central Asian Countries, Russia and China dominated by the latter two nations, while the South Asian Association for Regional Cooperation (SAARC) is a regional forum dominated by India. India and China tried to keep each other out of their respective denominations to contain greater regional influence by the other. But pressure from the other countries within the SAARC and SCO who have friendlier ties with the respective regional power eventually gave India SCO observer status in 2005 and as part of the deal China also became an observer in the SAARC. For India, as the economically and politically weaker party of the India-China power struggle, multilateral engagement can be a good tool to contain China's dominance outside the areas of India's interests.

Indo-American Alliance

Relations between India and the United States have continued to witness intensive engagement regarding a qualitative transformation over the past few years. Both the countries want to strengthen their ties further and develop a strategic partnership. They have been involved in institutional dialogues and interactions on issues of mutual concerns and interests—from the issues of defense, combating international terrorism to trade, and science and technology. They have also increased the number of military exchanges and have conducted joint exercises on a regular basis. However, Indo-American relations was affected by India's nuclear tests of 1998. In addition to postponing President Clinton's visit to India, Washington also put economic sanctions on India to force it to join the non-proliferation regime. But, India has since successfully repaired its relations with the United States by conducting formal consultations and resuming high-level visits. Indo-American relations came to a climax when President Clinton resumed his delayed visit to India and Pakistan in March 2000. He spent five days in India, but only five hours in Pakistan. During his visit, India and the United States signed a document entitled "India-US Relations: A Vision for the 21st Century", pledging to deepen the partnership through institutionalized dialogue and engagement in regular consultations. India and the United States were referred to as partners in peace, with a common interest in and complementary responsibility for ensuring regional and international security. Although the two countries failed to reach an agreement on nuclear non-proliferation, an issue that President Clinton termed important to realise the full potential of the Indo-American relationship, there is no denying that Indo-American relations have improved significantly.

Although the war against terrorism made the United States restore US-Pakistan strategic relations, the role of India has also been well-recognised by it, *i.e.*, it does not treat India on par with Pakistan, but does accept that India has much more strategic importance in the region. In an important manifestation of the qualitative change in India-US relations, the President George W. Bush and Prime Minister Vajpayee announced the Next Steps in the Strategic Partnership (NSSP) in January 2004, which covered cooperation in four areas—civilian space, civilian nuclear energy, dual-use items, and missile defence. Unlike its concerns over China's rise, the United States administration considered the rise of India as adding value to its strategic plot.

China was carefully observing the adjustment of the United States' policy towards India. The United States had soon waived economic sanctions upon India and Pakistan after the events of 11th September 2001 to seek the two countries' support. More significantly, the military cooperation between India and the United States also gained momentum after the September 11 terrorist attacks. In April 2002, India signed a US$ 146 million deal with the United States to purchase eight AN/TPQ-37 Fire finder weapon locating radars. This was the first major government-to-government weapons transaction in more than three decades between India and the United States. The United States Defense Department statement read, "This sale will contribute to the foreign policy and national security interests of the United States by helping to improve the security of a country that has been and continues to be a force for political stability and economic progress in South Asia". This significant improvement in the India-US military ties might not be directly aimed against China, but the development had cast a shadow on China's security environment.

The rise of China is one of the major factors that influence the United States' policy towards India. After the demise of the USSR, China has been a possible challenger to the United States in the future, and the United States has watched China's rise in international society and its military modernization with misgivings. It is thought that the United States would like to contain China by establishing an anti-China alliance. The perception of China's growing threat has made the United States lean more towards India. As China's military grows more formidable, there might be a greater coincidence of interests between India and the Western powers in thinking about a more effective balance to manage China. In pursuit of a shared objective of dissuading China from aggressive actions, India's counterbalance against China is seen as a visible interest in broadening the ambit of US-India defence cooperation. The Indo-US joint manoeuvres can be seen as efforts by a democratic coalition to contain the rise of China. The Indo-US nuclear deal can be seen as a significant step in this direction. The Indo-US strategic nexus is likely to continue and to be reinforced further with the growing rift between the United States and China or India and China.

China is keenly observing the increasing closeness of Indo-US relations, especially on issues concerning military cooperation. It seems to be increasingly worried about the formation of Indo-American strategic cooperation, which suggests a pattern of alliance-building activities that it cannot ignore. From China's perspective, the coming together of the United States and India could well serve the United States' plans to contain China's growing economic and military might in Asia. The shared security concerns regarding China's rise can be an incentive to boost relations between India and the United States. However, China does not believe that India will join the United States in confronting China. It deems that India will not blindly follow the lead of the United States. The considerations within the Chinese leadership are whether it should maintain some relations with India or let India unite with the United States on the international stage. Understanding the significance, China will engage with India if it senses that India would unite with the United States at the international level. It is believed that the difficulties in the relations between China and the United States will play an important role in encouraging the Chinese leadership to accelerate the process of normalizing relations with India.

It is believed that the United States' global security interests take priority over India's hope to become an independent power, *i.e.*, the United States wants to help India to become a power to fulfil Washington's own strategic goals, not to fulfil those of India. Therefore, the United States has been opposing the Iran-

India-Pakistan pipeline project, which is important for India's energy security. Pakistan-US relations and nuclear issues are also creating obstacles in developing a closer Indo-American friendship. The United States had no intention of developing Indo-American relations while ignoring Pakistan, no matter what kind of government was in power. However, India and the United States may also believe that the improvement of their bilateral relationship could generate greater foreign policy leverages for each other. The United States may use India's growing economic and military might to meet its strategic needs in Asia and to limit further Chinese influence in the region. No matter how China perceives India-US military relations, India wants to maintain good relations with the United States. Also, it is not in India's interests to spoil relations with China, *i.e.*, India is not ready to behave like Japan, a reliable ally of the United States in East Asia. Therefore, sometimes India jumps on the bandwagon with the United States, and sometimes it acts in pursuit of its own goals.

India-China-Russia Strategic Triangle

The idea of establishing a strategic triangle consisting of India, China and Russia was first proposed by the then Russian Prime Minister Yevgeny Primakov during his visit to India in December 1998 and since then, the idea of establishing an India-China-Russia strategic triangle and its implications surface occasionally, as people are concerned with the possibility that the three countries will transform the potential for an alliance into a formal alliance. Ties between the three nations have since grown dramatically and a series of bilateral pacts have been signed to define the direction of the relationship.

China has initiated "partnership diplomacy" with many countries and regions. As far as Russia-China relations and India-China relations are concerned, in 1994, Russia and China established a constructive partnership looking towards the 21st century and then a "partnership of strategic coordination" in April 1996, while India and China set up a "constructive cooperative partnership oriented towards the 21st century" in November 1996 and a "strategic and cooperative partnership for peace and prosperity" in April 2005. India and Russia have also continued the special relationship founded in the former Soviet Union era. An India-Russia strategic partnership was established in 1997, and the strategic partnership agreement was concluded in 2000. Therefore, it is believed that it would be neither strange nor difficult for these three countries to transform their declared bilateral strategic partnership into a triangular format.

Among the world's seven declared nuclear nations, three are India, Russia and China, and they combined have one-third of the world's population. Russia and China have already secured permanent membership of the United Nations Security Council while India is widely tipped to gain a new seat in the expanded United Nations Security Council. The combined strength of these three countries will increase and this group could act as a counterweight to the United States on the international arena. A strategic triangle alliance may bring about a new world order where the United States does not have such a preponderance of power. Even if they do not build up a strategic partnership to counterbalance the United States, they will find common areas for cooperation. As cooperation among these countries increases, so will their weight in international affairs. However, despite intense discussions among the three countries involved and the international community, the concept has not yet become a reality due to various constraints.

India-China-Russia cooperation has a rich and positive potential because they advocate a multi-polar world order and the establishment of a just and fair new international order, and object to the hegemonism and the United States dominated international order in the post-Cold War era. Thus, the similar viewpoints shared by India, China and Russia on major international issues can be seen as the basis for further development of their trilateral relationship and they are likely to work together in the international field in order to promote the establishment of an international order and a multi-polar world.

Policies of the United States provided a good setting and opportunities for India, China and Russia to voice their joint concerns about the global order. The concept of the strategic triangle came at a time when the United States and Britain launched the bombardment of Iraq, bypassing the United Nations Security Council. The need for such strategic triangle felt because of the unilateral nature of the United States' operation. Russia sensed the need to take countermeasures to check the United States' geopolitical "offensive" in Eurasia, such as NATO's eastward expansion right up to its borders. In sharp contrast to the concept of an Indo-American strategic partnership to counter China's increasing power, the idea of India-China-Russia strategic triangle reflected the thinking about the need to check the growing dominance by the United States.

Russia is engaged in bilateral ties with India and China along with actively promoting the trilateral cooperation among them. While, at the beginning, India and China demonstrated a relatively lukewarm attitude towards the strategic triangle. However, obstacles remain in moving towards a trilateral strategic partnership, but unilateral tendencies on the part of the United States are encouraging the three countries to move closer to each other. Attitudes of India and China have changed towards the triangle proposal after the military action in Kosovo in 1999. The Kosovo war reminds the three countries that they share common interests in international affairs. As a result, the idea of establishing a strategic triangle has been raised again and it won more positive responses from India and China.

The "strategic triangle" dilemma facing India, China and Russia is that they need a trilateral relationship with strategic significance to counterbalance the United States' unilateralism, but they do not want to provoke the United States needlessly. To deal with this dilemma, these countries have changed the phraseology for the concept—the term "trilateral coordination and cooperation" is now used to describe the efforts to promote the trilateral relationship, instead of the somewhat contentious "strategic triangle" phraseology. Under "trilateral coordination and cooperation", the trilateral interaction between India, China and Russia has vigorously developed in recent years, and an intensive political dialogue has been established. They have begun to conduct an informal consultative exercise to make sure that they can create and maintain the necessary coordination in international affairs. Since 2002, the Foreign Ministers of these countries have often held trilateral meetings on the sidelines of the United Nations General Assembly session in New York. Now, the trilateral meetings have evolved into a gathering of heads of state. In July 2006, the first India-China-Russia summit was held in St. Petersburg, Russia, to formulate the common agenda, the possibilities of joint cooperative actions to deal with issues such as terrorism and other global threats, energy security, and health and related matters. These countries then promptly held the second summit in New Delhi and issued a Joint Communique concerning their shared desire to work together on energy, terror, security and trade. Although China flatly refuses to describe its relationship with India and Russia as an alliance partnership, it has been keen to conduct joint manoeuvres. In October 1999, China and Russia held their first joint naval exercises in the East China Sea. Such an event had not been seen even during the 1950s when China adopted a "lean-to-one" policy of aligning with the Soviet Union. Similarly, for the first time in the history of relations between India and China, the India-China naval exercises took place in November 2003. Now it is the matter of time when the three countries will hold a trilateral exercise.

New Development Bank (NDB)

The NDB, headquartered in Shanghai, is a multilateral development bank established by Brazil, Russia. India, China, and South Africa with the objective of financing infrastructure and sustainable development projects in BRICS and other emerging economies and developing countries, complementing the efforts of multilateral and regional financial institutions toward global growth and development. It also supports infrastructure and sustainable development efforts in underserved and emerging economies for faster development through innovation and cutting-edge technology. It will partner nations through capital and knowledge, achieving development goals with transparency and empathy and creating an equal opportunity for the development of all countries. It will also provide technical assistance for projects and engage in information, cultural and personnel exchanges with the purpose of contributing to the achievement of environmental and social sustainability.

The main objectives of NDB operations are:

(a) Fostering development of member countries.
(b) Supporting economic growth.
(c) Promoting competitiveness and facilitating job creation.
(d) Building a knowledge sharing platform among developing countries.

To fulfill its purpose, the Bank will support public or private projects through loans, guarantees, equity participation and other financial instruments. In 2016, the NDB Board of Directors approved seven projects with loans aggregating over USD 1.5 billion.

The Bank's Articles of Agreement specify that all members of the United Nations could be members of the bank, however the share of the BRICS nations can never be less than 55 percent of voting power.

Countries by Shareholding at the New Development Bank

Country	Number of Shares	Share Holding (% of Total)	Voting Rights (% of Total)
Brazil	100,000	20	20
Russia	100,000	20	20
India	100,000	20	20
China	100,000	20	20
South Africa	100,000	20	20
Unallocated Shares	500,000	—	—
Grand Total	1000,000	100	100

The work of NDB complements the existing efforts of multilateral and regional financial institutions for global growth and development. To fulfill its purpose, the NDB supports public and private projects through loans, guarantees, equity participation and other financial instruments. It also cooperates with international organizations and other financial entities, and provides technical assistance for projects to be supported by the bank. In addition to financing development projects, it engages in informational, cultural and personnel exchanges with the purpose of contributing to the achievement of environmental and social sustainability. It believes that environmental and social sustainability are crucial to addressing the infrastructure gaps and sustainable development needs consistent with national laws and regulations, and its mandate.

China's Motives behind the NDB: An international institution is a representation of the balance of power in the international system, and a tool that great powers use to spread and project their influence over other states. China, as a rising power pursuing a more assertive foreign policy, is also developing and strengthening new institutional networks that could better defend its interests. China is working in several dimensions with projects such as the Shanghai Cooperation Organisation (SCO), in terms of security and economic cooperation, the Asian Infrastructure Investment Bank (AIIB), and the New Development Bank (NDB) of the BRICS, among others.

Although the NDB has fewer financial resources than the AIIB, it has become relevant to China's political aim considering that the NDB is the first attempt to develop an institutional framework as an alternative to Bretton Woods' financial order. Thus, the NDB is the first stable project emerging within the informal forum of the BRICS focused on the promotion and defence of the principle of sovereignty, which is opposed to the interventionist logic of the World Bank and the International Monetary Fund. In this way, the leading role that China is taking within the NDB could be considered as a proof of China's growing involvement in attempting to shape the rules of the international system for its own interests.

China's national interest can be organized around three main pillars:

(a) providing security and stability for its political system;

(b) assuring China's national unity and sovereignty; and

(c) protecting its economic growth as a guarantee of internal stability;

which can be translated into three principal sources of action:

(a) In terms of trade, China wants to engage in South-South cooperation, assure energy supply (energy security), and open new markets (for instance, through One Belt One Road initiative).

(b) In the field of diplomacy, China attempts to balance Western hegemony and gain recognition of the People's Republic of China under the One China policy.

(c) China tries to show itself as an alternative to the West for developing countries and promote value free win-win relations.

Besides, a certain degree of international stability and peace are considered as an indispensable precondition to assure the above-mentioned aims in China's foreign policy approach. Now, China has focused its foreign policy strategies on achieving the respect of sovereignty, multipolarity, economic cooperation, and avoiding military tensions with the United States.

Considering a scenario in which China is performing a hedging strategy without openly or progressively challenging the United States, the BRICS group is a convenient framework that enables China to divert the attention from its actions. Through the BRICS, China cannot be pointed by the other powers of acting unilaterally, it is indeed acting along the 43 percent of the world's population. With its participation in the forum, China drives an initiative for the promotion of sovereignty principle and equality among states in international relations. The model of a multilateral forum, not based on the imposition of ideological conditions among its members, allows China to apply and demonstrate the success of its view on diplomatic practices that it wants to promote. At the same time, it reinforces China's aims of presenting itself as a new great power committed to the democratization of the international system. Furthermore, the BRICS allows China to project its influence through the member countries overseas, Brazil and South Africa, deepening China's presence in Latin America and Africa.

Along with projecting its influence, the BRICS is also a framework that China can use to ease conflicts with one of its primary geopolitical competitors, India. The BRICS plays an essential role in deepening the India-China cooperation and trying to limit the United States' influence in India, as well as, developing shared projects among both countries which could restrict competition in reasonable terms. In addition, even when the BRICS is not an alliance, the existence and the enhancement of this multilateral forum sends the message that they are willing to defend their interests and to reach agreements with other partners to do so, even if they have significant differences among them. Besides and internally, the BRICS framework tries to advance from this joint defence of national interests in the development of common ventures which can mitigate the chances of conflict among forum members.

In the economic dimension, the group guarantees China's access to Russian, Brazilian and South African markets. Furthermore, due to its economic advantage, China has secured a leading role in the group, and the case of the NDB is the proper example of how China, even if it does not impose its demands, can obtain the most beneficial outcome of BRICS negotiations for its own interests. Nonetheless, China's leadership is far from being the same as the United States has reached among Western countries. Even though China is a *primus inter pares*, it is far from being able to present its interest as the one of the whole group.

In its financial dimension, due to its fewer resources, the NDB cannot aspire to be anything more than a complement to the World Bank (WB) or the International Monetary Fund (IMF) in a short/mid-term. On the contrary, looking to its political dimension, the atmosphere of distrust about the NDB can be understood taking it as an attempt to formulate a new governance logic based on the respect of sovereignty, which can be appealing for non-liberal countries over the world. Indeed, China needs this kind of institutional experience to strengthen its influence in the long-term strategy, and to prove its credibility as a global power. Through the NDB, China could lead the change of accepted norms and practices of development aid in the international system. Even in the least optimistic scenario for China, it could take advantage of the NDB as a tool for bargaining to achieve a reform of the system. Thus, the NDB can be considered as an asset for China's soft balancing strategy in its competition with the United States.

In addition, the NDB can also be a useful asset for China's foreign policy due to a set of factors:

(a) The NDB is an organization that China can use to increase its influence among developing countries.

(b) The NDB improves the dynamics of cooperation among BRICS. This is the first serious initiative in which the BRICS can cooperate in a long-term project, strengthening the cohesion of the group.

(c) From China's point of view, it is an opportunity to improve its know-how in managing international institutions. The NDB headquarter is based in Shanghai, and this gives China a decisive influence over this institution. Through the projects developed in the framework of the NDB, China not only can enhance the cohesion of the BRICS but also attach rival countries like India to China's economic plans, gaining centrality in the group.

(d) The NDB is the first materialization of BRICS multipolar ideology in institutional practice, as the NDB strategic documents stated. Through the NDB, China has the opportunity to demonstrate its capacity to provide alternative ways of dealing with international issues. This is a mechanism that China did not have until now and will be essential if its dream for leading the world is aimed to become real.

India, China, and the Emerging Global Order

The rise of India and China as major world powers promises to test the established global order in the coming years. As the two powers grow, they are bound to change the current international system with profound implications for themselves, the United States, and the world. And whether they agree on the changes to be made, especially when it comes to their relationship with the West, will influence the system's future character. A close examination of Indian and Chinese perspectives on the fundamentals of the emerging international order reveals that India-China differences on many issues of both bilateral and global significance are stark.

The parallel rise of India and China dramatically exemplifies Asia's resurgence in the global system. Although there has been a steady shift in the concentration of capabilities from West to East ever since the end of World War II, this transformation took a decisive turn when the smaller, early-industrializing nations of Asia—Japan, South Korea, Taiwan, and Singapore—were joined by the large, continental-sized states of India and China. The recent renaissance of India and China is owed in large measure to their productive integration into the liberal economic order built and sustained by American hegemony in the postwar period. As a result of that integration, both India and China have experienced dramatic levels of economic growth in recent decades. For example, China's economic performance has been simply meteoric, exceeding even the impressive record set by the first generation of Asian tigers between 1960 and 1990. During the last thirty or so years, China has demonstrated average real growth in excess of 9 percent annually, with growth rates touching 13 to 14 percent in peak years. As a result, China's per capita income rose by more than 6 percent every year from 1978 to 2003—much faster than that of any other Asian country, significantly better than the 1.8 percent per year in Western Europe and the United States, and four times as fast as the world average. This feat has made the Chinese economy, in purchasing-power-parity terms, the second largest in the world. It is believed that China will likely overtake the United States in GDP size at some point during the first half of the 21st century.

On the other hand, India's economic performance has not yet matched China's in either intensity or longevity. India's economic reforms, which have produced India's recent spurt in growth, began only in the early 1990s, over a decade after China's. However, these reforms have been neither comprehensive nor complete, and they have been hampered by the contestation inherent in India's democratic politics, the complexity of the Indian federal system, the lack of elite consensus on critical policy issues, and the persistence of important rent-seeking entities within the national polity. Despite these disadvantages, the Indian economy has grown at a rate of about 7.5 percent during the first decade of 21st century. Thus, India eclipsed its own historic underperformance and enabled a doubling of per capita income about every decade, placing the Indian economy, when measured by purchasing-power-parity methods, in the fourth place globally. More interestingly, India's growth, unlike China's, which relies extensively on foreign capital and export markets, has derived largely from internal sources. Accordingly, it can be concluded that continuing economic reforms will enable the country not only to reach its targeted objective of sustained double-digit growth but also to catch up with China in coming decades as China's own growth slows because of its incipient demographic transitions.

India and China are likely to sustain their relatively high levels of GDP growth for some time to come. This continual accretion of economic power will position them among the top three economies internationally by the year 2030, if not earlier, thus confirming their status as global giants. Propelled by the rapid economic growth achieved thus far, India and China are already extending their political influence as well as strengthening their military capabilities and reach. China is quickly closing in on its goal of becoming a major global power and India is likely to achieve global-power status in the next two decades. Indian and Chinese contributions to the expansion of the international economic system are generally welcomed, with growth in both nations promising to function as the motor of the international economy for several decades to come. They also share a common interest in ensuring that the international environment is peaceful to guarantee their continued economic consolidation and domestic political stability.

As India and China continue to grow, they shall want to progressively reshape the international system to advance their own interests—interests that may differ from those of the United States, the established hegemon that sustains the current global order. However, this does not imply that India and China invariably share common objectives in opposition to the United States. They are united by certain acknowledged aims—recovering the preeminence they once enjoyed as international entities of consequence; establishing a multipolar world with themselves as constituent poles; avoiding the costs of contributing to global public goods on the grounds that their vast developmental challenges are not yet overcome; and protecting their hard-won sovereignty in the face of new principles justifying foreign intervention in the internal affairs of states. Despite these convergent objectives, India and China are also divided by deep differences in the conduct of their political affairs. India's and China's divergent behaviours are shaped by the unique histories governing their formation as modern states, the stark contrasts in their respective political regimes, and their ongoing territorial disputes and geopolitical rivalries, which are exacerbated by their growing prominence in international politics.

Changing Global Order: India's and China's views on the current global order have evolved along a similar trajectory. In the aftermath of the Second World War, both states, driven by strong anti-colonialist impulses, opposed great-power politics and what was viewed as "superpower hegemony", calling instead for a multipolar world. However, since the end of the Cold War, both states have become increasingly integrated into the United States led international order. They recognize that this order has created a peaceful external environment within which they can safely develop, and they see globalization as a positive and, to some extent, inevitable trend. Therefore, India and China have abandoned calls for a complete overhaul of the global order and instead have come to support merely its revision.

Despite their engagement with the extant world order, both India and China remain concerned about this order's ability to protect their state sovereignty. As both states are still in the midst of major state-building projects, sovereignty is a key priority. India and China generally oppose Western-led interventions in the internal affairs of the developing world and identify another potential threat—the increasing empowerment of individuals and civil society at the expense of the state. Both states are suspicious of non-governmental organisations in their countries, in part because of their perceived links with foreign states, and they also harbor extensive reservations about international norms that seek to bind the hands of national leaders in domestic matters. Moreover, they watch the rise of new technologies, such as innovations in cyberspace and social media with some distrust. However, they yearn for a greater role in the global order and feel underrepresented in key international bodies, for example, China is not well represented in international economic institutions, while India is not a permanent member of the United Nations Security Council (UNSC). Neither India nor China opposes international legal institutions in principle, but in practice both states express strong reservations over the fact that institutions like the International Criminal Court can impinge on their sovereignty. In India's case, the opposition is compounded by its perception that these organizations often discriminate against states that are not permanent members of the UNSC.

It is assumed that India's and China's attitudes toward the future global order will not be affected by international institutions and norms as much as they will be decided by domestic and national political considerations. Therefore, their future relations with the global order will be determined more from within than from without, with sobering implications for American interests. Thus, their interests are often shaped by their relatively comparable levels of economic and political development. But the divergence in their positions is equally significant. While both countries are concerned, for example, about constraints on their sovereignty, the degree of concern differs greatly. China holds to the principle of state sovereignty absolutely—the most salient tenet in its foreign relations has long been the safeguarding of its sovereignty and territorial integrity. It sees many threats to its sovereignty as arising from the West, particularly the United States, and has firmly opposed them at every step.

On the other hand, India is becoming less concerned by threats posed by other states. It does not object to Western intervention on the absoluteness of state sovereignty since it recognizes the importance of states shedding some sovereignty to promote international cooperation, an evolving position shaped both by Indian democracy and its liberal political inheritance. It opposes the cavalier humanitarian interventions of the West mainly because it doubts their sincerity and efficacy. At times it places humanitarian concerns above state sovereignty, but it does so on the basis of pragmatic rather than ideological concerns.

While India and China are both suspicious of the empowerment of individuals and society relative to the state, their responses to that development are markedly different. China has made it clear that it sees this trend as "politically incorrect and unacceptable" and believes that sovereign rights will always be more valued than individual rights. Accordingly, it has positioned itself against the emergence of a robust civil society by committing to the reinforcement of state power, including through heavy regulation and control. Moreover, its attitude has affected its perceptions of other states and it does not distinguish between state actors and nonstate actors in the conduct of foreign relations.

On the other hand, India, which has struggled with the empowerment of civil society, has begun adapting to this reality. It has in fact embarked on state-supported efforts at empowering its citizenry through a variety of instruments ranging from acknowledging citizens' legal right to seek information about state actions to expanding the scope of public interest litigation to creating a gigantic rights-based welfare state.

The fact that both India and China desire greater representation in international institutions does not mean that they concur with each other's aspirations. In particular, they have clashed over the expansion of the United Nations Security Council (UNSC). India has prioritized permanent UNSC representation, arguing that the current structure is outmoded and ineffective.

For all their convergence at the international level, the geopolitical rivalry between India and China often impedes practical cooperation between the two states. China is fearful of American containment and thus wary of the United States' developing relationship with India. However, India is not necessarily moving closer to the United States, but that China is pushing the United States and India closer together by virtue of its adoption of potentially interventionist policies that threaten India's interest in its own neighbourhood. While India and China agree in the abstract on concepts such as state sovereignty and humanitarian intervention, they are divided by their perceptions of the threats facing the international system as well as by their concerns about their own security. China deeply fears American intrusions on its sovereignty and is acutely conscious of the leverage India possesses regarding Tibet's future as a Chinese province.

***International Economic System*:** Given India's and China's economic successes, it is not surprising that both the states support for an open economic order now and into the future. It is believed that China will surely continue to support an open, transparent, and rule-based global trade system; whereas India is committed to a free-market-based and liberal global economic order. India's and China's shared commitment to the global economic system is fundamentally rooted in the benefits that order has bestowed on their states. They have not only grown as a result of their integration into the global economic system but also used that integration as a force for beneficial domestic reforms. Both countries intend to continue their external integration and internal reform even as they simultaneously undergo consequential economic, social, and political transitions. However, despite the benefits offered by the liberal trading order, both the states are dissatisfied by the existing balance of power in many global institutions, especially those pertaining to international finance.

India and China are aware of their growing economic heft within the international trading system, and they see the rise of the G-20 and the BRICS as reflecting a larger shift in economic power from the developed to the developing world. Accordingly, they believe that developing nations are entitled to greater representation and rights within international finance institutions, especially the IMF and the World Bank, and that the fundamental structure of these organisations must be altered. They also agree that these institutions are becoming increasingly important in the current global climate. They fear of rising protectionism among developed countries, and emphasize that the West should not fence off its economies from globalization, given the importance of a universal free market.

India and China seek a greater leadership role in the maintenance of the international economic order, a position that derives from their growing economic power. However, both countries acknowledge that they will be unable to take a primary leadership role any time soon because of their still-significant economic, political, and social constraints. Domestic constraints are considered as a key obstacle to India and China replacing the United States, an intriguing counterpoint to most international discussions that presume India and China will step into such a role simply as a function of their increased relative economic power.

Given the expectation that India and China shall continue to benefit from the system, it is not surprising that both countries want to conclude the Doha Round of WTO negotiations expeditiously and in general strongly prioritize the expansion of the global economic order. They shall continue to support bilateral and regional arrangements, including free trade agreements (FTAs), that advance economic goals in a manner that complements global efforts. However, they prioritize global agreements over regional ones and are committed to not letting the latter become obstacles to the former. On the critical question of the geopolitical challenges posed by the differential rates of growth arising from an open international order, the core challenge for the United States today, India does not consider differential returns a threat because they are a direct product of integration into the global economy. Then for India, integration is the best option both because it limits the misuse of a state's power and because the alternative to open trade puts India in an even weaker position.

While both India and China support expanding the global trading system, they disagree on whether bilateral and regional FTAs are an obstacle. China considers regional arrangements to be incredibly important and takes interest in expanding them. It is feared that bilateral and regional trade agreements could undermine the multilateral trading order. Therefore, it is time for the WTO to play a greater role in monitoring these regional FTAs and ensuring they are not diverting trade.

Global Nonproliferation System: At the highest level of abstraction, both India and China concede that the Nuclear Nonproliferation Treaty (NPT) regime has advanced global nonproliferation goals, at least insofar as it has served as a brake on the runaway proliferation of nuclear weapons that might have occurred in the regime's absence. The choices of many states, the role of bipolarity in tamping down regional rivalries, the role of the United States as a security provider, and the high costs of nuclear-weapons programs also presumably all contributed to reducing the incentives for proliferation. Although, India continues to have significant disagreements with the NPT system, it is much more committed to the holistic purposes of the NPT than some of the signatories and has unilaterally implemented many significant measures to advance the NPT's nonproliferation and disarmament goals. This claim is anchored in India's unsullied record in regard to outward proliferation, which contrasts sharply with the records of both China and Pakistan. On the other hand, China's support of the nonproliferation system has strengthened since it signed the NPT in 1992, some twenty-two years after the treaty came into force.

Both India and China have strongly condemned North Korea's nuclear program. But given Chinese dilemmas and interests regarding North Korea, China has not prioritized compelling Pyongyang to give up its nuclear program. Lacking similar equities and given India's chagrin at North Korea's nuclear and missile cooperation with Pakistan, India's condemnation of the North Korean program has been more unequivocal. However, there is less disagreement with respect to Iran. Both India and China find themselves in a dilemma—they do not want to challenge Tehran's right to peaceful nuclear technology, but they are concerned about its nuclear program. Despite the differences between the North Korean and Iranian cases, both countries insisted on engaging with states challenging the NPT system. In part, this is because India and China recognize that North Korea's and Iran's decisions are driven by the larger political and security contexts in their respective regions. Accordingly, both India and China oppose the threat or use of force to coerce these nations and wish for an amicable resolution to the dispute through the improvement of overall international relations and appropriate settlement of regional security problems. Both India and China also maintain that they scrupulously follow international obligations over national interests when interacting with either North Korea or Iran. They are seeking less punitive international strategies not because they are self-serving but because they are more effective.

The superficial similarities in Indian and Chinese positions on proliferation mask deeper disagreements. India and China diverge sharply in their evaluation of the NPT system's success. Despite China's initial opposition to the NPT regime, it now sees the system as a success and views the treaty as "the cornerstone of the global nuclear nonproliferation system". This change of stand is linked closely to the treaty's recognition of China as a legitimate nuclear-weapon state. In contrast, the NPT treats India as a *de jure* outlier. Consequently, India has complaints about the flaws in the NPT system, claiming that the regime is under severe stress and in dire need of renewal and rejuvenation. India contends that while the system has positively affected global nonproliferation efforts to some extent, its contribution has been more limited than its admirers believe.

Indian and Chinese grievances about the NPT continue to be shaped by how the treaty treats the two countries legally. Although Chinese liberals still evince distaste for the regime's discriminatory aspects, a position once held by China as a whole, the country has since reconciled itself to the NPT regime and has consistently upheld it at least at a declaratory level since 1992. At the 1995 NPT Review Conference, China gave higher priority to its cooperation with other nuclear-weapon states than with other developing countries. However, India continues to harbor complaints about the treaty, though their public articulation has been muted considerably in recent years, particularly after the successful conclusion of the United States-India civilian nuclear cooperation agreement. Most importantly, India still believes, at least at a conceptual level, that the NPT regime remains fundamentally discriminatory, dividing states with nuclear weapons from those without.

India originally sought an NPT that would be a grand bargain—nonproliferation in exchange for disarmament, with the eventual goal of the total elimination of nuclear weapons. However, the NPT ended up holding nonproliferation as an end in and of itself. To some extent, even China agrees with this position since it maintains that all nuclear-weapon states should publicly commit to not seek permanent possession of nuclear weapons. But, in practice, China has passed the burden of disarmament on to the bigger nuclear-weapon states and will join the process only when appropriate conditions are met, or, in other words, when the larger United States and Russian nuclear arsenals are reduced to levels approaching parity with China's. Compounding India's objections is the permanence of the regime established during the 1995 Review Conference. India believes that the NPT should be a dynamic, flexible document that can adjust to developing situations. It also opposes the general exclusionary approach of the NPT system that, in its view, seeks to ostracize non-signatories. It believes that the regime needs to be more inclusive, with stronger compliance measures so that all commitments, including disarmament, are actively pursued. As part of this, India believes that the membership of groups such as the Nuclear Suppliers Group, a multinational body that regulates the import and export of materials used to make nuclear weapons, and the Missile Technology Control Regime, which seeks to prevent the proliferation of missile and drone technology, should be open to all interested countries, not just NPT signatories, in order to increase their efficacy.

India and China also diverge on how to manage the outlier states that never signed the NPT. Although China has never explicitly addressed this question, it appears to oppose the partial integration of some states as evinced by its opposition to the United States—India civilian nuclear cooperation agreement. Chinese liberals and realists opposed this agreement for different reasons—liberals because they felt that the deal subverted the universality of the NPT regime and realists because they saw the deal as the United States—Indian attempt to counterbalance

China's growing strength. But, the deal was made possible by India's impeccable nonproliferation record, and as a result, the deal proved to be a successful method of active partnership between India and members of the NPT regime, strengthening the system. Consequently, it remains a good example of how India has become a partner in the nonproliferation regime, rather than a target of it.

Despite the above disagreement, there is a small element of convergence between India and China as well. They agree that a similar deal should not be extended to other NPT outliers, but their reasons differ. China seems to believe that the United States—India deal was flawed in principle, whereas India believes that the deal was uniquely tailored to India's circumstances and thus cannot be successfully used in alternate situations. Therefore, where the outliers are concerned, China appears to stand fast by the canonical objectives of older United States' policy—namely, to integrate them eventually into the regime as non-nuclear-weapon states. Thus, for example, China has repeatedly endorsed a South Asian nuclear-weapons-free zone (presumably because it would imply India's nuclear disarmament) and strongly supports a Middle Eastern nuclear-weapons-free zone (which would entail Israel's nuclear disarmament). On the other hand, India believes that the NPT regime should treat outliers as partners in nonproliferation efforts by considering the threats they face and engaging with them.

Regional Security: From China's perspective, its most important security concerns are the confrontation on the Korean Peninsula, the South China Sea dispute, and the Iranian nuclear program. On the other hand, India's most important concerns are unresolved sovereignty and territorial disputes, terrorism, and the challenge of maintaining high economic growth. Both the states have prioritized economic growth even though they continue to pursue other long-standing objectives, such as national reunification and strategic autonomy. Both the countries are caught between the competing imperatives of security and economic growth. India's strategy satisfies the country's sovereignty and territorial integrity needs by gradually enhancing its conventional and strategic deterrence posture, while at the same time maintaining uninterrupted economic growth figures through mutually beneficial diplomatic, economic, and security arrangements.

In the pursuit of their strategies, India and China have adopted very similar means. Both stress the importance of international cooperation, collective security measures and multilateral security dialogues, diplomatic outreach, negotiation as the primary method of dispute resolution, and expanded economic ties. Both states generally eschew unilateral or coalitional attempts to address Asia's security challenges. Instead, they stress the importance of multilateral and regional fora while remaining cognizant that some security challenges are best dealt with at the bilateral level. Both states also envision a proactive and positive role for themselves in resolving the region's disputes and even guaranteeing their neighbours' security. In this context, they have primarily focused on nonmilitary instruments to advance Asian security. They see force as a last resort and argue that its use should be limited. Nevertheless, they are modernizing their militaries as a defensive hedge against external aggression, but with a marked difference in emphasis.

China is upgrading its military in part to deter military interference by other major powers, presumably the United States. In contrast, India's military is involved mostly in smaller conflicts in its neighbourhood. Thus, the two nations are slowly departing from their strict insularity of yesteryear and instead exploring how their military capabilities might serve emerging interests, including through the use of military instruments for nontraditional security operations (such as humanitarian relief and peacekeeping) and for collective-security measures. As they contemplate such departures, both countries agree that confidence-building measures have a crucial role in preventing conflict, which plays into their shared desire to avoid the use of force. However, both India and China see the United States as an indispensable actor in Asia, as they are well aware of the considerable American military strength in the region and the unlikelihood of its departure in the foreseeable future. They also accept the American presence, though with varying degrees of enthusiasm, and see it as being in their national interests.

Therefore, neither seeks to challenge the United States' leadership on this front. Despite the differences that both India and China have with the United States, they want it to play a constructive role in maintaining regional security and in promoting economic cooperation and integration.

For all the commonality in their approaches to Asian security, India's and China's national security strategies differ in three important aspects.

(a) China strongly opposes multilateral military alliances. Whereas India perceives the value of existing American alliances to its security. Although India will not join such organisations, it is less averse to bilateral military cooperation as long as it can maintain its strategic autonomy.

(b) China doubts that an Asia-wide organization can adequately represent such a geopolitically diverse region, but India sees potential in such initiatives despite their failure to resolve major security issues in the past.

(c) China seeks a United States that engages and cooperates with its rise, while India wants more resolute pushback against China's excesses and is wary of any United States' actions suggesting a Sino-American condominium in the form of a G-2.

China wants the United States to make it clear to smaller Asian countries that it is not balancing against China, therefore discouraging them from confronting China over territorial disputes on the assumption that the United States will back their claims. China also wants the United States to back away from its current militarization of regional issues, such as Taiwan, the China-Japan disputes, and the maritime squabbles in the South China Sea. In contrast, India expects the opposite—it wants the United States to act as a balancing force against China's irredentist encroachment on the global commons.

Stability in Southern Asia: Given the broad similarity in strategic objectives, at least at a formal level, it is not surprising that both India and China face many of the same security threats, ranging from unstable states to terrorism to the volatile

Indo-Pakistan relationship. The Indian and Chinese assessments of geopolitical threats continue to often be polite but pointed. The intimacy of the Sino-Pakistani relationship has been an irritant in the Sino-Indian relationship, and that in an ideal world the two relationships would be de-linked from each other. Therefore, India and China would like to separate their bilateral relationship from China's relationship with Pakistan. Since India and China have agreed to look at their relationship in a broader context and perceive a stable and cooperative partnership as a guarantee to their simultaneous rise, neither of them wants to see the Pakistan issue derailing their relations. Pure de-linkage is not a realistic prospect in the foreseeable future and that, in fact, if Pakistan's dependence on China increases in the years ahead, India may have to start thinking about Pakistan as a subset of the larger challenges posed by China. Thus, reflecting the complexity of regional geopolitics, China plays a significant and positive factor in Pakistan's recent decision to begin normalizing economic relations with India, thereby suggesting that China's relations with the smaller regional states cut in multiple directions.

There is a range of issues relating to the smaller Southern Asian states on which both India and China seem to agree. In particular, while both countries eye each other with some suspicion, they do not see themselves as fully locked into a zero-sum game for influence. Competition exists, but core strategic interests are not consistently diametrically opposed and sometimes they even align. For instance, both states welcome Myanmar's reform process and see each other's increasingly active role in Afghanistan as a positive development. Both are also aware of the great potential for misunderstanding, particularly from any Chinese moves in India's backyard, and they appear to be working carefully to create a constructive dynamic in these smaller states.

Indian and Chinese perceptions of security threats diverge most conspicuously in the nontraditional realm. While they share many mutual security threats, they emphasize different nontraditional security threats. China has focused on drug trafficking and organized crime emanating from the region, particularly from Afghanistan and Myanmar, while India has instead emphasized environmental and natural-resource issues. Both states see economic cooperation in Southern Asia as the principal instrument for achieving their strategic objectives. India, in particular, is willing to bear asymmetric burdens in order to do so and has accordingly entered into lopsided trade agreements, most likely a reflection of its greater investment and stakes in the region.

India and China have both supported efforts at diplomatic engagement and encouraged regional cooperation where possible. But there is an important difference as well, which is once again linked to the geographic locations of India and China and the stakes they perceive in Southern Asia. Significantly, they differ in their perspectives on the usefulness of force in the region to achieve their strategic objectives. China appears to have drawn the line at cooperative security measures, espousing a strong policy of noninterference in the domestic affairs of Southern Asian countries. While advocating similar principles as the preferred course, India has nevertheless built up its military and weighed the adoption of punitive strategies aimed primarily at Pakistan and rooted in its continued dalliance with terrorism. It should be noted that China has adopted a similar posture in East Asia where it has greater geopolitical stakes, but not in Southern Asia. From the Indian perspective, there is no reason to assume the futility of force in securing Indian strategic objectives, although the Indian use of military instruments is conditioned by a deep skepticism as to what they can actually achieve.

However, Indian and Chinese perspectives seem most sharply divided on their judgments about the role of the United States in Southern Asia. According to China, the American pivot to Asia is itself a potential security threat, perhaps because it is also perceived as implicating India. But, both India and China agree that the extant American role in the region has helped slow the spread of extremism and terrorism and prevent the Indo-Pakistani rivalry from spiraling out of control. It is believed that any differences between India and the United States are matters of emphases and priorities rather than objectives and that India seeks to continue working with the United States in areas of common strategic interest while managing operational differences. On the other hand, China sees the United States' increasing presence in Asia as a threat to Chinese interests and a possible prelude to containment. Therefore, it has adopted a dual strategy of playing up common interests with the United States while strengthening its regional ties and modernizing its military as a hedge against American threats.

Security in the Global Commons: The global maritime system is crucial to the continued prosperity of India and China. Of equal significance is their conviction that the United Nations Convention on the Law of the Sea (UNCLOS) remains both the core and the framework of that system and that upholding it is therefore incredibly important for continued stability. The strong convergence on this position indicates that India and China, like many other developing countries, see only benefits in supporting a regime that offers strong national control and jurisdiction over ever-increasing ocean areas, especially those subject to the most intense human use. This expanding jurisdiction over broad expanses of ocean waters—a national enclosure of what was previously treated as the high seas—sets both India and China, along with many other Third World states, apart from traditional maritime powers such as the United States.

Both India and China see UNCLOS as codifying, not rejecting, the inheritance of customary international law while also expanding upon it in various significant and welcome ways. In particular, both countries value the fact that UNCLOS expanded states' jurisdiction over their continental shelves and exclusive economic zones, the area over which a state has certain special rights to maritime access and resources. UNCLOS also added new rules about the passage of vessels, including the activities of naval and research ships, in waters where India and China now enjoy jurisdiction. Although, India and China strongly support UNCLOS as the new foundation for the maritime regime, they emphasize different aspects of it. China focuses on the freedom of the seas and supports UNCLOS because it is viewed as equitable and reasonable. In China's interpretation, UNCLOS's primary virtue is that it allows all countries to pursue their interests in a fair way. China greatly fears the United States' ability to interfere in the rights of other states by virtue of the conjunction of its superior might and its rejection of the Chinese interpretation of what UNCLOS permits with respect to national jurisdiction. On the other hand, Indian concerns about the maritime commons are largely oriented around the mounting security challenges fueled by maritime disputes.

However, neither China nor India seeks to find a replacement for UNCLOS as the foundation for the global maritime order. Both view UNCLOS as indispensable and argue that most current maritime challenges arise from the omissions in UNCLOS rather than from its affirmative provisions. For that reason, both India and China believe that any changes to the global maritime order should occur through revisions and additions to the UNCLOS regime. In considering potential changes, both countries support a move toward maritime multilateralism in order to better protect their interests. In this context, India and China have developed similar approaches to managing their maritime disputes, both strongly supporting the process of diplomatic negotiation as the primary tool for dispute resolution. They have also cautioned that maritime disputes are not simply the result of differing interpretations of UNCLOS and that they often incorporate complicated historical, political, economic, and social factors that make them difficult to settle. It should be noted that UNCLOS cannot be used as a legal foundation to make new claims over territorial sovereignty since it only applies to maritime boundaries. In other words, a state's territorial claims predetermine what UNCLOS may ratify, and the new jurisdictions extended by the convention do not permit the assertion of any new territorial claims.

India and China agree that the use of force is inconsistent with the rules established by UNCLOS. All the rights endowed by UNCLOS are on the basis of peaceful purposes. Therefore, the exercise of the rights endowed by UNCLOS must be done in a peaceful way. While force may be inappropriate to protect UNCLOS-derived rights, India and China reserve the right to use force to protect their territorial sovereignty, including their ownership of any islands that are the center of maritime disputes. UNCLOS does not override this basic right. The both sides support diplomatic negotiations as the primary tool for resolving maritime disputes, however, there appears to be some distance between them on the issue of alternatives to diplomacy. China may find collaborative, multilateral efforts appropriate in some areas of nontraditional maritime security. This suggests that, consistent with China's current approach to the disputes in the East and South China Seas, China is willing to not press its claims to permit either joint exploration or exploitation of the resources at issue among the disputants. But as it does so, it retains the right to employ force if necessary to resolve the elements of contested sovereignty that may be inherent in the quarrel. On the other hand, India enthusiastically embraces international arbitration under UNCLOS if no resolution through diplomatic negotiation is possible.

The disagreements between India and China extend to their perceptions of the role of the United States in the global maritime order as well. They disagree with the United States interpretation of UNCLOS. They have different views than the United States about what military activities are permissible in other states' exclusive economic zones, especially on the issues of surveys, probes, and reconnaissance. They also look askance at American maritime initiatives that might interfere with their sovereignty or the freedom of the seas.

In addition to the disagreements between India and China vis-à-vis the United States, there are significant differences in the behaviours of the two Asian powers. While China routinely confronts the United States' naval vessels and aircraft operating in its exclusive economic zones, India studiously avoids such confrontations. Thus, although the two powers reject the American legal justification for its military operations, their practical responses to these activities are vastly different. This difference can be explained only by the fact that for all their ideational solidarity over UNCLOS, India and China view the role of the United States in the global maritime order through very different lenses. China suspects that the United States is using its naval power to meddle in China's territorial and maritime disputes and to infringe upon the UNCLOS-derived rights of all nations. Specifically, China sees the United States' Navy as a powerful tool for the United States to pursue American global hegemony and intervene in regional affairs. On the other hand, India has extensively engaged with the United States' Navy, has a robust program of joint exercises, and is exploring more expansive forms of military-to-military cooperation with the United States' sea services. India believes that the United States' Navy is providing an important global public good by maintaining maritime order and stability.

***Space Security*:** It is a subject of great interest in light of both China's antisatellite tests and the growing international recognition of the importance of space for economic and military activities. India and China view space as a critical arena for advancing their economic and national security goals. Consequently, both states are accelerating their space programs, which are in many ways exemplars of national achievement, and both are increasingly devoting resources as well as political and bureaucratic attention to the issue of space security. However, there are conspicuous differences in the two national programs. The Indian space program has been from its inception an entirely civilian endeavor, and it has only recently been pressed by its national security managers into supporting some military tasks. However, this reorientation is still extremely modest, and the strategic components of the Indian space program pale in comparison to its emphasis on development.

On the other hand, China's space program has been a military effort from the start. It does not have a clearly defined civilian space component. Instead, it has seamlessly integrated the civilian and military dimensions of space into one program. Many of its current programs, from space launchers to space systems, serve the operations of the People's Liberation Army in a way that has no comparable analog in India. Thus, although China pursues a wide set of objectives that include exploring space and making discoveries for the benefit of humanity as a whole, these activities are natural progressions of various organizational endeavors that have, at their base, a strong military complexion. India's space organization, in contrast, is still fundamentally focused on exploiting space for peaceful purposes through the development of various space systems for communications, remote sensing, meteorology, and space science, with a newer and more limited set of national security objectives now embedded in the larger civilian effort. These narrower objectives are focused on providing support capabilities for the military, countering China's burgeoning ASAT program, developing an independent space situational awareness program to counter the threat posed by space debris, and debating an International Code of Conduct for Outer Space Activities for activities in space. These broad differences in orientation are reflected in the fundamentally divergent approaches that India and China have pursued toward their strategic objectives in space. Chinese government's involvement in promoting space research and exploration suggests that China's central-planning approach has allowed it to advance quickly in terms of space-technology development. In general, China appears willing to pursue many different technological avenues in the course of its research and development process—an approach that takes advantage of the country's growing wealth and national resources. It has tested many weapons systems that have explicitly counterspace functions, which again indicates a predominantly military space program.

On the other hand, India has been both slow to promote space-technology development for national security purposes and hesitant to test and field space weapons. Instead, it has adopted a wait-and-see approach, settling for creating some retaliatory capabilities but refusing to test or demonstrate them until other states force India's hand. Moreover, India has taken a measured and exploratory approach to space-technology development, focusing on a few specific areas rather than advancing its technological capabilities at every level. In part, this is because India's space industry is smaller than China's. Both programs are government-directed, but the Indian Government lacks the resources available to its Chinese counterpart. Thus, unlike China, which has invested in its military space programs across the board, India has specifically prioritized improving mainly its space imagery and surveillance, position and navigation, and communication systems.

Thus, although both India and China remain opposed to the militarization of space and have strongly advocated the use of space for exclusively peaceful ends, neither country is optimistic about preventing such a development and both are engaged in exactly those activities normally associated with militarization. While India and China contend that any militarization will be in response to threats posted by others, they disagree sharply on the sources of those threats. It is believed that the greatest threat to China emerges from the United States' space dominance because it upsets the balance of power in outer space, thereby affecting the terrestrial power balance as well.

India and China have stressed the development of an international space regime that incorporates the use of multilateral forums as part of their efforts to deal with the dangers associated with the ongoing militarization of space. However, both states are skeptical about these organizations' chance of success, and they have accordingly also pursued bilateral and regional options. Ultimately, though, India and China believe that only unilateral actions can adequately protect their security.

There are revealing differences in Indian and Chinese attitudes toward the United States' space superiority. Both India and China acknowledge the technological sophistication of the United States in space. They hope to cooperate with the United States to maximize mutual commercial and technological gains while simultaneously tamping down security competition. But both Asian countries are skeptical about the extent of possible cooperation. However, their reasons for this skepticism vary greatly. China is concerned about competing militarily with the United States in space, but it fears American space hegemony even more than that competition. On the other hand, India is suspicious of cooperating with the United States not because of any geopolitical rivalry but due to the legacy of American technological sanctions against Indian entities. In other words, India does not see the United States' space dominance as an inherent threat but is instead concerned about the consequences of becoming too dependent on the United States given its fickle attitudes toward friendship with India.

Cyber Security: It is the most pernicious problem of the contemporary age given the ubiquity of computer connectivity, the high level of network integration that ties together all the key sectors of the modern economy, and the inherent difficulties in detecting, attributing, and neutralizing cyberattacks. The significance of these problems acquires added impetus because of the pervasive evidence that China is one of the few countries that has a highly dedicated, state-supported "cyber corps" of civilian and military specialists focusing on what the People's Liberation Army calls its Integrated Network Electronic Warfare strategy.

Given India's emergence as an information-technology powerhouse and China's rise as a major industrial entity, they have steadily growing cyberspace programs that are of mounting importance to their national economies. Cyberspace is the central nervous system of India and China. The increasing importance of cyberspace has been accompanied by an increasing number of threats against it in both countries. Normally, there are four types of cyberthreats—hacking, illegal online activities, cyberterrorism, and the militarization of cyber space. In addition, both India and China confront actions in cyberspace that threaten their political stability, thus leading both to expansively treat such activities as cyberattacks. In this environment, India and China have increasingly prioritized cyber security, albeit in fits and starts. Both states have worked hard to first establish and then to fine-tune a legal regime that adequately addresses cybercrimes. They have also struggled to manage a multi-actor governmental system in which different agencies have different cyber security responsibilities and powers—a system not entirely different from that of the United States—and have actively cooperated in bilateral and multilateral cyber-security efforts with other countries.

Both India and China have recognized the importance of public-private partnerships in overcoming national cyber security challenges, a critical step forward for countries with large economies and many major private enterprises. There are differences in India's and China's views on the role of industry in cyberspace. China has approached the issue of cyber security by linking government, industry, nongovernmental organisations, and individuals. It has encouraged industry to work toward national technological autonomy to prevent China from depending on the technology of foreign powers and thus being open to sabotage. In China, industry works closely with regulators and often self-regulates, but in India, private actors generally work at the behest of the government rather than independently. Although, such unilateral efforts to protect cyberspace are certain to become more common in both the countries, they recognize both the difficulty and the necessity of broader international cooperation in this area. They are well aware that there are major disagreements between states with respect to the perceptions of cyberthreats and priorities in addressing them. These divergences are compounded by differing legal systems, law enforcement capabilities, and stages of development. Nevertheless, India and China both recognize that the transnational nature of cyberspace means that states should have common objectives.

Since both countries view cyberspace as a global public good, it is believed that formal regulation under the auspices of the United Nations and the creation of new multilateral treaties to govern the system is called for. This new regime should be informed by the United Nations Charter and the laws of armed conflict, and it should respect state sovereignty and the necessity of resolving international disputes through peaceful means. States should complement these official efforts through multilateral cooperation and initiatives to create mutual trust in cyberspace. A legal regime may create definitions of unacceptable behaviour, but whether it could effectively deter or penalize misuses of cyberspace is highly questionable in the absence of a strong supranational authority, which India and China are unlikely to support. China values an open Internet but recognizes that complete freedom is impossible whether online or offline. On the other hand, India is constitutionally committed to the freedom of speech and expression, but the freedom is not unlimited and must be balanced against other concerns, including national security.

It is argued that cyberwarfare and espionage conducted in cyberspace are likely to be used by states in the future and that such a development is not illegal under international law. India and China disavow the use of surrogates in cyberspace or nationalist hackers as means of cyberwarfare, noting that they contravene the international conventions on war. However, it is assumed that India and China will soon develop offensive capabilities in this area precisely because many elements that would otherwise help deter such development, including the clarity and speed of attribution as well as the certitude of a devastating response, remain unclear. India and China differ somewhat when it comes to taking responsibility for attacks that emanate from within their borders. China thinks that it is unfair and unrealistic to ask states to take responsibility for any attack that originates inside their territory. On the other hand, India seems poised to sign an agreement that mentions the duty of states to prevent their territories from being used by non-state actors to conduct cyberattacks against other states.

Non-traditional Security: This section deals with two issues that would traditionally be treated as outside the realm of "high politics" but that have recently assumed enormous significance not only for India's and China's economic growth but also for general international stability. Firstly, this section will focus on energy security, a subject of importance for any economy and especially for those growing at a particularly rapid rate. Secondly, the discussion of non-traditional security concerns will be made by examining the environmental challenges facing India and China and their responses. This section will address Indian and Chinese perceptions of national and global environmental challenges, their strategies for dealing with these challenges, the role of international agreements in this context, and how both states seek to balance economic growth with environmental responsibility.

Both India and China rely heavily on coal, and this reliance is unlikely to decrease substantially in either country. They are also optimistic about making use of their domestic shale-gas reserves in light of recent technological advances, but they remain unsure about whether they have the ability—for technological, political, and regulatory reasons—to access these reserves in the near future. While both India and China will use more and more energy, but there are differences in both countries' abilities to indigenously meet their increasing energy needs. China is largely self-sufficient in all energy sources and saves oil, and therefore its dependence on foreign sources of energy will largely be limited to this sphere. In contrast, India already depends heavily on foreign sources of oil, coal and natural gas, and this dependence is likely to intensify in the future. This comparatively greater dependence on global sources of energy will have consequences for India's geopolitical autonomy.

Given the rising demand for energy in both countries, it is not surprising that India's and China's energy security objectives are similar, but there are important differences in accentuation. China has strongly emphasized expanding indigenous sources of energy in accordance with its ideological preference for self-reliance. In other words, China has particularly concerned itself with the sources of supply. On the other hand, India's energy security goal is defined as seeking to supply lifeline energy to all citizens irrespective of their ability to pay for it as well as meet their effective demand for safe and convenient energy to satisfy their various needs at competitive prices. The pressures of Indian democracy and the objectives of its developmental state suggest that India's primary concern is ensuring universal access qualified somewhat by price. Obviously, issues of access, source, and price are all intimately connected. But the different focuses in India and China highlight important dissimilarities in underlying philosophy that emerge from the two countries' varying stages of development and differing regime types.

In their effort to achieve energy security goal domestically, both India and China have adopted hybrid, market-state domestic energy systems where market prices are paired with government price controls, regulation, and subsidies. However, these similar systems have different focuses. China focuses fundamentally on reducing its energy intensity to allow for both continuing economic growth and decreasing energy consumption, and it emphasizes the rapid domestic development of its energy assets. India has also concentrated on the domestic development of energy assets but not at China's frenetic pace and, most importantly, with less attention paid to energy intensity. Moreover, India's efforts to expand its domestic energy production base and increase energy efficiency have been mired in the complicated dynamics of its democratic politics. In both countries the efforts to expand internal energy sources have run up against rising domestic concerns about safety, especially in a democratic polity such as India. For example, Japan's 2011 Fukushima Daiichi Nuclear Power Station accident has led to an uptick in concern about nuclear technology in India and China. Both countries emphasize nuclear energy as an important component of energy security, but their central governments have become increasingly wary about approving new projects. India has even seen direct civil action and violent protests against nuclear plants (as well as hydropower projects), although similar occurrences do not appear to have broken out in China. Yet the differences in the two governments' responses have been remarkable. China has used the rising concerns about nuclear safety to ensure that China's new nuclear plants conform to the very latest Western designs. Meanwhile India has allowed its compromised nuclear-liability legislation, the culture of secrecy pervading its atomic-energy establishment, and its leisurely decision-making to ensure that its dreams of large-scale investments in nuclear energy will take even longer to come to fruition than its leaders originally imagined.

The quest for energy security inevitably takes both India and China toward international sources and markets. Therefore, they have internationalized their energy security by actively pursuing foreign sources of energy through their national energy companies (NECs). They have balanced a mix of market-based and statist behaviour to address their general apprehensions about reliance on foreign markets. On the one hand, the two states continue to maintain a high degree of control and influence over their NECs through various political and bureaucratic instruments. On the other hand, the NECs are also subject to the concerns and imperatives of other nonstate investors. Partially because of this, Indian and Chinese NECs are typically driven by commercial concerns much more than they are by national security interests. But there is an important difference in how the NECs are situated in each country elative to their parent government. In China, the relationship between the state and the NECs is a close one, and the NECs look to the government for state financing. In China's view, this financing corrects market biases and allows the NECs to compete more successfully against other established oil companies. However, in India, the NECs are wary of government appropriation and incompetence, which leads them to exploit the rhetoric of national security for protection while also underwriting their preference for overseas investment rather than investments in the riskier climes at home. Indian NECs are often pushed into aggressive behaviour abroad that is commercially unwise and to the detriment of overall competition in the energy market.

The two countries also differ when it comes to state political support for NEC deals. While China uses its diplomatic heft to support its NECs' overseas deals, it is caught in a tussle of allegiance between those states that demand diplomatic support, the United States and its political and security allies, which argue that China should be proactive in effecting positive political change. In contrast, India's NECs shun diplomatic support, largely because oilmen often do not have too much faith in diplomacy and are always wary of commercial details of the deal becoming available to the public, or worse, to competitors.

The Indian and Chinese presence in foreign energy markets will remain a fact of life for the foreseeable future. To the extent that India and China have invested in foreign energy assets, however, they have often done so primarily in states that enjoy little foreign investment either due to their political pariah status or a risky investment climate. Despite India's and China's growing shares of world energy consumption, they are not seriously involved in world energy governance mechanisms. In addition to the lack of routine contacts, China often disagrees with these energy governance institutions' analyses and distrusts their motives. In response to this situation, China has tried to initiate multilateral discussions with all major energy-relevant countries. India has a similar perspective, believing that bodies like the International Energy Agency (IEA) need to undergo basic structural changes to increase the representation of countries like India and China.

On the issue of the utility of military instruments for energy security, the elements of convergence and divergence between India and China reflect their larger approach to how global-order issues intersect with their geopolitical interests. Both India and China are concerned about the safety of their energy sea lines of communication focusing on chokepoints such as the Strait of Hormuz. To combat these perceived insecurities, India and China have committed themselves to international collective-security efforts aimed at redressing specific security threats such as piracy. Energy concerns have fueled naval-modernization debates in India and China, for example, India's growing overseas energy assets have contributed to the steady increase in its expeditionary capability. Both the states are intensely aware of their significant military shortcomings, which generally preclude the employment of their armed services in unilateral actions aimed at safeguarding their energy assets.

While India and China share concerns about the security of their sea lines of communication, they have divergent views of the role of the United States and its Navy, in protecting them. Chinese are anxious about the leverage of the United States' Navy and fear that it might blockade China in the event of a conflict. On the other hand, India is apprehensive about the withdrawal and retrenchment of American naval capabilities, especially as United States' domestic problems threaten its defense budgets and its larger force structure. India is perceived to have been free-riding on United States Naval forces and any United States' withdrawal or reduction in capabilities could increase India's vulnerability.

Environmental Issues: India and China have encountered severe domestic environmental stress as a result of their national concentration on rapid economic growth. Health and environmental problems are pervasive in India and China, caused by the intense use of resources in production coupled with rising consumption. Among many challenges, both countries see pollution and the deterioration of domestic environmental quality as the greatest immediate threats. Threats to natural resources and global environmental problems are other major challenges in India. Despite some successes in improving the quality of the environment, India and China believe that persistently scare resources, high economic growth, and rapid social development will aggravate these challenges. In China, the impacts of pollution on human health are widely recognized, and public debate is growing over the price China has paid for blindly pursuing economic growth. In India, the links between environmental quality, material use, public health, and quality of life are still not well understood, although civil society is making growing demands to moderate or alter the strategies and quality of growth to accommodate environmental concerns, much as in China. Both India and China have sought to address these challenges through a wide variety of legislation and regulation aimed at ameliorating environmental degradation. In general, it seems that both countries have adopted primarily command-and-control measures, but there has also been a limited movement toward market-based regulation supplemented by a focus on raising public awareness. However, despite these broad resemblances, both states appear to have invested dissimilar amounts of resources in environmental management.

China has spent significant sums in an effort to clean up the environment. While the current programs are still insufficient, they nonetheless represent a genuine effort to resolve the problem. China consciously seeks to improve its efficiency, restructure its economy, and change its long-term growth path in order to guarantee its sustainability. In contrast, India is still vacillating between green growth strategies and no strategy at all. In India, the political class and the bureaucracy itself increasingly see the environment as a secondary objective to growth, in fact as a threat to growth, even though civil society is increasingly pushing back. It is believed that environmental challenges may fall even more by the wayside as India's economic growth slows. To the extent that the government has attempted to address the problem (often as a byproduct of other efforts such as energy security), its writ is frequently ignored at the level of enforcement, meaning that India has a long way to go before it successfully mitigates its environmental threats.

Both India and China have tried to strike a balance between economic growth and environmental health by concentrating on areas where the two issues do not conflict. China has focused on improving its efficiency and promoting "leapfrog development". On the other hand, India displays a clear development bias, although many in India would disagree with framing the issue as one involving tradeoffs between growth and environmental health. Despite their best intentions, therefore, both India and China at some level appear to have prioritized economic growth over environmental health. Indian and Chinese struggles to manage environmental issues within their countries occur within the context of larger global environmental challenges. There is widespread public awareness in both countries of these transnational environmental problems, especially climate change. But both India and China view this hazard as emerging from the excess and unsustainable consumption and lifestyles of the developed world. They believe the best way to deal with the critical challenges facing the global environment is through international negotiations among all states and through the existing institutions of global governance. This will require some series of international agreements, but their character, enforceability, and division of burdens remain issues of great contention. Additionally, neither India nor China has staked out a clear position on whether international environmental agreements should generally entail a high degree of formal obligation, presumably because any position on this question would depend on how the responsibilities were apportioned between developed and developing countries. India, for instance, would balance the loss of sovereignty against the fairness of an agreement in deciding to sign it.

India and China diverge over the degree of external authority that is acceptable in international environmental agreements. China may support an enforcement mechanism that is managed by an international legal authority or at least guided by meaningful rules to ensure compliance, giving the example of common accounting practices. In contrast, India finds the notion of delegating external authority troubling. It believes that ensuring equity in the governance of any external authority would be problematic and would therefore prefer distributed governance among existing institutions in the United Nations system. Given the difficulties in reaching an acceptable international consensus on these issues, India and China do not expect concerted global action to appear for some time and are therefore likely to stay focused on pursuing independent national solutions. They strongly emphasize the importance of historical equity and the principle of "common but differentiated responsibilities (CBDR)". They firmly believe that any international climate change agreement should take into account countries' historical per capita emissions, which would put a high proportion of the burden on the developed nations. Similarly, they refuse to take on any onerous responsibility before the developed world acts. For instance, if the developed countries are willing to shoulder their responsibilities for their share of historical emissions, China, too, would be morally constrained to directly face its future emissions and try harder to carry out domestic policies for industrial restructuring and upgrade. On the other hand, India cannot moderate its growth for the sake of global environmental concerns; rather, the view is that it is India's turn to grow and it is the duty of the world to create ecological space for that growth.

India and China will need to undertake serious efforts to curb their emissions, but they will do so only after the developed world has committed itself to stringent caps on emissions and in a way that does not hinder development in emerging countries. They also stress the importance of measuring per capita emissions as opposed to national ones, which is unsurprising given their continental sizes. Given the mutual focus on CBDR and the needs of developing countries, India and China both strongly support the continuation of the Kyoto process begun with the Kyoto Protocol and the use of the United Nations Framework Convention on Climate Change for a future global climate agreement. As Indian and Chinese positions are generally in accord on the issue of managing the environment, it is unsurprising that the two countries have diverged only slightly in their perspectives on past climate change conferences. China may have been slightly more definitive about the outcomes of the 2009 Copenhagen Conference, claiming that it reflected the political willingness of all parties to address climate change.

The Conference achieved some consensus among the parties and clarified the direction for future negotiations. On the other hand, India's feelings about the results of the Conference may have been more mixed, but it does not fundamentally disagree with the Chinese view that the effectiveness of these discussions is open to debate. China criticized the Durban Conference on the same grounds, viewing the outcome as acceptable but not sufficiently satisfying.

India-China Relations in a Nutshell

A close examination of Indian and Chinese perceptions of different aspects of the global order reveals that the conventional wisdom about an India-China convergence on transnational issues vis-à-vis the West is considerably exaggerated. The differences between the two Asian giants on bilateral matters are well known, but a careful study of their positions on these major issues leads inevitably to the conclusion that the divide between them may be just as significant on matters of global magnitude. Outside of the international economic system, energy security, and environmental issues, India-China differences on all other subjects, such as the global order, the nonproliferation system, Asian security, regional stability in Southern Asia, and security in the maritime commons, space, and cyberspace, are considerable even though those differences may not always be apparent in public discussions.

Differences in Indian and Chinese positions sometimes arise from the two countries' competing visions but more often from their underlying geopolitical rivalry, which appears to be sufficiently deep-rooted to prevent the two states from realizing any natural accommodation. Both the Asian giants bend over backward to conceal their differences in public, and both have often struggled to reach some accommodation that might permit occasional practical cooperation. But the differences in national power and performance between India and China, the seeming disdain with which China treats India, and the deep fears that India harbors about China's policies and intentions lead to a never-ending contest for securing strategic advantages. And that contest takes on critical significance as both India and China seek to manipulate their bilateral relationship and ties to the

United States and other Western countries for national gain. The ensuing interactions, which implicate both India's and China's engagements with one another and their separate affiliations with the United States and others, then make for a complex dynamic of cooperation and competition that transcends simple categories like partnership or rivalry. But the dynamic does not generate the unqualified cooperation that many believe defines the India-China relationship with respect to global issues. This reality leads to three important conclusions.

(a) Despite the superficial convergence between India and China on many global issues, there are deeper disagreements that—though sometimes subtle (especially when compared to the differences in Indian and Chinese views on the United States)—are nevertheless likely to preclude the development of a meaningful partnership between India and China.

(b) The disagreements among India, China, and the United States on many global issues are often rooted in, and reinforced by, structural constraints that are significant enough not only to prevent a meaningful resolution of many transnational problems but also to generate potentially pernicious consequences for both the global order and individual states. A possible exception to this generalization might be the international economy, where the interests of all three powers may align on many of the major issues.

(c) The bilateral problems that plague the India-China relationship are so serious that even their outwardly optimistic and polite rhetoric cannot mask their underlying suspicions and corrosive rivalry. This security dilemma, in turn, frustrates whatever possibilities may otherwise have opened up for bilateral cooperation on global issues.

Thus, the problems inherent in the complicated interactions between India and China suggest that a better understanding of the India-China rivalry remains the critical research task for the future.